The First Voyage of the *Joshua*

The First Voyage of the *Joshua*

by Bernard Moitessier

Translated by Inge Moore

William Morrow & Company, Inc.
New York *1973*

Published in the United States in 1973.
This translation copyright © 1969 by Adlard Coles Ltd.
Translation published in Great Britain in 1969 under the title
Cape Horn: The Logical Route.

French edition, under the title *Cap Horn à la Voile,* published by
B. Arthaud, Paris, copyright © 1967 by B. Arthaud, Paris.

Printed in the United States of America.

Moitessier, Bernard.
      The first voyage of the Joshua.

      Translation of Cap Horn à la voile.
         1. Joshua (Ship). 2. Voyages and travels—1951-   I. Title.
G464.M5713 1973   910'.41   77-170220
ISBN 0-688-00023-1

Contents

Foreword

There isn't a sailor who doesn't shudder at the thought of Cape Horn. The great sailing ships of bygone days have left too many victims there. The yachtsmen who have dared to take their boats through these stormy waters are few: Conor O'Brian, Vito Dumas, Marcel Bardiaux, Nancy and Bob Griffith, Bill Nance. Only one, Al Hansen, has rounded the Horn from east to west, well off shore, before being wrecked on the coast of Patagonia.

In November 1965 a French yachting couple, Bernard and Françoise Moitessier, joined the ranks of these outstanding navigators by setting out from Tahiti and rounding the Cape 49 days later.

Who were these new 'Cape Horners'? Françoise, the first woman to round the Horn in a yacht, was still a novice, but Bernard was a seasoned mariner.

A vagabond in search of congenial company, he had one day, many years before, left his native Indo-China aboard *Marie-Thérèse*, a junk so dilapidated that in the middle of the Indian Ocean he had to dive underwater to stop up the worst of the leaks. After 85 days of tough sailing into the teeth of the monsoon Moitessier, through lack of navigational instruments, ran aground and wrecked his ship. It took him three years' hard work on the island of Mauritius before he could sail again in a new boat, *Marie-Thérèse II*, built with his own hands.

At the end of a tiring Atlantic crossing Bernard, overcome by fatigue, having stayed at the helm too long through the Antilles, was once again shipwrecked; he lost *Marie-Thérèse II*, his sole possession, his reason for living. An error of navigation, one might simply say. But behind this bald statement there also lies a human drama.

Moitessier has given a fascinating account of his roving existence as an aimless and penniless vagabond in his book *Un Vagabond des Mers du Sud*.

This new book by Bernard Moitessier begins in the Antilles following the loss of *Marie-Thérèse II*. Left without a boat, without money, without a job, without friends or family, Bernard was faced with having to rebuild his whole life. Anyone less determined would have given up. He returned to France in 1958 and four years later was the owner of a new boat, bigger and more seaworthy. He had even saved enough to allow him to think about another long voyage.

Meanwhile the vagabond had got married, and he decided to offer his wife the most wonderful of wedding presents: an Atlantic crossing through the Trade Winds, a long holiday in the secluded coves of the Galapagos Islands and among the colourful atolls of the Tuamotu Archipelago. On the ocean highways they met many of their old friends: the amazing Henry Wakelam, Pierre Deshumeurs, the companion of many trips on board the old *Snark* back in Indo-China, Joseph and Madeleine Merlot, first met in Durban, Jim and Adolfo and many more. They also made new friends, all of them vagabonds of the seas.

From Tahiti the Moitessiers had the choice of two classic routes by which to return to Europe; via the Red Sea or via the Cape of Good Hope.

But it was a third route that Bernard chose; the route which led them through the terrible winds of the South Pacific and the enormous seas of the Roaring Forties, round Cape Horn.

It is the most difficult, the most dangerous route, but also the fastest, the most direct and the most logical one. It is grandiose and magnificent in its impartiality. And in their 39 ft ketch, Bernard and Françoise Moitessier accomplished an incredible performance; in 126 days at sea, without port of call, the two covered 14,216 miles from Moorea to Alicante.

Others might have told the story of this extraordinary adventure and made it sound commonplace. But Bernard Moitessier possesses a rare talent of perception; with great sensitivity he sees, feels and describes things which would escape most people. Modest and helpful, he never fails to give hints and tips from which other yachtsmen, both inshore and offshore sailors, might benefit. Bernard Moitessier is not only a great seaman, a man of exceptional strength of character, he is also a great writer.

The classics of nautical literature are rare. Bernard Moitessier's book, by virtue of the magnitude of the exploit as well as for the wealth of human experience which may be gained from it, deserves to become one of them.

Jean-Michel Barrault

The First Voyage of the *Joshua*

Part 1 *Birds of Passage*

I

My Paper Boat

'My child, the ways of the Lord are wonderful'. The words of peace which the Honolulu missionary offered Eric de Bishop after he had wrecked his yacht *Phu-Po* came to my mind as I tried desperately to come to terms with my misfortune. But I had not even the will-power left to resist it as de Bishop had. I was completely stunned; nothing mattered except to go to sleep and never wake up again.

'Take it easy, Bernard, let time solve your problems. Come and have a drink with me. I've got some money'.

This was the advice of Adolfo, my Argentinian friend, who had heard about the shipwreck of my boat, *Marie-Thérèse II*, on Radio Cocotier, and had come to meet me off the local launch that brought me back to Trinidad. A real friend, Adolfo. But he could not understand that my will was broken for good this time.

'Come now, Bernard, you aren't going to let this get you down ... Let's have a bottle together, and tomorrow we'll see. Come along now ... or I'll kick you! You are married to life for better or worse. So come on!'

Good old Adolfo, you had no idea what it meant to lose a boat, you had never been through it ... Imagine a hermit crab whose shell has been smashed by someone, doing it 'no harm, apart from that'. Watch it fight against its fate. To think that as a child I played this cruel game myself! I hate to admit it, but I did. And now it was my turn to find myself lying on the beach without a shell. I had already lost my previous boat, at Diego-Garcia. But that was nothing compared to what I was suffering now in the Antilles.

'Listen, Bernard, you have lost your boat, and that's a hard blow, but you've still got the most important thing of all – your life. Not to speak of your freedom. Think of the blind people who find it quite natural to sing in their eternal night. For you tomorrow will be another day. You ought to be ashamed of yourself!'

And suddenly I found myself sobbing on my friend's shoulder without feeling the slightest bit ashamed. The abscess had finally broken. From the depths of my being a spark of life was released, as I remembered some verses by Musset which my father used to read to us as children:

> *As I walked through the valley*
> *A bird sat singing on its nest.*
> *All his young, his treasured brood,*
> *Had perished in the night.*
> *And still it sang to greet the dawn.*

A week later I was over the worst of the crisis, whether thanks to Adolfo or Musset, I do not know. But I knew only too well that I was not going to recover from this second shipwreck in a hurry. A mistake of such magnitude cannot be wiped out with a mere wave of the hand. I had well and truly committed a crime towards my boat by ignoring the sacred laws of the sea, the first of which is to keep watch, and the second never to relax one's efforts.

When Toumelin was nearly dropping with fatigue as he nego-tiated the reef-infested Torres Straits, he pricked his leg with the point of his knife so that the pain would keep him awake. I should have done the same, or chosen another profession.

Still, there was no point in looking back. What was done was done. Besides, it is not in my nature to think of the past – nor of the future, for that matter. But this time things were more serious than usual.

'You have the mentality of a cork – nothing can keep you under', a friend in Mauritius had said to me when he saw the speed with which I got myself back in fighting trim after my first shipwreck in the Indian Ocean. That may have been so at the time, but then the island of Mauritius is a land of good fairies where sympathy abounds, and all my problems were solved as if by magic, thanks to generous friends who had found a good job for me, so that I could get down to building *Marie-Thérèse II* without much delay.

But there I was at Trinidad, and here the cork met with almost insurmountable difficulties in its efforts to get back on top, despite some good friends; all the more so since in this part of the world my friends were not exactly well-off. Although this by no means reflected on their characters, it was nevertheless a grave incon-venience when someone was in need of a well-paid job and wanted to build a boat. And anyway, I could not impose myself on friends all the time, they had their own problems; Jim, Ruth and Juda needed all their energies for finishing *Rongo*. As for Adolfo, he put me up in his little room for a week, but I didn't want to plant myself on him; that would have served no purpose and only annoyed him in the end. Me too.

One afternoon Adolfo took me to the Hotel de Paris to cheer me up over a drink, and we got down to brass tacks.

To start with, I had sixty dollars in my pocket and it was out of the question to find a well-paid job in the Antilles. Adolfo, who is as artful as a monkey, hit the nail right on the head. If I stayed there I would always be a penniless 'bum', and for many years to come, too. This would never do, because I was already thirty-three, and had always been in favour of early retirement.

In that part of the world (like any other) a millionaire can double his money in a relatively short time, providing of course that he gets down to it. But a vagabond possessing nothing but a pair of pants and a shirt (even if there are sixty dollars in the pocket) can go a long time before he can afford to buy another pair of pants and a new shirt. This is an accepted law, and I am not the one who invented it. It sums up the financial aspects of my problem.

As for the spiritual aspects, they were as follows: I had to have a change of air, I had to leave the Antilles at all costs and start from scratch in another country, preferably France, where money flowed like water and where the ghost of *Marie-Thérèse II* might fade and finally disappear behind new impressions and a new occupation.

For ever since the day of the shipwreck, *Marie-Thérèse* had come to haunt me nearly every night and crush my chest, as though demanding justice. I would wake up in a panic, drenched in perspiration and almost demented. I *must* turn the page for good, and without delay, otherwise the outcome would be tragic, in spite of Musset's verse which I remembered during the day, but promptly forgot at night.

Sitting peacefully on the shady terrace of the inner courtyard of the Hotel de Paris, cheered by the long dissertations of the sparrows and blackbirds, I explained all this to my friend. Then I told him my solution, the only one which I was sure would get me back to France.

At first Adolfo turned pale. Then gradually he concentrated his attention and his eyes lit up with delight as he realised that, for the first time since my arrival in Trinidad, I was saved.

My idea was to build a boat out of newspaper over a wooden frame, light but strong. This is not as silly as it may sound. In fact, some of the junks in Indo-China are made of a bamboo wicker-work which is then covered with a mixture of cow dung and oil, mixed with resin. This skin, which is perfectly watertight, though somewhat ... flexible, is then reinforced with what at first sight (and even upon closer inspection) looks a rather rudimentary frame.

Yet these bamboo boats built on the coast of Annam, the largest of which can carry fifty to sixty tons of cargo, have gigantic rudders which serve as centre-plates in deep water. They move in a groove in the stern and can be raised when the boat is beached.

These disproportionally large rudders hanging down way below the bottom of the boats seem to defy our European logic, for the strain imposed on the stern post and transmitted by it to the thin skin of interwoven bamboo is quite considerable.

But after having sailed on these junks I can only insist that they are by no means just feeble tubs that keep themselves afloat as if by a miracle on quiet rivers, but large, proud seaboats. They sail with heavy cargoes in their holds, often covering close on a thousand miles on one passage with the Monsoon filling their palm-leaf sails. And, I might add, they are equipped with a type of roller reefing which is much more efficient than any of the European methods, for to my way of thinking extreme simplicity comes closer to perfection than ratchets and gears made of gunmetal. It is true that in this respect twenty-six years spent in Indo-China have made me thoroughly biased in favour of Asian methods. They do have their merits!

'And yet it turns,' said Galileo.

'And still they sail,' the Vietnamese sailors on the coast of Annam might say about their junks. Still, I agree with most Westerners on one point: they do not sail as well as the earth manages to turn. But they do sail, despite their flat bottoms which are compensated for by those incredible hung rudders which seem to be specially made for wrenching off the stern posts.

'I tell you, Adolfo, this won't pose any problems: I'll build a very strong frame, out of planks of roofing timber, for a 5-metre hard-chine boat: a keel, a straight stem, a stern post, and no more than six or seven frames. If I put in twelve hours of work a day I bet you I can finish the framework in three days for no more than ten dollars' worth of wood. And I can guarantee that my frame will be much stronger than that of any boat on the Annam coast. But it will still be slightly flexible, that's the secret of these bamboo junks.'

'I agree with you about the framework, but what will happen if your layers of newspaper peel off like onion skins when your pitch starts to melt? That'll be a damned nuisance, won't it?'

'Don't worry: we'll put on one layer of paper, one layer of pitch (but first you'll help me turn the framework keel up) one layer of paper, another layer of pitch, and so on. After twenty-five to thirty layers of paper I'll have a strong enough skin which I'll then finish off with an outer cover of jute sacking, sewn together and plastered with pitch. Just like covering a kayak. By the way, you have just given me an idea: I'll start off with an inner skin of sacking, too, then the newspaper will not be able to escape on either side. You never know.'

'Brilliant ... absolutely brilliant! A paper boat crosses the Atlantic! Only you could have thought of it ...'

'Nonsense, it's the most logical thing in the world, Henry and I discussed it once before. There was this young boy without two pennies to rub together who wanted to do some sailing in Durban harbour. He thought we were off our heads, but it was the only solution. To think that Rommer crossed the Atlantic in a kayak and others in dories and rowing boats, and this little lad would not even hear of a paper boat, just for tacking around inside the harbour ... there's nothing worse than lack of imagination!'

'Ah well, Bernard, we all do what we can, and this lad was not really set on going to sea. There's a world of difference between saying "I want to" and "I will". But what about your deck, how are you going to build that?'

'Fred Rebel crossed the Pacific from Sydney to California, mostly against the Trade Winds, in a centreboard boat decked with a tarpaulin. I don't quite know yet how I'm going to knock a deck together, but that isn't really important. Maybe I won't need more than a half-deck with an awning over the cabin. Several chaps have crossed the North Atlantic in open dories and, believe me, they weren't fools. Their boats were simply very light, and they knew it.'

There remained one small snag, though. I had given my sextant and Neufville tables to the black skipper of the schooner that had brought me back from St Vincent to Trinidad. The reader may wonder what possessed me to let such a precious instrument go. But it seemed quite logical; having a boat no longer I needed no sextant either, and it seemed natural that the instrument (which, by the way, I had had given to me and therefore could not really call mine anyway) should benefit someone else.

This black skipper, whom I had taught to use the sextant during our short crossing, was beside himself with joy at the thought of knowing a great secret which was, he believed, only known to a chosen few. I advised him to treat the sextant with extreme care so as not to put the mirrors out of alignment and to have it checked from time to time by an officer on a cargo ship at Trinidad.

When I told him: 'Take it, it's yours,' he did not understand, it was too much at once. As I insisted the realisation slowly dawned on him and his hands started to tremble and caress the magic box. From a simple skipper he had suddenly become Captain, he could find Barbados by placing himself on the same latitude, in spite of Trade Winds and contrary currents. I explained it all to him.

'First the black people at St Vincent pillage your boat and then you give your sextant to a black man, after having taught him how to use it! It's enough to make me ashamed of my race!'

'Don't you think I would have pillaged the *Queen Mary* if she had been wrecked in front of me? And without being ashamed either of myself or of my race! It's quite normal to pillage a boat stupid enough to get wrecked ...'

While waiting to come across the *Queen Mary* on the rocks I would still have to manage without a sextant. But there was a way out, simple if not perfect.

When Cassiopeia and the Great Bear are on the same level above the horizon, the position of the Polar Star marks your latitude almost exactly. So I would make myself a kind of cross-staff such as the earliest navigators used, with coloured glasses from a pair of sunglasses. This instrument would be marked in two-degree steps as accurately as possible by checking the angles against Jim's sextant.

Besides, I had kept my chronometer and could indulge in the luxury of navigating on longitude by the method of equal circum-meridian altitudes. The figures for the declination and equation of time for the next two months I would copy from Jim's Nautical Almanac or on board a freighter.

True, I would be navigating with a possible error of between 150 and 200 miles. That was far from perfect, but it would at least be better than in the days of *Marie-Thérèse I* when my longitude calculations were completely haywire. Still, I would always have to bear in mind the average limits of this approximation because I should first have to head north along the coast, along the chain of the Antilles, before meeting the Westerlies which would blow me straight to Gibraltar. From there on there was a chance that someone might present me with a sextant. Some yachts have two, and solidarity among yachtsmen is not just a myth. So navigation would present no real problem.

Neither would the question of drinking water. Eight to ten jerricans would do the trick, giving me a normal daily ration of half a gallon. I was sure I could get these jerricans for nothing; I had done so before.

Food presented an obvious financial problem which I hoped to solve partly thanks to the low price of rice. I also hoped that fishing would be good, because fish hooks are cheaper than tins of corned beef! In any case, I would not suffer a tenth of what Bombard had gone through, and Jim had mentioned a box of tinned sardines which a friend had mentioned to him etc. Eventually I would get to France, in the middle of summer.

'A country rotten with money,' I was assured by Adolfo, who had motored through France two years previously and spoke the language quite well. 'If you write a book I bet you'll be off in another boat within five years,' he added with conviction.

I had no intention whatever of writing a book, thinking that one had to be very gifted to be able to write. All I wanted was to get lost among people, make a niche for myself among them, not too deep but very wide so that I could get out of it quickly in a real boat, made of real wood, not a rotting tub like … like *Marie-Thérèse II*, who so nearly became my coffin.

'The ways of the Lord are wonderful.' It seemed to me that I was beginning to understand them. I had lost a boat, but in exchange I had gained a lot, not to speak of ... my freedom. And I would have to see what I could do with this freedom in a country which I scarcely knew, having spent only six months' holiday there ten years before. The thought of French winters filled me with fear like the great unknown, but after all forty-five million French managed to put up with it, so it must be a question of adaptation. In France I could thoroughly forget the Tropics until my feathers had grown again.

2

Like a Well-trained Monkey

I had been at Trinidad for exactly eight days, and in two days I was to start building my boat, next to Jim's catamaran *Rongo*.

The outcome of that scorching hot morning was encouraging: the editor of the local newspaper offered to let me have as many old newspapers as I needed, but that was not all: as soon as the boat was launched he would give me a hundred dollars out of his own pocket to buy provisions with. And all that because he liked my face! ...

In return for this invaluable service he would get from me a letter of at least twenty pages, written in English, giving an account of my crossing. He could do with it what he wanted, blow it up to a hundred pages if it suited him, or throw it into the wastepaper basket. It wouldn't concern me, and we would be quits. There is something nice about this kind of mutual trust, especially if it is the other chap who makes the first move ... But I did hope that he was not going to quote me saying too many stupid things in this letter. In the meantime the hundred dollars from this kind gentleman would suit me admirably.

As for the wood I was going to buy from Donald, that would be fifteen dollars, cost price (he insisted on showing me his bills), and he would deliver it free. I was going to see him that afternoon to pay him cash, true to my principles but also to be sure of clinching the deal.

No doubt, the good star which had guided me since my birth was shining again as bright as ever. It had never yet abandoned me, except for momentary eclipses. And *Marie-Thérèse II* had not come to haunt me the night before. Could she have forgiven me already?

Life was beautiful! And to think that there are chaps who make mountains out of molehills ... !

It was almost midday when Adolfo rushed up to me just as I was leaving Donald's place savouring my dream.

'Bernard! The Norwegian Consul 'phoned at about ten to ask you to go round there urgently.'

'Let's go, Adolfo, I'll explain to you on the way.'

Life is funny. The consequences of a chance gesture, an encounter, even a simple word can bring the most concrete plans tumbling down without warning. In my case it all started with the sextant. After having stowed it under his berth and covered it up with a piece of sailcloth as carefully as if he were covering up a baby, the captain of the schooner had talked to me like a brother:

'If you stay in the Antilles you will always be poor. Go to Europe where people are rich. Go and see the Norwegian Consul in Trinidad, he will fix you up on an oil tanker in the place of a deserter, and as soon as you get to the other side, you desert. You are poor now, so go and stay with my father at Trinidad. I will give him money for your keep and you can go and see the consul every morning. In the end he will get you on a ship. If you stay in the Antilles you will be a Poor White Man all your life.'

I had gone and seen the Norwegian Consul, a man in his sixties, tall and square, who had been a Cape Horner in the days of the sailing ships. He had listened to my story with compassion, not bothered about my nationality but asking the kind of questions a seaman would ask. Then he had taken Adolfo's telephone number, 'just in case', telling me quite frankly that it would be difficult but not altogether impossible.

That had been on the very evening of my arrival in Trinidad, and I had forgotten all about it, the paper boat seeming so much more tangible and real than the possibility of becoming a stopgap in the crew of some Norwegian tanker.

And lo, here was my paper boat going up in smoke in the Norwegian Consul's office. I felt like a hunter who has spent a whole morning stalking a deer and suddenly finds a fat buffalo in his line of fire. He doesn't have to think twice to realise that it will pay him to shoot the buffalo ...

Nor did I. I fired without hesitation and cut off my own retreat with a determined stroke of the pen, for the tanker was loading her cargo of crude oil some six miles south of Port-of-Spain and would weigh anchor in two hours. I had enough time left, all the same, to take a taxi with Adolfo and go back to his place to fetch my rusty old sea chest, witness to many heavy blows, which I had lugged around with me since my days in Indo-China. It contained clothing, letters, a boat's compass and some improbable bits and pieces every one of which held a memory for me. These were all my earthly possessions, and I meant to keep them. Provided this vestige of my past did not bring my tanker bad luck ...

What a world of difference there was between a small sailing boat and this 16,000-tonner! And I don't just mean the difference in size or behaviour at sea, that goes without saying.

Only a month ago I had been a sailor, living in close contact with the sea, forever trying to read its face to interpret its little frowns, its smiles, its moods. And here I was, a ... exactly what was I? I did not know and it did not matter, maybe a kind of unskilled worker occupied eight hours a day with chores like washing, scraping, painting and from time to time coiling down a few hawsers just to remind me that despite everything I was still on a seagoing vessel.

I no longer had to tell myself that this or that needed doing, or ask myself how on earth I was going to manage some job or what the devil I could have with my rice today. There was a boss to work things out and make all the decisions for his crew. It was up to him to rack his brains over whether it was better to start painting at the front or at the back. All we had to do was follow. Very convenient. As for the soup, it was excellent and always on time, and I started to put on weight.

It was an extraordinary contrast which surprised me whenever I thought of it. But I thought of it less and less, for that page of my past was well and truly turned without any effort on my part.

I was having a holiday on board this great tub that was growling like some animal as it covered its 350 miles a day, its belly full of oil which it was going to discharge at New York. What surprised me a bit (but basically I couldn't have cared less) was to see it embark again for Trinidad with yet another cargo of oil without pausing for breath, discharge at top speed, fill up again at the same quay from another pipe-line, dash off to New York to discharge, re-load and return to Trinidad, always full of oil ... just like perpetual motion or the Circle Line.

Since my lively mind takes an interest in anything, I finally discovered that there are a great number of different types of oil: crude oil, lubricating oil, light fuel oil, etc.

So at least we weren't tramping the same stuff around all the time.

Our tramp at last set course for Europe after receiving a radio message: 'Discharge at Stockholm and drydock at Hamburg.' Always provided that in Stockholm the company did not find an urgent cargo for Yokohama and a more interesting drydock in Japan!

'You have all the damn luck,' Bill said to me, 'and here's me trying to get back to Australia for the past four years, and I've changed ship five times.'

We were buddies, Bill and I, having shared a two-berth cabin since I embarked, and he explained to me how to go about it: 'Don't breathe a word of your plans. Wait till we get to Hamburg. There'll be a lot of commotion in the dock. I'll take your chest ashore saying it's mine and I want to sell it. In the meantime you wait for me at the station, with your ticket, and you beat it without anyone being any the wiser.'

The only snag was my passport: it was under lock and key in the captain's safe, like all the crew's. Occasionally sailors in dire need of money sold their passports in cold blood (I cannot remember exactly how much I was offered for mine in New York, but it was quite a tidy sum).

To remove the risk of temptation all passports were kept out of harm's way, and we were issued with temporary passes by an immigration officer every time we docked. I would thus have to cross the border without being able to show my papers and would have to tell the French police that I had lost my case on the journey. But … was I making a mountain out of a molehill?

While I was waiting for Europe to come my way, the tanker offered me unexpected opportunities to improve my nautical education under the direction of real *professionals*. So far I had accumulated knowledge in a jumbled mass and much of it lacked the firm foundation which is so necessary to well-constructed edifices. Now I could sort out some of this jumble and add to it some new material made available to me by a first-class crew. In a way I was about to become westernised on this ship which smelled as much of Europe as it's bilges smelled of oil.

Up forward, in the officers' quarters, the second officer and a young pilot who had taken a liking to me helped me penetrate the secrets of the night sky, the laws of the stars, the planets and the moon. I had imagined it to be a book with seven seals, and now all my complexes dissolved after just a few systematic study sessions on the bridge. 'You are ready for great things, but make use of every opportunity to perfect your knowledge of astro-navigation, it is a much wider subject than you think.' I was yet to understand the full implication of what the second officer told me then.

As for the poop (reserved for the crew) it was simply teeming with objects of interest, none the less difficult to absorb, for only the boss seemed to know what was going on, everybody else being busy following instructions.

All the same, I learned that the topsides of a ship do not rust if they are maintained in the time-honoured manner of the merchant navy: paint, paint and paint again, with quick drying paints because ships are always in a hurry to sail. The thicker the coats of paint, the better the steel is protected: the stern, for example, which is not exposed to wear, had about 6 mm of paint on it which it had accumulated over the years. Under this thick protective layer the steel was as good as new (I chipped it to find out) even though the ship was sixteen years old. The metal deck, on the other hand, presented a problem because the paint never had time to harden under the crew's boots. I also learned that the sun is good for something.

Sticking my nose into everything, trying to understand why things were done one way and not another, I started to realise that a properly built steel yacht without any inaccessible corners could be maintained by a well-trained monkey. Honestly, on this ship I had to have no more intelligence than a chimpanzee to do my day's work.

I realised, of course, that it was dangerous to become wildly enthusiastic on the basis of appearances which I had not had time to study thoroughly, yet the advantages of steel impressed me despite my instinctive mistrust.

The maintenance of my wooden boats had always confronted me with delicate problems and required real qualifications, for I had had to be 'Doctor of Rot', 'Doctor of Teredos' and 'Doctor of Leaks'.

Here a scraper, a can of paint and a large brush took the place of three doctorates and no other qualification was needed except a little elbow grease. Besides, I noticed that there were only five of us to do the painting, and the five of us painted this 16,000-ton hull in nine hours (with paint rollers) from water-line to deck, before leaving New York.

Five men, that is just 700 lb of human flesh to maintain 16,000 tons of steel in 8 working hours per day ... That would mean how many pounds of human flesh to do the same to a 5-ton yacht, but at a rate of 8 working hours a month? But I was being ridiculous. I could build a wooden boat myself, under a tree, but a steel hull would have to be built by a yard and cost a lot more money than I had ever owned in my life. I had better not bore my readers with my daydreams, for they did not hold water.

From the early hours of the morning we had been sailing in calm water among a shoal of islands shimmering in the July sun. This was the entry to the large bay at the end of which lies Stockholm, neat and proper, probably one of the most beautiful pleasure-grounds in the world.

Twenty-seven hours in port, that was a lot for a tanker. 'I chose the sea to see the world, but all we do is cross the water to get from one night-club to another,' Bill complained.

Several days later we entered the wet dock in Hamburg, and my heart beat faster: soon I would be in France, if everything went without a hitch ...

When Bill had talked about commotion in the dock I had had but little idea of what it would really be like: the ship was immediately besieged by some ten men who gave a hand with the heavy hawsers with such abounding eagerness that despite my innocence, I could not imagine them to be paid hands. They were in fact members of the famous fraternity of beachcombers, paid-off sailors of indeterminate nationality, not altogether commendable but very likeable – and also very talkative. They wanted news of this chap and that, who had signed-on on such and such a ship, they asked and replied to an avalanche of questions shouted to them by their old shipmates, and all the while never stopped taking in the slack. Having been at it for many years, these old-timers know just about every ship, the good ones and the bad ones, and always hope to find a berth on the ship of their choice, although they would probably be satisfied with any old tub provided she left quickly. They shared our table, which is normal practice, but we thought it wise to lock our cabins. All the same, they were a likeable crew in a rough and ready way, living from one day to the next, and I would have liked to join them for a little while. But one cannot do everything in life, one life simply isn't long enough.

Besides, on the following day I was sitting in the train to Paris, with my sea chest and my passport. I had had it handed back to me as had the rest of the crew, some of whom had joined the ranks of the beachcombers, because the company who owned the tanker had decided that it needed some extensive and lengthy work doing to it. So everybody found themselves out on the street except for a few mechanics.

Adieu, tanker of my heart, I had once again fallen on my feet. No wonder, with my star!

3
Like a Lost Dog

Paris ... I had been there for three weeks, feeling terribly out of place in spite of my adaptability, this secret weapon of all who spend their life roughing it. There was something which made me feel ill at ease: all those unknown hearts and faces seemed closed to me, hardened by the ruthless struggle for the daily bread.

What a change from the warm tropics, where the warmth comes not only from the sun. How far away they were, my tropics. It was foolish to keep thinking of them now that the page was turned, but I couldn't help casting my mind back, feeling, as I did, like a lost dog without a master in this immense desert of a capital.

I had always thought I was solitary by nature, because I could not imagine going to sea any other way than alone. I realised now that solitude at sea was steeped in rich colours, sometimes violent, but always warm, which had nothing in common with this greyness, this total emptiness a man feels without a friend, lost in an indifferent and perpetually hurrying crowd.

In order to face what others call solitude a man must first attain a very high spiritual level – like Buddha, or the Apostles. As for myself ... poor chap, I would gladly have given ten years of my life to be able to sit for five minutes by the side of a good friend. Well, maybe not ten years, one mustn't exaggerate, but I would joyfully have given my precious sea chest to be able to warm my hand in Henry Wakelam's.

I believe that ashore, just like at sea, a man sometimes runs into periods of very heavy weather when he has to heave to unless he wants to come to grief. At sea it is all very simple: all you need is enough sea-room, and if anything goes there is always a way to repair the damage. But on land the manœuvre is made complicated by the fact that instead of sea-room you need bank notes, and they cannot be run off a duplicating machine.

Since my arrival I had written some twenty carefully worded letters in reply to advertisements for jobs in the *France-Soir*. But I was obviously not the only one offering his talents on the labour market, for so far there had been no reply from my prospective employers. True, my curriculum vitae was perhaps, not the most impressive in this civilised country!

Of course, I could always have found a labourer's job, but then I would almost certainly have been stuck, with very little chance of getting myself out into something else later on. No, a white-collar job is what I wanted, not because I am a snob – I was long past that stage, anyway – but because I could then look further than the end of my nose. I wanted a job which would give me time to look around me and from which I didn't get home dog-tired at night. Working in a factory may be charming if you already own your boat, but much too much like hard work if you have to build one from scratch.

Still … as Pierre Deshumeurs said quite rightly on board the *Snark* the day I broke the pricker for the primus inside the pressure valve: 'It's only the rich who worry.'

Now him I would really have liked to see again. I knew that he was in France, for a fellow I had known in Indo-China and into whom I had run by chance in the Jardin du Luxembourg, by the edge of the pond on which the children sail their boats, had told me that my old companion off the *Snark* was now growing roses in Grasse. I wrote to him at once, but the letter was 're-turned to sender', to the shabby little hotel in the 6th arondisse-ment where I had parked my precious sea chest on the first floor, waiting for better days. The disappointment shattered me com-pletely. Alone. Completely alone.

I wrote off to all the places along the coast where flowers are grown, and all I hoped was that the postmen knew their job: Menton, Nice, Saint, Jeannet, Vence, Cannes, Antibes, etc., and a week later a heavy envelope arrived, addressed in a hand which was familiar. Ten pages, and I read them breathlessly, again … and again. 'If you are broke write at once, and I will send you some money. France is a wonderful country, but tough, very tough. If you do not find work in Paris let me know immediately, I am your last hope whether you like it or not. And don't forget, old chap, your home is at Vence.'

An enormous ray of sunshine … an immense rainbow across the grey sky of Paris.

The wheel was starting to turn. It moved a fraction, for there, miraculously, in reply to one of my applications for a job, was a letter asking me to come for an interview on Monday at eight.

It came from the Laboratoires Midy (makers of Antigrippine, Algipan, etc.) where, from my very first visit, I sensed that atmosphere of respectablity and reliability which made me keen to get that job at all costs. But there were thirty-five of us applying for four vacancies!

On the following day twenty were already eliminated. This looked a bit like the battle for survival which I had heard people talk about, and I was beginning to understand why the French wear, like a mourning robe, that *serious* air to which I was not quite used yet. They obviously had plenty of reason!

At the end of the first week there were seven of us left in the running. If I had arrived in France slightly drowsy from having spent over thirty years in the tropics, watching the coconut palms sprout, my compatriots had certainly taken it upon themselves to wake me up with a start.

Finally, after two months' strict probation, I found myself one of the four survivors, promoted to the rank of 'Medical Visitor' (which deserves to be spelt with capital letters).

The weather had broken, the barometer was high. Not only had I found a pleasant employment with a firm of impeccable reputation which relieved me of material worry, but I found pleasant colleagues, people with a proper place in life. This lifted me out of the roaming existence I had led for so many years but for which I no longer had the slightest inclination, for I was heartily tired of never knowing what tomorrow was going to be like. Now, tomorrow was just like today, and I asked for no more. My pay dropped in as regular as clockwork at the end of each month, and I meant it when I told my employers that the desire to go to sea had left me, that it was part of the past, a colourful past, yes, but it interested me no longer, for France was a very beautiful country and a man could have friends here, too. So why look beyond the horizon?

I had found Pierre Deshumeurs again, that was great. And now I had another friend: Jean-Michel Barrault. We met quite by chance, but then it is nearly always by chance that one makes a friend. He took me to his home where I found children, a family, a warmth, something like a haven or refuge. Here I could spend an evening now and then, dropping in casually after work. It felt good to have a place like that to go to and hear the laughter of children.

My work was very active and gave me plenty of opportunity to walk and get back into good physical and mental condition. It consisted of visiting doctors and introducing them to the firm's products. This also involved answering technical questions on the use of new products, hence the probation period I mentioned earlier on.

Not only was the job as active as I could wish for, it also left me enough peace of mind to write my *Vagabond des Mers du Sud*. In fact, doctors only receive callers in the afternoons, rarely before two and only in exceptional cases after six, the happy medium lying between three and five o'clock.

So I had once again landed a job of solid gold, one of the very few professions which might enable me to see Henry and the other pals in the tropics again. Meanwhile it had turned winter in France and I was soon to see the snow fall for the first time in my life.

Let the snow descend in large flakes from a grey sky, I noticed it not; let the mud of the north (my territory) stick to the soles of my shoes, I didn't care. While I sat snug and warm in a cafe at the end of a day's work the mud and cold outside became my allies because they made me dream of *Marie-Thérèse's* bow wave casting out luminous rainbows under the sun of the Trade Winds, while her hull carved a wake of blue water studded with pearls. And from it there gradually emerged the vision of my new boat, more beautiful than all my other boats put together.

I could feel this boat growing within myself. A really fine boat, built to western standards, not from rotten planks tied together with string. Sea-fever ... no man can ever be cured of it, but I realised that it was better that way. I also understood that Jean-Michel and Dany Barrault were only too right when they said: 'Write your book while you can still see things with the eyes of an Easterner. Once France has absorbed you this may no longer be possible. You were born down there in the tropics, you will feel the need to go back there.'

4

The Wheel Turns

A year passed. With the manuscript finished and accepted by my publisher I quit my job as a medical rep to find another in the South of France where there was sun and ports full of boats.

I was now employed with the Yacht-Méditerranée agency where I proved to be a poor salesman: it is not enough to be able to haul on a sheet to sparkle as a salesman of second-hand boats, and I soon realised that for once I had not landed a plum job. That was the reverse of the coin whose other side was rather more attractive, for I had countless opportunities to brush up my knowledge of seamanship by handling a large number of yachts and sailing with friends. It is surprising how quickly one learns to sail on other people's boats and to take part in races under the command of a good skipper.

Finally, and above all, there was in Marseille a little slip of a woman called Françoise ...

When anyone asks her how we met, she gaily replies: 'At the cinema'. The fact is that our parents had been friends since childhood and used to explore Corsica together in their holidays. I remember well looking at the photograph of a little girl with curly hair in my father's album back in Indo-China. The little girl had grown up since those days and the fate which guides us all unbeknown to ourselves took it upon itself to bring us together. Though not 'at the cinema' as Françoise jokingly says, she had become my wife for better or for worse.

Now there were two of us working in the same direction, each with a lucky star over our heads, the wheel was starting to turn faster, and more smoothly, too, since the day I had run quite by chance (no, not by chance!) into this extraordinary little woman: apart from possessing all the necessary qualities that make an ideal wife, Françoise had solved all family problems with a single stroke by presenting me with three children by a previous marriage: three handsome, healthy youngsters who adopted me at once and aroused in me all the paternal feeling that had for so long lain dormant. So here I was at last with a complete family, all the lost time made up for. If this wasn't perfect bliss: slippers, a corner by the fire ...

But I have never been one to sit back and relax for long in the whole of my tumultuous life. Nor has Françoise either. She went to work, of course, because she did not feel that a married woman ought to be a 'kept woman'. I didn't disagree with her, for now the wheel was really turning and something told us that we had entered a period of fair winds during which we had to crowd on canvas to round the Cape before the weather turned ...

My *Vagabond des Mers du Sud* had just been published and the royalties started coming in. I had never seen so much money in all my life! Then the naval architect, Jean Knocker, introduced himself to us and proposed that he should design our new boat. He made his offer on one condition, which was extremely sensible and revealed him to be a man of great experience: that I, the owner, should first draw up a design unaided and then he, the architect, would make a proper plan out of my rough draft, taking into account all the principles of naval architecture.

Jean Knocker has experience in racing round the buoys, ocean racing and pure cruising. He is, therefore, not biased towards, and restricted by, just one aspect of sailing (like myself) but is sufficiently far-sighted to comprehend the complexity of problems involved in long-distance cruising, where a boat has to combine, as harmoniously as possible, the four fundamental elements which are the secret of all good sailing boats: strength, simplicity, safety and speed on all points of sailing. At least, this is Jean Knocker's view, and I share it.

Nevertheless, the final plans did not go altogether smoothly for the architect, owing to certain requirements which were difficult to reconcile.

After much deliberation we decided on a 34 ft double-ender, ketch-rigged, fast on all points (we hoped!) despite having as moderate a draught as possible. The prospect of extended cruising and the desire to take the children made me want very ample cabin space, with an after cabin protecting the central cockpit (the reasons for this choice are given in the appendix).

All this sounds very simple, but the correspondence exchanged over the planning of this boat would fill a small book, and the final plans dragged on for a whole year.

I would have to build the boat myself, of course. It would be in wood, cold moulded, which is convenient for amateur construction. But the first skin would be in 6 mm marine ply, laid straight over the final frames. This would make work easier by doing away with the bumps and hollows which are nearly always unavoidable when the first skin of laminations is laid on a mould which has insufficient members, and I would save a lot of time. The remaining skins would be made up of 3 mm laminations.

But it wasn't enough for me to dream about this boat; first of all Françoise and I would have to earn every penny towards building it. Nearly all the wood necessary was already bought ...

'If you write a book I bet you'll be off in another boat within five years.'

The words of Adolfo's prophecy danced before my windscreen and the roadside rushed past as I sped towards Chauffailles with my foot hard down, for it was a long drive from La Rochelle to Chauffailles (Saône-et-Loire). Something told me that he may have been right, provided we didn't drag our heels.

Françoise must have felt the same for I had had the impression that her voice trembled when she told me on the 'phone the night before: 'Bernard, I think this is really *important*, and I like the way he writes.'

Then she read me a letter consisting of six lines, a letter which sent a shock, like an electric current, running through my veins. I blew a kiss to my wife, settled my hotel bill and set off well before dawn behind the wheel of my big car.

For I now moved about in a big car like a respectable citizen, and like most street vendors I even had an official street vendor's licence which I needed to sell these cans of mine in public squares. As to what they contained, I should have liked to know that myself. Clear water, no doubt, with a little mysterious something added which made cars shine, provided a good dose of elbow grease was applied. In order to sell this product I found it convenient to express myself in hesitant French, because it sounded more respectable and people always liked listening to a 'noble stranger'. People are like that. In any case, I was better suited to selling cans than to selling boats.

And now, at last ... my sixth sense told me that it would soon be over, this roving life, always on the road, always in a different hotel, always away from Françoise and the children whom I could only see for two days every fortnight. True, France is a wonderful country, and I was only too ready to admit it, but I had so far not had the time even to listen to the birds singing.

'If you write a book ...' And I had written it. Jean Knocker had read it and offered to design a boat for me. And now there was this six-line letter, the gist of which was: 'I have read your book, come and see me, I think I can help.' Signed: J. Fricaud.

Three hundred pages to my book, six lines to Fricaud's letter. Six lines ... and a boat.

Driving as if in a dream, yet not too fast for I wanted to arrive in Marseille in one piece, I kept telling myself that it was true, without being able to believe it. And yet it *was* true. I did not telephone Françoise with the news, it was just too simple and, at the same time, too fantastic: thanks to Fricaud we were now emerging from a long, dark tunnel as though someone had waved a magic wand.

Jean Fricaud showed me round his large boiler works (250 employees), then he showed me *Sainte-Marthe*, a 36 ft steel boat (designed by Maurice Amiet), built ten years ago by his workmen and later brought back to Chauffailles for some alterations to the cockpit. And I had been astounded to see *for the first time* a steel yacht built properly: hoop-iron frames welded on edge instead of the traditional angle irons which are veritable rust traps. In this hull there was not a single corner which was inaccessible to the scraper and brush. After ten years in the Mediterranean the hull was still absolutely sound, without any of the little corners into which the owner of a steel boat dare not put his nose for fear of meeting the devil (rust).

Aboard *Sainte-Marthe* everything was simple, neat, solid and without surprises, like Fricaud himself, who reminded me of Henry Wakelam: a bulldozer capable of barging through a concrete wall if there was no way round it.

It was now mid-July, the factory was due to close in August and I was to spend that month on holiday aboard *Sainte-Marthe*, crewing for J. Fricaud. In this way I should have plenty of time to nose about the boat and let my impressions settle, so Fricaud, who did not want to influence me, had said. If, after spending a month on board the boat I felt that I was 'ripe for a steel hull' we would get to work when the factory re-opened and on the first of September I would join the two workmen who had built *Sainte-Marthe* to make up the team. Fricaud reckoned that the hull, decked and fitted with the two cabin tops, could be ready to be loaded on a trailer at the end of the year; that would be four months after starting the hull ...

As for the price ... here the *patron* had once more waved his magic wand: just the cost of the metal and the electrodes needed for welding, that would be all ... 'In this way,' Fricaud had explained, 'you will only have to make the masts and the sails.' Fortunately, I was already sitting down!

What's more, this boat would measure 39 ft instead of 36 ft! So much excitement, and all in one day, that's why I wanted to get to Marseille before telling Françoise.

I shall not go into great detail trying to explain to my readers why I suddenly condemned what I had worshipped before ... To start with, I have never 'worshipped' timber. I just 'put up with it', with all its major inconveniences like rot, ship-worms and leaks.

Besides, one cannot compare wood and steel from the point of view of strength: coming into the dry-dock at Hamburg our tanker had lightly scraped the edge of the dock, crushing a lifeboat hung in davits. This lifeboat, made of thin steel, had been repaired on board by jacking out the hull, which had been pushed in on one side as far as the centreline. True, there were several holes in it, but they were repaired with rivets. If it had been clinker-built, or made of moulded ply or fibreglass, this 28 ft boat would have been a total write-off, and I had had the feeling that it was saying to me: 'You have lost two wooden boats. Had they been steel, you could perhaps have saved the first, and certainly the second ...'

True, steel rusts if it is not adequately protected, but I had seen how big ships are maintained: nothing elaborate (a well-trained chimpanzee ... etc).

As for *Sainte-Marthe*, she had been deliberately neglected for ten years, because Jean Fricaud 'wanted to see what would happen'. Well, nothing had happened: the bottom showed some superficial pitting, especially round the waterline, but the topsides were absolutely sound. 'Just a coat of paint at the end of each season,' Fricaud said jokingly. But his workmen confirmed that it was true.

When the Van de Wieles returned from their trip round the world in *Omoo* they considered that a steel hull was not to be recommended for warm waters. But paints have been improved since then, and chemists, on behalf of the leading shipping companies, are continuously searching for better, more adhesive and more resistant paints.

Omoo's paint came off in big sheets at times, and when it came to cleaning the bottom the couple had to scrape the hull right down to the metal several times.

But the paint on the tanker which brought me to Europe never flaked. Still, we used to spend several hours painting her before every trip, and she did fifteen knots. Other ships do twenty knots and are always painted before they leave again, for freighters cannot afford to waste any time. But they use high-quality products and I would simply have to do what they do and turn straight away to the makers of 'marine' paints. After some years of trial and error I would be sure to find a good make to which I could stick.

One might argue that in the case of merchant ships the thickness of their hulls alone is protection against corrosion. That is true: 15 or 20 mm steel as used in ships lasts longer than 5 or 6 mm steel as used in yachts. But I have learned that during the last war small escort vessels and submarine hunters were built in 5 or 6 mm steel (over strong frames) and that those which escaped the torpedoes are still afloat. And they get scant attention by comparison with the care a man can bestow on his yacht (without actually going round with a brush in his hand from morning to night!).

As planned, work on the boat got under way at the beginning of September. The first three days were taken up with the drawing of the plans in all their glory. One week later I finished the last frames. They were of 50 × 5 mm hoop iron, bent edgewise in a small worm screw press operated by hand like a vice.

Meanwhile, Alexandre, the team foreman, and Démurger, the welder, built the keel: 15 mm for the sides and 20 mm steel for the bottom, with a partition to coincide with each floor frame.

It all looked nice and strong and the work progressed fast, for we worked nine hours a day, five and a half days a week.

We then passed on to assembling the floor frames, and two weeks after the first whistle had sounded the keel was placed between two large wheels set up vertically on a level floor. Then the frames were fitted in place. Next came the stem and stern, both in 100 × 20 mm hoop iron. I pitied the quayside that was going to be clouted by that stem. Plumb line, spirit level ... and when Françoise came for a long weekend to see the dear child three weeks after work was first started, she could hardly believe her eyes: the frame was welded, the first sheet of the garboard strake (6 mm) already aligned with the keel and the stringers.

I have seen workmen work in my time, but never before like this. The whole thing was crazy! The factory was humming like a beehive, but there was no idle chatter; and it took me five weeks to discover that there was actually a foreman. He did not stroll round the works with a pencil behind his ear and a spanner in his left hand, but he worked like the other two hundred and forty-nine workers. And here was I believing quite sincerely that I deserved a medal for having moved myself a bit in a factory in Durban! Françoise thought that I had lost some weight ...

Three weeks to the day after Françoise's brief visit the final skin went on (5 mm) and we now got down to the deck frames, 50 × 5 mm hoop iron and set on edge like the frames.

Up till now the sheets of metal had been spot welded by electric arc, that is to say held in place against each other by spots of welding wire (at Chauffailles they call it 'seam tacking'). Only when the deck and hull were completely assembled were the seams, inside and out, to be sealed by continuous welding. All seams were welded in a horizontal position, which meant under optimum conditions, thanks to the hoops which allowed the boat to be turned at will.

The steel sheets for the hull were first of all sand-blasted on both sides with the help of a hand-held electric sander with an abrasive disk which rotates at 6,000 rpm. This method, while being as efficient as granite sand blasting, is much cheaper: it took me 50 hours to sand all the hull sheets on both sides. Scale is well-known for setting up electrolytic action in salt water due to the difference in potential between it and steel. It is therefore wise to get rid of it before painting the hull.

Alexandre, Démurger and I forged ahead as far as the laying of the deck, but when we started on the superstructure the mad pace slowed down a bit, because we were now entering a phase of details which took time. We had to 'think' more. We could not afford any mistakes in welding on a sheet cleat or a mooring bitt; the angle at which the cockpit drains were to be installed needed working out, etc.

At last ... in mid-December she was finished, complete with hatches, mooring bitts (five in all), sheet cleats and hand rails on either side of both cabins, horses for both mizzen and staysail, two watertight bulkheads and four built-in lockers, each fitted with an inspection hatch to permit regular painting. These four watertight lockers (with a total volume of 1,200 litres) would be used as reserve fresh water tanks and for storage of some of the provisions. But their main purpose was to contribute to the safety of the boat in case that particular part of the hull should ever happen to be banged on the rocks for too long ...

The keel was hollow, as on all metal hulls, but instead of filling it with concrete mixed with shot (the traditional method) I intended to fill it with pigs of iron held in place by strong bars across the floor stringers, so that they couldn't be dislodged in case of a capsize. Why did I choose to have this internal ballast?

First of all, the boat could then be careened[1] in a spot where there was no slipway or which was not tidal. Besides, it would make it possible to do long repair jobs very cheaply: in the Antilles I had seen a schooner of some hundred tons which had had all her planks and frames replaced while she was afloat! They had careened her for nearly two months ...

But the great asset of removable ballast lies in the fact that it can be jettisoned to save the boat if she runs aground. Three

---

[1] To careen a boat means to lay her on her side in the water by pulling down on the mast(s) till the keel emerges. This cannot be done if the keel contains fixed ballast. The big sailing ships of the past employed this method of careening in tideless waters or where there was no dry dock.

or four tons less can work miracles. Just a small detail one thinks of when one has lost two boats in that way.

I fervently hoped that I should never have to face that sort of emergency, but it was safer to leave myself enough elbow room from the start, for one never knows beforehand what fate may have in store, and it may turn out rather tough.

'The ways of the Lord are wonderful ...' But this time I would prove myself worthy of this boat, which Françoise and I christened *Joshua*, in honour of the great yachtsman Joshua Slocum.

5
Afloat at Last

Icy roads in the Chauffailles region put Joshua's transport by lorry to Lyon back until mid-February. In Lyon *Joshua* took her first bath in the river Saône and then had to wait for some ten days for a tow down river, because she had no engine.

Finally we reached Marseille on the 2nd March after an uneventful trip down the Rhône, behind a barge. We experienced a few twinges of anxiety, perhaps, passing through the locks in a mistral, but those barge skippers are past masters in the art of manœuvring!

The 2nd March came and went sooner than expected ... I had to press on as never before. People always say that, but this time it was really true, for the first lot of pupils for our sailing school were due to come on board on the 1st May, roughly two months from then.

At that time *Joshua* resembled a gigantic lobster (she was painted red), hideously high in the water, without ballast, without mast, completely bare inside. As for the motor, well, we intended to make do without one for that first season. You can't do everything in two months. Four sturdy oars would solve the problem of getting in and out of the harbour in calms, we thought. And apart from flat calms, we wanted ours to be an out and out sailing school. It is certainly not an ideal state of affairs to be without an engine in the Mediterranean, but during this critical stage in my life the main thing was to work quickly and for things to be strong. This principle was sacred, so far as the rigging was concerned. Everything else could be left to scull along as best it might, but not the rigging. One thing was certain, I was going to have to keep my nose to the grindstone if I wanted to be ready in time ...

Thank goodness I was not short of funds, for my prospective crew members had paid deposits. This enabled me to hire a chap to give me a hand, the only one available in the entire vicinity of the Vieux Port (the yacht harbour of Marseille). I soon found out why he was available and nearly passed out at the sight of his tools: a small plane the size of a child's toy, a saw that had not been set for goodness knows how long, and completely rusty at that, an extraordinary screwdriver that was both hammer and gimlet at the same time, not to speak of some saw-toothed chisels (two in all, which was a bit better at least). Still ... this fine fellow reminded me vaguely of the time when I was a chippy at Durban...

As it happened, Philippe Puisais moored up alongside *Joshua* a week later. He had built his cold-moulded hull (a Cape Horn class) somewhere near Tours and sailed her to Martinique. But for Philippe my May crew would have had to sleep on bare floor boards!

Little by little the accommodation took shape, as did the outside, but there it was very much touch and go: there were no masts to be found anywhere. I had had the feeling that it was going to be difficult, but not as bad as that. Eventually the situation was saved by M. Romieux, director of the Saint-Nicolas boat yard, who remembered a 58 ft telegraph pole which he thought might possibly make a temporary main mast. I didn't need asking twice! On with the track, the crosstrees, the shrouds made with wire clamps – life is too short to start splicing wire rope.

One week later *Joshua*'s main mast pointed proudly towards the sky. It was stepped on the keel and measured 57 ft, 49 ft above deck. The mizzen mast was to follow shortly, thanks to a friend who worked with E. D. F. But here again, it was touch and go. Phew! What a relief it was to have her rigged.

Joshua's masts were solid poles, then, a bit heavy perhaps, but at least there was no danger of them coming unglued as hollow masts can do. The mizzen mast (that is the one from E.D.F.) had been impregnated with creosote under pressure like a telegraph pole. This was to protect it from rot. As for M. Romieux's main mast, I smothered it in Cuprinol to protect it from rot until it might be replaced.

'I have a feeling that this is a permanent make-shift', M. Romieux said to me when he came to inspect the work ... 'In any case, no-one made a fuss about it in the old days: all masts were solid, and they didn't often break.'

I feel the same way about it: a solid mast has to bend like a fishing rod before it breaks. Besides, the difference in price counts for something – telegraph poles only cost 10 francs a metre!

Work on the boat had never let up since it started; it was like perpetually running for the last bus. But a fortnight before the

first crew was due to come on board Henry Wakelam dropped his
hook alongside *Joshua*, thank goodness ... Henry, that tower of
strength, had come just in time to lend a hand in the final spurt:
  'You French bastard, I'll bet you could do with a hand ...'
  'You bet!'

We had parted at Martinique four years before. Since then, Henry
had sailed *Wanda* to England, found a job there and met Ann.
And here they were at Marseille, married, and finding *Wanda*
rather cramped.

The two women took to each other on sight, and Henry and I
were pleased. They gossipped and showed each other their
clothes; it was quite touching. Then they passed on to more
serious matters, sewing sleeping bags out of old sheets for the
crews of our sailing school, making curtains, cushions and bed-
spreads for *Joshua*. Meanwhile I got down to splicing and rigging
up sheet tackles, and Henry saw to the engine.

An engine indeed ... a small 7 h.p., two-stroke *Sotecma*, a present
from a pal who did not need it any more.

Having decided that I would not have the time that year to
bother myself over installing an engine I had shelved the idea,
but Henry insisted that he could instal it in less than ten days,
including the shaft and propeller, and without putting the boat
on the slip! Knowing Henry, I gave him *carte blanche* ...

Those pleasant evenings in our flat, which we shared with
Henry and Ann, were spent talking and planning in the way you
do sitting snugly in the cabin of a sailing boat moored safely at
the end of her chain. The Wakelams' plans were precise enough:
they wanted to find an old steel hull somewhere in the Mediterranean, fit it out, sell *Wanda* which had become too cramped for
two, and with their new boat do one or two seasons' sailing
instruction on the sunny coasts of France.

The continual whirl in which we had lived for the past two
months was coming to an end. One evening the cabins were
ready, swept, scrubbed and tidied. The engine was installed, the
shaft aligned, the propeller fitted. But the stern gland posed a
a problem which Henry had not entirely solved up till then:
we left it till the next day.

Still, *Joshua* was ready, engine or no engine. The sails, delivered by Mezza the night before, as promised, four days before the deadline, were bent on. But what a crazy rush! It was incredible what an effort three people have to make to transform a naked steel hull into a finished boat in two months.

It was a very fine morning with a light northerly breeze when we went out under sail for the first time. Up until then *Joshua* had just been a work site in the Vieux Port. That day, she became 'my boat'. This moment when a skipper first takes possession of his boat is sweet and at the same time terrible. A feeling of great peace sweeps over you, and that is why I wanted to be alone with Henry. He can hear a boat speak and participated with me in the communion without uttering a word that was not absolutely neccessary for manœuvring. You have to be able to listen to the silence, the apparent silence as the wind glides through the sails, the murmur of the water running along the hull and leaving a turbulence behind the rudder, this silence filled with all the small, scarcely audible sounds emitted by a boat that is coming to life. All this you can only appreciate in solitude, or in the company of one who knows how to listen to silence and comprehend the meaning in it.

It is only the real seaman who can make himself part of the wonderful state of equilibrium which surrounds him and understand, bit by bit, the meaning of the long conversations between the hull and the sea, the sails and the wind.

Joshua tacked well and was quick on the helm. She gathered speed as soon as a puff made her heel a bit more. Listening to the sounds of my beautiful boat, looking at her slicing bow and her rushing wake, I knew that we had, indeed, emerged from the long tunnel. True, the struggle was not over, it never is, that is quite normal, and it is better that way, but the worst of the medicine had been swallowed, to the last mouthful, just over three years from the demise of *Marie-Thérèse II* ... a miracle.

In a few days the first of my sailing school crews were due to descend on my 'sanctuary', and then the spell would probably be broken for a while, depending on my crew; if they turned out to be sailors, *Joshua* would remain 'my boat' and become theirs. For 'the others' *Joshua* would simply be a piece of apparatus for getting to know the sea, and I hoped that they too would learn to listen to the Silence in which you can hear the Wind, the Sea and the Boat.

The first group deposited their sacks on board on the morning of the 1st May. I must admit that I was almost sick with worry, expecting to see a lot of landlubbers step on deck ... But my lucky star was watching over me: three of my first crew were real seamen who immediately hit the right note. Phew! They took to leaving and entering the harbour and coming alongside the jetty under sail alone, without a hitch. My crew was keen and so was I, and we got the best out of *Joshua*, who was as keen as the rest of us put together. What extraordinary luck to hit on the best crew of the season during the very first week! The engine worked, but we ignored it – it was so much like more the *real* thing to check her way by using the sails, and to drop astern alongside the jetty by backing the staysails and the mizzen.

The season ended in October. What a relief it was to know that *Joshua* would not budge for another six months, and barnacles would be growing peacefully on her mooring chain ... Françoise, too, was exhausted from her work at the hospital, plus several tiring jobs for the sailing school (provisioning, looking after latecomers, etc.,) and we dreamed more than ever of the Pacific, the Pacific which we did not yet know, with its eternal sun, its atolls and green lagoons of crystal-clear water. It was certainly wonderful to be able to dream in peace, knowing that the children were well-fed ...

Early in May the following year *Shafhai*, the Wakelam's new ketch, began her first sailing school season, *Joshua* her second. Our two boats kept close together, much as Henry and I had done in the old days. Occasionally we met up with Jean Bluche's *Chimère*, Fred Debel's *Tereva* and Pierre Deshumeur's *Vencia*. During nocturnal reunions at various ports between Marseille and Corsica we would all make plans for sailing to the Antilles and the Pacific, leading that happy life of gregarious sea birds of which Henry and I had dreamt for so long. At last our dreams were coming true! *Joshua*, in any case, was to leave at the end of the season and wait for the others in the Canary Islands.

6

Towards the Tropics

Joshua had to be fitted out during September if she was to try and
get out of the Mediterranean before the onset of winter. That was
without allowing for the countless small details which always
have to be seen to before a long voyage ... True, after two seasons
of sailing instruction our boat was ready from truck to keel, as
one says. But this is only a manner of speaking, for a sailing boat
is never really ready, as any cruising man well knows. But he also
knows that by trying to prepare things too well does, in fact, do
no more than continue to polish what is already bright, while
losing sight of what *really matters*: to go to sea with everything fair
and square, not to be a maniac for perfection. For he will always
find sufficient time at sea and in his first ports of call to put right
any small details that have been left unfinished.

Joshua was ready to set out on her trip round the world reasonably
well prepared in mid-September, but her crew was still bogged
down with financial and family problems which could not be
sorted out inside a week.

Our two boys went back to their boarding school near Albi
(promising solemnly to work hard), our daughter was put in
charge of Françoise's sister, and relatives offered to look after
all three during their school holidays.

In the end, everything fell neatly into place, Françoise found
a tenant for her flat and ... we bought a piece of land in the Midi
so that we could have a corner which really belonged to us, where
we could pitch our tent afterwards ... But why in France, instead
of finding a nice little atoll in the Pacific? Because, let's face it,
France is a very beautiful country, one of the most beautiful
countries in the world, and we sensed it subconsciously. And,
anyway, roaming just for the sake of it meant nothing to us.
That is roughly what I used to do in the days when I sailed single-
handed, and I only found it half-satisfactory.

On our wedding day, a friend said to me sadly:

'Poor old Bernard, now your goose is cooked. Women are like cats, they like walls ...'

Quite likely, but I, too, like walls, so long as I don't feel imprisoned by them. After all, freedom is largely a matter of personal interpretation. I had plenty of time to learn that in the days when I roamed the seas like a vagabond, without any fixed aim.

Well, here I was, no longer a vagabond, having put down roots, and I did not regret it. For it was nice to have a wife, children, a house (not yet built, so my friend might still live in hope ...)

One splendid night, on 13th October 1963, to be exact, Françoise and I left Marseille, happy but completely exhausted. The weather forecast promised fine weather, and *Joshua* glided towards Gibraltar in a light northwesterly breeze, as soft as the caressing touch of a gentle Trade Wind, on a sea as calm as a millpond. This is how we like to get under way: in fine weather.

Two days later, after a spell of dead calm, *Joshua* rushed headlong back to Marseille, her tail between her legs, chased by a very angry mistral that had dropped on us as we left the Gulf of Foss. Confounded Mediterranean!

At first we hove-to comfortably with the staysail aback and the mizzen close-reefed, a pressure lamp of 250 candle-power lashed to the shrouds. But this state of affairs became dangerous when, in the middle of the night, a small freighter took it into her head that she *must* 'render assistance'.

I suppose there is a light signal which says: 'All's well on board, leave us in peace and give us a wide berth.' But, unfortunately, we did not know it, so we turned off our lamp, eased the sheets and fled towards Marseille to put our precious *Joshua* safely out of the reach of any well-intentioned freighters who might be overflowing with sympathy for nutshells battling against the unleashed elements ... Phew! Nevertheless, we felt better tucked away in the yacht harbour of the Vieux Port.

Some ships put you in mind of a fable by La Fontaine: watching over his sleeping friend, a bear, with the best intentions, crushed a fly sitting on the farmer's nose with a sweep of his mighty paw.

This is how Harry Pidgeon was run down, in the middle of the night, by a friendly freighter that insisted on 'rescuing' him while he was sailing along peacefully with the helm lashed, not bothering anybody. The result was that *Islander*'s bowsprit was smashed.

The same kind of surprise was meted out on one occasion in bright daylight: *Yan*, a 40 ft steel ketch, had three shrouds sliced through by a ship seeking to 'render assistance' while the Housiauxs were having a siesta down below and *Yan*, with her helm lashed, was idling towards the Antilles before the Trades.

The rules of Safety at Sea demand that yachts shall carry the cold flag N–C ('I need assistance'). This is a very wise precaution in view of the steady flow of newcomers to the sport of yachting.

But surely there must be another code (I am ashamed to say that I don't know of it) which says: 'All's well, do not disturb.'

Joshua left Marseille once more on 20th October in fine weather and with a favourable, or rather a non-committal forecast: light, variable winds with no gales in the offing. We were hoping that the weather would hold and no depression would sneak in and pounce on us in the Gulf of Lions. Meteorologists do their best, but their task is not an easy one in this part of the world. We accordingly adopted the technique of 'port hopping' which is very desirable in the Mediterranean, where the weather can deteriorate with disconcerting rapidity, especially at the onset of winter.

We crossed the Gulf of Lions without incident in conditions of feeble breezes and occasional fog, helped by the engine which pushed us along at 2·2 knots in a dead calm. We called first at Sète, then at Rosas on the other side of the Cap de Creus, where we discovered the joys of exploring all the little bars on our first contact with Spanish soil. The wine was excellent and very cheap and the cost of living nothing compared with France.

With our ears glued to the radio to pick up the weather forecasts we continued to hug the coast, running for shelter at the slightest grimace in the sky. What an absurd stretch of water! It is marvellous when seen from the safety of a jetty, but possessed of the devil as soon as you want to get somewhere.

Gerbault made the long passage from Cannes to Gibraltar in one go and without an engine. I must take off my hat to him, for the Mediterranean is an exhausting sea, even if there are two of you: you have to trim sails all the time, watch for the slightest

Bernard Moitessier with Youki

Joshua under construction at Chauffailles

TOP *Joshua*'s main cabin

BOTTOM The 'perch'

ABOVE Françoise Moitessier
at Tahiti

LEFT *Joshua* under sail

OPPOSITE A sailing-boat hull
of the same type as *Joshua*
in the hoops with her keel in
the air

ABOVE Coupling up the wheel steering to the tiller

BELOW The hollow keel

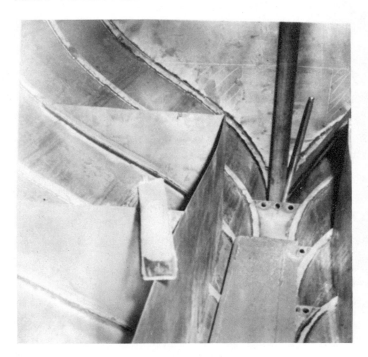

ABOVE Boats at Annam made of braided bamboo, their rudders raised

LEFT On board my first junk, repairing a piece of rigging at sea

LEFT Careening the *Snark*
in Indonesia

BELOW LEFT *Marie-Thérèse II*
before leaving for Mauritius

OPPOSITE *Marie-Thérèse*

ABOVE Las Palmas: our three children in the dinghy

BELOW Paul Johnson's *Venus*

RIGHT Pierre Deshumeur connecting the steering vane

BELOW Henry and Ann Wakelam

ABOVE A turtle harpooned from the dinghy

LEFT At Barrington

OPPOSITE TOP At Barrington

OPPOSITE BOTTOM Pelicans

ABOVE A sea iguana

BELOW A large green iguana

OPPOSITE Gale in the South Atlantic

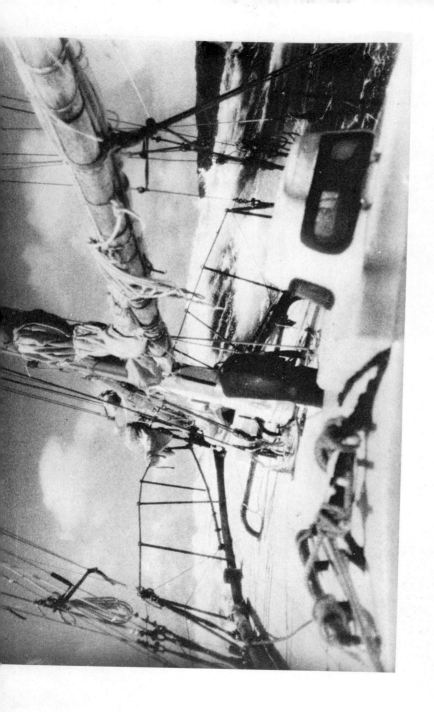

ABOVE Gale in the Atlantic

BELOW Wave

puffs, keep your eyes open for ships and above all fishermen, of whom there are a great number along the Spanish coast.

In my opinion a yacht's lights are neither bright enough nor *explicit enough* to ward off all danger of collision.

For this reason we left no exterior lights burning on board *Joshua* while we were sailing offshore and had some wind (which meant we could manœuvre), and while we were awake. (But we always put lights on for entering a port.)

Imagine a car with its headlights on driving along a straight road while a pedestrian ahead of it is walking on the road or about to cross it. To avoid being run over our pedestrian 'goes about' before the car reaches him and then 'goes about' again to cross the road behind the car. The car steering a straight course is a ship with all its regulation lights on and visible from far off, while the pedestrian represents a sailing yacht with all her lights extinguished.

This one-way game of hide-and-seek is made easy by the fact that all moving ships carry two white lights, high above the water and visible through an angle of 220°.

These two white lights, which can be made out from some ten miles off, are placed at different heights, the after light being higher than the forward one, so that they indicate at a single glance the ship's course. They make it possible to visualize the ship as though it were plain daylight. And one can never go wrong by passing astern of a vessel larger than one's own. (If all pedestrians passed behind cars …)

Naturally this only applies if the wind conditions allow the yacht to make headway and to manœuvre. If not (in a dead calm or with the boat hove-to) we used to hang a 250 candle-power paraffin lamp of the Alladin or Optimus type in the shrouds. This was visible from 8 to 10 miles off and gave ships plenty of time to take their bearings and keep clear of what was then a *visible object*.

As for the custom, which is very popular among yachtsmen, of shining a torch at the sails to warn a vessel that has come too close, this can have dangerous consequences.

A friend of mine, an officer in the Merchant Navy, once saw a conical shape vaguely lit by the moonlight, rear up about 200 yards off his bows. There aren't any rocks between Marseille and the Balearics, but he obeyed the natural reflex of a seaman who suddenly notices a danger dead ahead and put the helm hard down!

He then had a look through his binoculars and made out the sails of a small yacht lit intermittently by a torch, about 60 to 100 yards away off one bow.[1]

'If that clot had signalled long beforehand by shining the beam of his torch at the ship instead of playing at phantoms I would not have had any cause for anxiety. And there is another important fact which I would like you to point out to your yachting friends: *this yacht was carrying full regulation lights*, I noticed this after the first shock had passed, but they appeared so dim in the moonlight that I had not noticed them ...'

Moonlight ... *there's a danger* to all small yachts. It brings to mind the case of *Kurun* who was run down at dawn, from astern, despite showing a stern light and with her cabin lights shining through the port-holes. This happened off Madeira, and the Portuguese captain threw up his arms repeating 'La luna ... la luna ...'

Indeed, 'la luna ...' is our worst enemy when we encounter a ship, for the glow from an oil lamp is indistinguishable from the reflection of moonlight on the sea.

Pierre Auboirous and René Blondeau, two single-handed yachtsmen whom we were to meet in the Canaries later on, narrowly missed being run down in the moonlight though they, too, were showing a white light. But their light was provided by a storm-lantern of very low candle-power, and the first thing Blondeau bought at Las Palmas was a 250 candle-power pressure lamp, the only reliable defence against ships, particularly if the moon joins in.

I hope that the authorities who decide on measures for safety

---

[1] A good pair of binoculars help to remove any doubts once the lights of a ship have been spotted with the naked eye. Our binoculars are 7 × 50. They have very good luminosity, and though they are 15 years old (Krauss) they have rendered us invaluable services on entering ports at night. In my opinion good-quality binoculars of large magnifi- make navigation much safer. But it is best not to go for a magnification greater than 7 × 50 if one wants a good luminosity, which is indispensable for night sailing.

at sea will pardon us if we adopted measure which did not always conform with the rules, but of all the dangers which threaten a yacht, collision with a ship is probably the only crime for which fate, though habitually easy-going, may inflict the death penalty without reprieve.

Once again taking our hats off (metaphorically) to Gerbault, we reached Gibraltar on the last day of the year, having spent Christmas off Alicante ... What a business this fantastic Mediterranean is! Still, we didn't complain too much, for it can also be kind during its good moments (which are short in winter). As for Spanish ports, we found them good on the whole, especially Alicante, which is very sheltered and where yachts are allocated a berth at a safe distance from the 40 to 60 ton trawlers.

Another advantage which Spain offers is that along this coast-line where fishing is so important slipways are good and well-organised. We shipped the boat and cleaned her bottom at Tarragona for an incredibly reasonable figure: about 150 Francs (the equivalent of roughly £13) for 10 days out of the water and doing all the work ourselves.

What else is there to say? Not much except that we were happy to have at last reached the Atlantic coast, where sailing would be more enjoyable, much less tiring and nerve-racking, in other words much more like the real thing. (Françoise was waiting for proof ...)

As for land-locked seas, we had had enough of them!

7
In the Open Sea

Here we were at last at the gates to the Atlantic. Our morale was high, even though it was winter: no more coastal navigation, at least not for a long time, and then it would be different from what we had done so far. Long live the Ocean with its sea-room, its unbroken horizon and the promise of long daily runs which it held out to us.

But not so fast – first there would be Casablanca, our next port of call, where my parents lived. That is always providing bad weather along the African coast did not force us to point our bows to sea, towards Madeira or the Canaries. How nice it was to be able to say to yourself: 'If all goes well, we will go into Casa. If not, out to sea we go, to the open sea that stretches as far as the Canaries.'

It is almost impossible to beat out of the Straits into the Atlantic because the general current flows into the Mediterranean at an average speed of 1·5 knots and becomes stronger under the influence of a westerly wind. Eric Hiscock, well-known through his books and his long trips round the world, was beaten back to Gibraltar six or seven times in succession trying to leave that port during a spell of southwesterly winds, which would have enabled *Wanderer* to make a cracking passage to England, once through the Strait. But first you have to get through ...

After a week's stay at Gibraltar, where we were watching the clouds racing towards Marseille, we suddenly got a nice easterly breeze with a good weather forecast.[1]

---

[1] The weather report is posted up at the Harbourmaster's Office. You can also telephone from the small look-out on top of the office and ask for a weather forecast from the central met office. The officials there are very helpful. Besides, radio-signal chart No. 6253 shows the times and wave-lengths on which weather reports from various ports are broadcast, among them Tangier, Casablanca and Agadir. Finally, volumes 195 and 196 on meteorological broadcasts give general information and a list of stations broadcasting regular weather forecasts (for the whole world, I believe, but we had not yet got these on board).

'Quick Françoise, we're leaving!'

'But I've still got some potatoes to buy, and a bottle of perfume for your mother ...'

'Forget it, we're leaving.'

Françoise sulked a bit, but she knew that it would be fatal not to take immediate advantage of a fair wind.

We were lucky and got out into the Atlantic before sunset, still pushed along by a nice little breeze which died away during the second half of the night. The following day was calm, but *Joshua* was already far out. Then the wind came up again, heading us, of course, and we settled down to a beat with the coast to port and the open sea to starboard. In fact, there wasn't really any wind to speak of, just a gentle breeze, hardly rippling the sea.

What relaxing sailing compared to what we did in the Mediterranean! All down the Moroccan coast, everything was so simple and uncomplicated: *Joshua* made one board towards the coast during the day, and another towards the open sea after nightfall. This coast with its barely identifiable landmarks, bordered by low dunes which are hidden in the mornings by fine-weather mist, is downright dangerous if flirted with at close quarters. The white sand dunes in the south-east fail to reflect the sun during the first half of the day, and they come surging up suddenly quite close at hand from behind a line of breakers. Many ships have found this out very much to their cost and have given rise in others to 'a holy fear of the low coasts and the sound custom of getting out the sextant several times a day'.

After an eneventful passage which once again reconciled us with the sea, *Joshua* rounded the harbour mole of Casablanca around midnight, full and by in a nice force 2 to 3 breeze.

Pleasant sailing ... well, that was true in a way. But I had hardly ever since my beginnings in Indo-China felt as insecure as I did during the hour before that night entry into an unknown port. For we remembered the terrible drama that befell our friends of the yacht *Altair* several years earlier, when she was battered to pieces in these selfsame waters by an enormous roller, which came from nowhere and washed two members of the crew overboard before driving the boat ashore. There were about 4 fathoms of water under her keel, but it was nevertheless enough to knock up some freak waves amid the general swell.

On our left, there was the low, dangerous coast. It is *very dangerous* because it lacks any landmarks, and judging distance at night is difficult. (The weather bureau at Casablanca had promised no swell, otherwise we would have moored in 10 fathoms and waited till dawn).

Ahead of us were the harbour lights, completely merged with the lights of the town behind and difficult to identify despite our good night glasses. There were several lit buoys outside the harbour, but they played at hide-and-seek in the swell (there was some swell, of course) and their flashing signals could not be seen from the deck of a small yacht until they were quite close.

Of course there was also the hand-bearing compass, which has not been invented for nothing, but one cannot rely on it for very accurate angles. At last we were moored in a good port, and I dreamed of a transistorised echo sounder running on dry batteries which would enable me simply to read a dial rather than stop the boat as I have to do with *Joshua*'s traditional sounding method.

On board my last boat, *Marie-Thérèse II*, I had a cheap, home-made job, a cigar-shaped piece of lead weighing 5 or 6 lbs with small fins to keep it down without stopping the boat (like certain sinkers used for mackerel fishing).

When approaching land the device was lowered at the end of some 20 fathoms of very thin stainless steel wire run from a drum. The vibrations transmitted by the line when the lead touched the mud was warning that the coast was approaching. The line was then adjusted to a minimum depth.

But I hoped to equip *Joshua* with an echo-sounder less clumsy than my home-made lead cigar ...

There was no hurry now. *Joshua* was to spend the winter in Casablanca, where the local yacht club had provided us with a safe mooring in pleasant and extremely gay company. The club members are really keen sailors who go out every weekend even if a howling gale whistles through the rigging, and many of them perform quite admirable feats of seamanship in leaving their moorings under sail alone, without a hitch and as though it were the most natural thing in the world. A real pleasure to watch.

We felt at home in this nautical atmosphere, and since we were now on the right side of the straits we could afford to spend several pleasant months there before once again pointing *Joshua*'s nose towards the horizon.

But life was all go, and here we went again: finances were worrying us. We should have to find some extra cash quickly.

So off I went to find some work, as in the days of *Marie-Thérèse II*. The trouble in Morocco is that it is illegal for a noble foreigner to take a paid employment without a work permit, and they are issued in a mere trickle. But it all worked out in the end, thanks to the fact that there are no definite provisions made in Moroccan law for those who do odd jobs, which is not classified as work. It is nevertheless wise not to attract the authorities' attention by excessive zeal. So I pottered with discretion and without overdoing it.

Françoise, for her part, contributed actively towards keeping the pot boiling, for she found a temporary job and worked away in her white overalls with such optimism that it was a pleasure to watch. But I considered it wise to remind her of the advice given to me by an old Chinese who was my friend when I was a young man: 'My young friend,' he said, 'remember that money is saved in two ways: first you get it, and then you hang on to it.'

Four months passed and we used them to the full. Our daughter, Beatrice, was to join us before her summer holidays started. The kitty was replenished, the bilges were full of rice and tins. What's more, I expected to get a cheque from my publishers, and then our two boys were going to join us by plane at Las Palmas (in the Canaries) at the beginning of the summer holidays.

At the beginning of May everything was ready: we had scrubbed the boat on the ebb (this is easy in the harbour at Casablanca where the tidal fall is over 6 feet). The rest of the boat had received two coats of paint, and two water tanks out of four were filled with fresh water (165 gallons in all), for there were to be five of us on board: besides Beatrice, who had arrived the week before, Loick Fougeron and Claude Laffon were coming with us to the Canaries.

Loick, a dyed-in-the-wool seaman, is one of those friends whom we are just glad to see after a week as after ten years: 'Françoise! It's Loick! Have you eaten? Sit down, we'll cook you some eggs ... Here's the key, come back when you like ... Oh come on now, you must be out of your mind, you're not staying at a hotel! ...'

He had crossed the Atlantic with Jean Lemasson in a decked whaler. After an interlude at Dakar (to find a job and get in funds again) and a stay at the Cape Verde Islands they had sailed on as far as Martinique. Now that he was a family man Loick lived in Casablanca, but from time to time he accompanied a cruising yacht as far as Las Palmas to rediscover the uninterrupted horizon and the taste of salt water which no seaman can ever forget.

Claude, once a pilot in the war, was now a dentist in Morocco and went in for dinghy sailing, hoping to have a cruising boat some time in the future.

We did not regret having taken him on as a crew for he was untiring, always cheerful and certainly good at handling a heavy boat.

But I am surprised to see that I have forgotten to introduce the most important member of our crew: Youki. She was a small bitch which a friend in Gibraltar had given us. I became so attached to her that the yacht club members called her 'Youki Moitessier'!

8

The Fickle Trades

All was ready except the wind, which had been obstinately contrary for over a week. Despite the approaching summer, depressions were chasing each other almost without interruption to the
north of the Azores, bringing dull weather with sou'westerly
winds to the Moroccan coast, interrupted by very short clear
periods. These were too short for us to 'sneak out' without being
caught.

Map in hand so that we could follow the path of the depressions
Loick and I telephoned the central weather bureau twice a day.
One of the boffins seemed to have taken a personal interest in
presenting *Joshua* with good weather conditions. He now recognised our voices at the other end of the line ...

'Ah, it's you, *Joshua* ... It's a good thing you called me early
this morning, I've news for you ...'

'Is it moving off at last?'

'It' was the stationary low which had been sitting north of the
Azores for several days, undermining our morale.

'Yes, it has quite unmistakably moved towards Portugal since
last night, and the other one is about to break up, the report is
definite on that.'

'The other one' was a slow-moving depression which had been
forming north-west of the Azores.

'And ... there won't be a third one, creeping up on us, from
further west, will there? The barometer has hardly risen since
yesterday ...'

'Nothing is forecast from the west. Not for the moment ... Listen,
Joshua, if you want my advice, I think this is the green light.'

Loick hurriedly telephoned Claude, then dashed off to get
some round loaves from a baker he knew. Meanwhile, Françoise
and I saw to all those final details which precede every departure,
while 13-year old Beatrice finished the domestic chores.

Getting out of this narrow harbour under sail alone was made
easier by the fact that we were moored to two bouys. There
was no anchor to be weighed just at the right moment, while
all the time the jib would be in danger of being taken aback by

some vicious eddy. Everything was simple: we hoisted the sails with the sheets paid off and let the mooring ropes slip through the rings on the buoys at the precise moment when everything was ready. But true to the ancient traditions of sailing men we kept our anchor ready to drop at the end of the long mole which encloses the harbour.

Outside we found a nice little force 3 from the sou'west, and *Joshua* bowled along close-hauled on a sea which had clearly been going down since the day before. The weather was dull and cheerless, far from pleasant, but we had confidence in our un-known friend: 'If you want my advice, I think that this is the green light ...' Loick, too, thought that this was the green light. As for myself, I thought about nothing at all, I merely noted that we were beating into a head-wind, that it was not too strong (that was something at least), and the rest I left to faith. Anyway, everything went well on board, despite my unholy terror of passages which start with a head-wind.

The watches were worked out: Françoise would do the cook-ing; Beatrice and Youki would help her, and the men would share the watches in shifts of three hours each during the night, four hours during the day. Why three hours at night instead of the logical four which would have given everybody eight hours of sleep at a stretch? Honestly, I don't know, but it was un-important, for the watch rota was necessarily upset anyway as soon as we met the first of the Trades. The 'watch at the helm' then became the 'watch on deck' (because of ships) and we all blessed that marvellous little contraption, the self-steering vane. The automatic self-steering works as well close-hauled as on all other points of sailing (including before the wind), but we helmed the boat ourselves the first day in order to get the best out of the feeble breeze.

In the late afternoon the wind went round westerly, force 2, and the sky cleared. *Joshua* went onto the starboard tack, standing inshore. Then the breeze died ... and sprang up again lightly from the sou'west. *Joshua* stood out to sea on the port tack, then tacked again at dawn because the breeze, still light, veered. The sea became smooth, quite smooth, so that the sails remained nicely filled and converted every puff of this weekend sailor's breeze into energy. Now we knew that it was true: the green light for the Trades ...

Our noon position on the 3rd June (the day after our departure) placed us only 42 miles north-west of Casablanca, well away from the land. But the wind unfortunately went round to the west sou'west. Then it blew from due west, easing off, and finally with its dying breath from the west-nor'west. Towards midnight it was dead calm with the barometer falling, the sky completely overcast and a light drizzle. What a life! Then the breeze sprang up again, steadied and freshened from the sou'west. We thought it advisable to take a timely reef in the mainsail, another in the mizzen, and to watch for squalls as *Joshua*, with her lee rail under, bowled along on the port tack to gain searoom.

'I say, Bernard, is this some cunning depression that has crept up on us?'

'Let me close the hatch, Françoise, it's teeming down ...'

Yes, this certainly looked like the cunning depression whose existence we had vaguely suspected all along. But that didn't necessarily mean a lot, for there are always depressions about, either active or in the making, north of the 40th parallel. What's more, I could be wrong, I thought, which would please everybody, most of all myself!

My turn to take a watch came round, in sweater and oilskins. It was raining solidly from a very dark sky across which massive, invisible clouds were racing. But the sea was almost luminous, for the rain whipping up the surface of the water was throwing up phosphorescent sparks. The breeze was very fresh and forced me to bear away slightly in the gusts to stop the sails from flapping. But it was not too bad, just a rain squall with a little wind, no really heavy stuff, and *Joshua* was not carrying too much canvas.

In the main cabin Françoise was lying on our large berth with a bolster wedged under the mattress to stop her from sliding off when the boat heeled. I expect she was listening to the patter of the big drops of rain on the iron deck and asking herself if it was going to turn really nasty. As for Beatrice, who was tucked up to leeward in the little starboard berth, she was probably asleep by then and Youki had crept in with her.

Loick and Claude, who shared the after cabin, were sure to be keeping their ears cocked for all the noises going on outside, ready to dash out at the first shout. Françoise might well have envied them, for the after part of a yacht beating to windward in a fairly rough sea has less movement than the central part.

In another hour it was Claude's watch, but I let him sleep and did his watch for him. Not that I lacked confidence in Claude, on the contrary: Claude is a sturdy, reliable chap, one can depend on him. He 'feels' the sea, I noticed that on the very first day. If he was on watch he would not fail to open the hatch and tell me in good time that something was in the offing. That is what I call being able to rely on a chap, and Claude was certainly reliable.

But our sneaking depression had not yet made up its mind what it was going to do, and I had to wait and see – that is a skipper's job. Either it would remain stationary and make life difficult for us, or it would move off to the east and wake up the Portuguese fishermen. My job as the skipper was to remain in the cockpit, to stay with my ship and listen to what she was telling me, my head bare in the rain to be able to hear better, for *Joshua*, like all boats, expressed herself in scarcely whispered monosyllables. Just then, for example, *Joshua* told me that it was probably going to settle down, because, if there was a real depression, the swell from the west would have reached us by then. But it hadn't. I nevertheless felt like handing the large staysail and put up, instead, the boomed staysail which was much smaller and could be shortened further by reefing if things did get really hot. This was a simple manœuvre to accomplish without waking the others, for the small staysail was already hanked to the second forestay ... but my boat whispered that it would be a tactical error, for even if the wind increased I could always change the staysail without difficulty. If I did it at once and the wind eased (which it probably would) I would have the bother of rehoisting the large staysail. There was some truth in this; *Joshua* was not altogether wrong. On the other hand, my boat approved of the reefs in the mainsail and mizzen, for she sailed well under this rig, and if I had to heave-to in a hurry, to wait and see while I smoked a cigarette, there would be no problem under this slightly reduced canvas.

But *Joshua* thought that it was going to ease off soon. While you could not call it fine weather, it wasn't really bad weather either. Maybe it was just a kind of 'front' (what exactly *is* a 'front'? I don't know ...) Anyway, the rain started to ease off and there weren't any gusts for ten minutes.

'Shall I take over? It will be daylight in two hours.'

'No, it's alright, Loick ... I'm not tired ... light me a cigarette, there's a good chap.'

'If there's anything, call me. I've got my oilskins on. Here's your cigarette.'

Good old Loick ... He meant it, but he *knew* that the skipper has the right to lie on his back for a week if everything is going according to plan and the course has been worked out in advance. He also *knew* that when it blows or looks like blowing the skipper's place is on deck, for forty-eight hours or several days if need be, those are the rules of the game ... He had stuck his head out because a sailor is never completely asleep. He sensed that the weather was improving, and maybe he thought I wanted to shake out a reef. But if Loick had been the skipper he, too, would have liked to stay a little longer in the cockpit, alone, and not to have this communion between a man and his boat disturbed.

'Françoise ... are you asleep?'

'I'll come up and sit next to you for a bit. It is almost daylight, and the weather looks like improving ... Wouldn't you like to get some sleep? Claude will take over from me in an hour while I cook breakfast.'

'No, it's alright ... How's the barometer?'

'It hasn't fallen since last night ... The weather is definitely improving ... I'll light you a cigarette and make you some hot coffee.'

'Oh, yes, please!'

What a gem ... a rare gem ...

'Ahoy down there! ... It's getting light and the weather is improving. Let's shake the reef out of the mizzen!'

Around six o'clock the sky had almost cleared and we were back to fine weather. *Joshua* bowled along with all her canvas set in a nor'westerly breeze force 2 to 3, veering gradually to north and becoming a steady nor'easterly Trade, force 3, in the course of the night. So it was, after all, 'the green light'. Thank you Aeolus, and thank you, unknown friend at the other end of the line at Casablanca ...!

Our noon position was only sixty-two miles on from the day before, but now *Joshua* quickly gained in latitude, heading straight for Las Palmas, and with every mile we got nearer the centre of the Trade wind belt. We left the steering to the self-steering vane, that ingenious, simple little gadget which seemed to say to us: 'Leave it to me, just enjoy yourselves, I'm here.'

The watch rota was changed: four-hour watches became the rule of the men at night (because of possible shipping), but no watches were kept during the day, because there was always somebody on deck to enjoy the splendid sail. We settled down to a very broad reach, with the wind almost from aft. The mizzen was paid out till it touched the shrouds, the mainsail sheeted in a bit further, but held down taut by a vang, and the small genoa hauled in until it was just short of lifting. The staysail was lowered because it would have blanketed the small genoa and be itself blanketed by the mainsail. This was not yet the best possible arrangement for we lacked twin staysails, but for the moment *Joshua* sailed herself very well. Our twin staysails were to materialise during our stay in the Canary Islands. If one always waited till everything was absolutely ready before going offshore one would never get to sea! *Joshua*'s sail wardrobe was still incomplete: apart from our basic Terylene sails (main 377 sq. ft, mizzen 215 sq. ft, No. 1 jib 236 sq. ft and boomed staysail 126 sq. ft) we only had two cotton sails which we had bought second-hand before leaving Marseille: a small genoa of 323 sq. ft and a staysail of 193 sq. ft. We would have to complete this outfit with one staysail of between 430 and 480 sq. ft, a medium-sized jib of between 150 and 170 sq. ft, *and, above all, a storm-jib*. We would have to get down to making all of these in the Canary Islands, for a large roll of Terylene had been sent there in advance and was awaiting our arrival.

Our noon position on the 5th June showed that we had covered 122 miles the day before. The Trade wind was now a steady force 4, and *Joshua* was making 6 knots. The sea had become regular under a sky full of fair-weather cumulus, round and plump, which are typical of this zone of steady winds. Seeing this cumulus cloud again after so many years – so many years spent in foreign waters – stirred a strange new emotion in me. 'You were born down there in the tropics, you will feel the need to go back there.' How true that was!

Another 146 miles to go on the 6th June and we were now fairly tramping along at seven knots under a sky of cumulus clouds which had grown a bit too large since the previous day. Hm ... We gave the little island of Allegranza a wide berth. Her lighthouse, not very powerful, cannot be seen in time through rain showers. Besides, there can be some pretty vicious currents in these latitudes.

Towards midnight we altered course and headed straight for Las Palmas, prudently leaving Allegranza some twenty miles to port. It was a dark night, the weather uncertain, but ahead it was clear and in the early hours of the morning the sky cleared while the wind was definitely dropping. *Joshua* was only doing 5½ knots now, but she had nevertheless covered 155 miles in the previous 24 hours. We were looking out for the island of Gran Canaria with its harbour of Las Palmas. There was nothing to be seen. Claude checked our calculations. They were correct.

I could navigate for a thousand years and still never shake off the kind of anguish which comes over most navigators when they are about to make a landfall. My sights were good, I checked them, the chronometer was correct to the second, we picked up W.W.V., every evening, and just to make sure I checked everything again before daybreak, so land must be a mere 30 miles away. I ought to have been able to see it as large as life, yet it wasn't there, and I knew that it must be.

'Laaaaand!'

'Where?'

'There ... look ... just to the right of the jib ... can't you see it? It's staring you in the face!'

'So it is! ... good heavens, it's enormous!'

Ten minutes later the land had become so 'enormous' that we could see nothing else. This is a strange phenomenon often experienced on approaching land: a scarcely distinguishable bluish line becomes a solid, bluish-grey mass in another mile, as though there were a kind of net curtain beyond which everything becomes suddenly visible.

The wind started to drop gradually as the sun sank below the horizon and it was not till 10 p.m., that *Joshua* sailed into the calm waters inside the big mole. The CQR anchor was ready, hooked onto the bob-stay, its chain wedged in a groove in the top of the mooring bitts. All it took was a sharp tug to release the chain and let go the anchor a split-second after the skipper shouted 'Let go!' Be ready to let go the anchor on leaving harbour ... be ready to let it go on entering, that is the old maxim of sailing men. The halyards were ready, too, coiled flat on deck so that they could run out freely without any kinks.

The binoculars, stowed by the cockpit coaming on the right of the helmsman always helped to identify lights in good time, to make out un-lit buoys, to pick out a dark jetty as plainly as if it were daylight. Everything becomes clearer with the binoculars. Off went *Joshua* on her first tack, at 5½ knots, towards a ship moored 300 yards away.

We passed astern of her and intended to weather her on the next board ... no ... we weren't going to make it, there was another freighter moored behind the first, I could see it clearly through the binoculars.

'Ready about ... Lee-o ...'

It is wonderful to enter a harbour at night. A hundred times better than in the day. For in daylight you're always a bit inhibited by the presence of onlookers who might think that you want to show-off or demonstrate how well you can handle a boat. You try in vain not to care, you still feel ill at ease. At night, on the other hand, everyone does his job, without fuss, because he likes doing it well, with the boat as the only witness.

'Ready about ... Lee-o ...'

The green flashing light on the buoy which marked the limit of the underwater works on the extension of the central jetty was left to port. Ahead of us, within 200 yards, was the Santa-Catarina Mole with a red light at the end of it. And behind that mole we should find the small harbour marked on the chart, safe in all weathers, where *Joshua* would be able to sleep in peace. But we could not quite lay it on this tack.

'Ready about ... Lee-o ...'

An electric torch and a fog-horn were within reach in case a fisherman should come shooting out of the harbour, skimming round the end of the Santa-Catarina Mole. But we took care not to pass too close so that we could bear away or luff up if necessary, and still have plenty of elbow room ... Good ... all clear now, we should moor on the next tack.

To think that a lot of people consider it very difficult to enter a harbour without an engine ... It depends on the harbour, of course, but if they would only try it, perhaps they would never again press the starter. It is so much more genuine to come in under sail, listening to the silence, without unnecessary words or gestures.

'Ready about ... Lee-o ...'

And *Joshua* went off on the port tack, gliding towards her moorings. The entrance to the little harbour grew wider as it drew closer. Everything was fine, for we were well to weather, in a good position if the wind should start to head us. Everything could be clearly seen through the binoculars: on the left the small coasters were moored, along the Santa-Catarina pier. On the extreme right, there was the fishing fleet, packed in so close that it was difficult to imagine how they could manage to get out. And there, in the middle, were only three yachts, with lots of beautiful room for us to moor among them.

We were almost there ... luff up ... the jib and staysail came down ... the main followed soon after ... the mizzen stayed up a little longer to push her along.

'Let go the anchor!'

9

Meeting Place of Ocean Birds

What in the night looked like a fishing fleet turned out to be something like a gipsy colony made up of old schooners that had been laid up out of commission for years. There were about thirty of them, destined to lie moored there side by side till the end of their days, inhabited by whole families ranging from grandmothers to grandchildren, and dogs, dogs, dogs. Two of these could sing on great occasions, and another artist (a great hairy beast who was really talented) even managed to miaow when he reached a certain stage of exasperation: we only had to approach slowly in the dinghy and he found the right note. The fourth star in this canine chorus was a dumb mastiff who barked without uttering a sound, bounding up and down on the spot rhythmically. Poor old thing ... he must have suffered a lot. As for the human population of this village, they seemed extremely pleasant, gay and smiling. In any case, they were well guarded. So were we: whether Youki liked it or not, she had to sleep on deck.

So far as the harbour itself was concerned we were being spoilt: we were completely sheltered from all weathers, and the bottom was first-class holding ground. Nearby there were cafés shaded by big trees, where I could sit in the open and write my articles in peace whilst listening to birds singing. Three minutes' walk away there was a wonderful beach facing a lagoon formed by a reef, which was as ideal for the children as it was for us parents. And finally there was a yacht club as we like them: big, deserted, built in the 19th century luxury style, with an impressive lounge, a ballroom whose parquet floor was arranged in an artistic pattern to include compass roses, a lavish stairway on which a prince would have felt at home, and enormous but beautiful furniture covered with dust. There was also a labyrinth of corridors where our children could play at treasure-hunts. Here the 'ocean birds' could feel at home, really at home. The building was in the process (slowly, very slowly) of being demolished to make room for a future ring-road.

The new club house had already been built, resplendent with luxury, a swimming pool and ladies' hairdresser, but its anchorage outside the little harbour was not so safe. We birds of passage prefered the quiet old club, where we could loft our sails on the parquet floor, out of the sun and out of draughts.

The twin staysails were already in hand, cut from our roll of Terylene, and Françoise and Beatrice sewed the panels on our sewing machine (three seams, sewn with Terylene thread). It was a very old Kohler machine whose handle I used to turn when I was Beatrice's age to help my mother sew her dresses.[1]

Leaving the women to their sewing, I went off to a café to write and try to maintain the level of our finances. This was relatively easy in a country where living is so much cheaper than in France or Gibraltar (1964) or in any of the ports at which we were to call later. Besides, Las Palmas enjoys special customs regulations (similar to a free port). All tinned food is very cheap there, so we filled up our bilges.

Our twin staysails (215 sq. ft) were finished four days later. Don Pedro, the sailmaker round the corner, who dropped in out of curiosity, did the boltropes for us at an amazing speed and a price which was more than reasonable.

And, having agreed on a lump sum, he immediately got down to making the small jib of 86 sq. ft and then another one of 150 sq. ft with two rows of reef points. They were made with *impeccable* workmanship, such as one rarely sees, all hand-sewn in 10 oz Terylene. Apart from the Genoa of which we still dreamed, *Joshua* was now ready, and we felt much happier.

Our two boys arrived, and time passed quickly. It always does in these sunny countries: as for myself, I frequented the terrace of my favourite café to do my scribbling, chewing my pen when 'it wouldn't come', while the sparrows kept me company.

---

[1] A sewing machine is no luxury on board. Despite *Wanda*'s cramped cabin, Henry Wakelam would not have parted with his sewing machine. Ours rendered us *invaluable* service working on *Joshua*'s sails later on, for *worn Terylene is extremely difficult to sew by hand*. Besides, this machine helped with innumerable small jobs in which women delight: making dresses, pillow slips, bunk covers etc. One can find second-hand sewing machines very cheaply at Casablanca, and they are amazingly robust.

Meanwhile the rest of the family, Youki included, enjoyed themselves swimming in the lagoon, where I went and joined them whenever the muse left me despite the little birds.

Several days later we set sail for a change of scenery and cruised for a week among the islands of the archipelago, stopping at Tenerife, Palma, again at Tenerife and finally sailing back to Las Palmas to pick up our mail and see whether Bluche, Deshumeurs or Henry had arrived ...

A week back in Las Palmas, long enough to write an article for the magazine *Bateaux*, and *Joshua* was off again, this time heading for Fuerteventura some fifty miles away. At last we were living, to the full, unhampered by that feeling that we had no time for

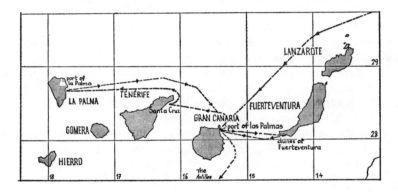

anything except eternally running to catch the last bus by the skin of our teeth. Since we had arrived in the Canaries all that had changed: there was no longer a last bus, it was no longer time that dictated but we alone who made the decisions.

At Fuerteventura it was love at first sight, for all of us, even Youki. This island impressed us with a sense of grandeur, with its solitude, its vast deserted beaches, its high dunes of white sand, its clear waters which are so full of fish that I could feed my small family with the help of my underwater harpoon, and virtually choose my catch. The children were almost deliriously happy, collecting shells by the bucketful and sorting them like treasure. Like us they got back on board ship at night dead-tired, famished and happy.

When we had run out of fresh food we sailed *Joshua* back to

Las Palmas, filled her up with drinking water and fresh vegetables and hurried back to anchor close to the beach of Fuerteventura, almost under the dunes, where time still flowed in its own natural rhythm. These dunes of fine sand which run along the coast for miles and miles, dazzlingly white beaches as far as the eye can see, all this sand we were looking at, had come from the African desert, brought there by winter gales which carried it over the sea. In the face of this great undertaking of nature, who goes about her tasks so quietly, grain by grain, without ever tiring, we felt very small and impressed by the power and triviality of time.

The holidays were soon over, at least for the children, who had to return to their boarding schools in France. They left on board the *Ancerville*, gorged with sun and wonderful memories, taking their shells and their treasures with them.

'You will come home soon, Mummy, won't you?'

'Yes, my pets ... we shall come back by way of the Red Sea instead of the Cape of Good Hope, that'll be shorter.'

It was sad to see them part, holding back their tears and clutching their shells. But learning is so important in this age. Later, when they had passed their exams, they could choose: medicine, law, industry ... or a gipsy life. But it was for them to choose, not for us. True, we could have kept one of them and taught him (or her) on board as the Bluches did on board *Chimère*. But that would have been too unfair to the other two, with grave repercussions on their morale and their studies.

In any case, we were well aware that we must not dally in the Pacific, this ocean of our dreams, for children of their age – almost adolescent – must not be separated for too long from their families. Beatrice was already thirteen, Emmanuel and Hervé were twelve and eleven respectively. We must not dally on our route ... no matter how beautiful it might be.

The harbour of Las Palmas, now crowded with yachts, resembled a small cosmopolitan village. They had arrived one by one and were waiting to set out across the Atlantic after the cyclone season in the Antilles had come to an end in mid-November. Everyone in this little community was messing about on board or in the ballroom, doing a bit of painting, getting their boats ready without working too hard, for the bad days of the Channel and the

Bay of Biscay had been left far behind. And ahead of us were the Trade Winds and everlasting fine weather (or almost).

We were now fifteen boats, sitting on the water like gulls waiting to take off. Englishmen, Americans, two Germans, a Dutchman, a Norwegian, an Australian, two Frenchmen (René Blondeau's *Aigle de Mer* and *Joshua*). We were still waiting for *Chimère* (Bluche), *Aventure* (Alain Hervé), *Vencia* (Pierre and Cathy Deshumeurs) and *Pheb*, Henry and Ann Wakelam's new 55 ft ketch, the story of which is little short of miraculous.

Everybody eventually arrived, one by one, in high spirits: first Bluche, then Pierre and Catherine Deshumeurs, Henry and Ann the following day; finally everyone with the exception of *Aventure* (Alain Hervé) who was still at Casablanca when last heard of. Alain was to bring us the 1965 Nautical Almanac, but one day after another passed with a nice little breeze ... should I leave ... should I wait? If I left I might not be able to get the Almanac at Martinique. A cruel dilemma for a skipper who has to sit and watch all the nice little Trade-wind clouds go by. Well, that's just too bad; we decided to wait a little longer.

And we weren't sorry, for another boat joined our small floating community, the English ketch *Venus*,[1] sailed single-handed by Paul Erling Johnson (aged 24), a really first-class seaman who had been all round England and to Norway in his minute boat without an auxiliary engine. A tough mariner, whose acquaintance was more than rewarding.

Finally, one last boat entered the harbour: *Néo Vent*, sailed by the French single-hander Pierre Auboiroux. He is a classic example of complete relaxation in a man and has managed to cram all the essentials of life into one word: go. At times this surpasses the understanding of the average weekend yachtsman, and yet it works alright for Auboiroux, for everything always sorts itself out as the voyage proceeds.

An evening with Auboiroux is like a breath of fresh air, a cure for nervous tension, better than all the pills in the world against

---

[1] *Venus* is a clinker-built whaler type of remarkably beautiful lines. Her dimensions are: LOA 18 ft 9 in, beam 5 ft 10 in, draught 2 ft 10 in, sail area 260 sq. ft. She carries internal ballast which cannot be dislodged if she capsizes.

congestion of the liver. And when I think of that chap, I cannot remember where it was, who wondered whether he ought to install an outboard 1 ft 5 in or 1 ft 5½ in long, while we ... ah, well, here we were, all pals together, in the Canaries where life is great.

The fine season had now begun and several boats had already left. *Pheb* had left her mooring that day, under full sail, making two boards to leave the harbour, and she is a boat of over thirty tons! She had come in under sail, but I had not expected her to do the same on leaving, for that is much more tricky, especially with a boat that size. Well done!

Aigle de Mer, too, had been gone for some three weeks so that she could call at the Cape Verde Islands, where she wanted to wait for the end of the cyclone season. She would certainly have left again.

At the end of November the harbour was almost empty. Only five boats were left, among them *Vencia* and *Néo Vent*. But my old pal from the *Snark* wasn't going to cross the Atlantic that year. Pierre thought it wiser to go into Dakar and restore his financial position. This was a great pity, for we had hoped to cruise in company as far as the Galapagos Islands, then meet again at the Marquesas and finally Tahiti. But Pierre was right, it is difficult to get funds in the Antilles, and as for later on in the Pacific – it is impossible except by an extraordinary stroke of luck.

The day of departure drew near. Françoise had finished buying provisions, I had checked all the sails and halyards, we would leave on the morrow, Almanac or no Almanac. *Aventure* had not arrived, but the weather was really too fine to miss, so we decided to weigh anchor at daybreak.

'Good night Pierre, good night Cathy ...'

'You really are leaving tomorrow?'

'Yes, old chap ...'

Atlantic

No doubt day broke radiantly on the 9th November, but *Joshua*'s crew were still asleep. We had been up late the night before, sitting in *Vencia*'s cabin and swapping memories as though sitting by the fireside. So it was not until a little after midday that *Joshua* left harbour.

By mooring to *Vencia*'s stern we were able to take in the anchor at leisure, scrub the chain, wash the mud off the decks and hoist sail on a clean boat. Then we backed the staysail to pay off on the right tack.

'Okay, Pierre, cast off ...'

There it was ... we had met ... we had parted again ... for a long period this time. There would be so many turtles and lobsters in the Galapagos ... but Pierre and Cathy would not be there to share them with us.

Outside the weather was at its best, a force 3 Trade which looked like holding, and *Joshua* stood out to sea with her sails well filled to get away from the land as quickly as possible and escape, before nightfall, from the influence of thermal winds which might counteract the trade and becalm her.

There was a patch of calm towards midnight: *Joshua* rolled abominably in a cross sea knocked up by swells from two different directions, one from the north-east (the direction of the Trade wind), another from the north-west, coming round the island of Gran Canaria.

We had to sheet all the sails in to damp down the infernal rolling a little. The self-steering vane had already been clouted by the mizzen boom and looked a bit bent and sorry. It was nothing serious, though. I unhitched it and lashed it to a stancheon to wait for the wind to return. All three of us felt ill, Françoise and Youki because the movement was really too violent, myself because I was a bit ashamed of not having set sail two days earlier when the Trade was blowing full force. The limits of the Trade wind belt vary according to the position of the Azores High – a bit to the north, a bit to the south. There are no fixed limits, and I had the feeling that we had missed the boat for a good start, the Trade wind having shifted south of its mean limits. To think that *Pheb* and *Chimère* were bowling along on the 14th parallel with the full Trade behind them, while Lacombe had had to plug into a westerly in what is, in theory, the Trade wind belt, because the Trade wind had gone down south ... the thought in itself made me ill. Yes, we had missed the boat by just one day. Still, it was done now, and if we had to pay, pay we would. But I would certainly try to remember never to let a fair wind go begging again.

But all was well. After three hours of unrest and recriminations the wind sprang up again, timidly at first, then steadying to the old Trade wind, and *Joshua* sauntered along southward without any more ado.

'Run, *Joshua*, run before the wind changes its mind ...'

And *Joshua*, on the port tack and with 1,125 sq. ft of canvas set forged ahead in a strengthening Trade, hoping to stick with it as far as Martinique. The sea was still choppy, slowing us down but we were gaining in latitude, heading sou'sou'west towards the Cape Verde Islands while the wind steadied and the sea settled down, becoming regular after two days.

On the 10th November, one day after we had set out, *Joshua*'s daily run at noon was only 101 miles. On the 11th it was 117 miles, on the 12th 156 miles and on the 13th (Friday) 150 miles, the wind having been a steady force 4 during the latter two days.

Flying fish were now shooting up from under the bows, soaring for a moment then launching themselves again off the back of a wave with the stroke of their tails and soaring for another sixty feet or so. The spectacle was always new and we could watch it all morning, sitting on the forward hatch or standing in front of the windlass and holding the forestay so that we could see further. And we always watched with the same amazement these brilliant little playthings, like fan-shaped mirrors, who seemed to come up from under the bobstay.

'Françoise, a rainbow ... quick ... it will be gone in a minute ...'

With her chin on the cockpit coaming, hypnotised, Françoise looked for the first time in her life at this jewel suspended like an apparition in the fine spray of the bow-wave ... the Trade wind rainbow.

It played just above the bow-wave, disappeared, re-appeared, lit up, faded away and re-appeared again, threw out shafts of light and was gone.

I had occasionally seen momentary rainbows in the Mediterranean when *Joshua* was sailing in a mistral between Porquerolles and Corsica, miserable looking things in which the blue and the yellow, watered down to a pale green, could hardly be distinguished from each other.

Only the miracle of the Trade wind could have produced a rainbow as radiant as the one we saw then. Maybe it is due to the particular limpidity of the tropical sky, or to the sun being so much higher and hotter than in Northern latitudes. Perhaps it is also due to the special backcloth of the Trade wind sea. I don't know, and it isn't important. I was simply happy that the Trade wind had presented Françoise with such a beautiful rainbow that day.

The richness of the colours varies a bit according to the angle at which the sun strikes the bow wave, and also depends on the quality of the particles of spray, spray which is as fine as mist. Under optimum conditions the rainbow at the bow can glow like a crown of jewels, and then the red appears, flashing like lightning. I mean the real red, the colour of blood, not merely orange tinted with red.

It is very rare to see the red. Much rarer than the green gleaming over the setting sun. I have seen the red only once, in the Indian Ocean on board *Marie-Thérèse*. It was like a blast from a trumpet, like looking into the heart of the Trade wind.

Françoise was beginning to discover the rhythm of life which I had described to her before we left the Mediterranean, a rhythm in which she would not believe during those exhausting days and which anybody who has not sailed in the tropics finds difficult to imagine: *the rhythm of the Trade wind*, days with nothing to do ... absolutely nothing, and yet as full of life as a phosphorescent wake. And a happy boat, happy to be alive, happy to be free, happy to have all that water to sail in with her sails full of wind and the flying fish darting from under her bows. A happy boat feeling at home in the Trade wind.

To say that we did nothing at all would give the wrong impression of what a Trade wind crossing is like. For example, we stayed awake at night because we were in the shipping lanes as far as the Cape Verde Islands. In fact, we were really only half-awake so comfortable were we, lying on a mattress in the cockpit with a cover over us, dozing under the stars and opening an eye from time to time to cast a look around.

We also used the splendid weather for studying the stars and identified them one by one thanks to a marvellous little booklet by Post Captain Pierre Sizaire.

'Hullo! I've found Arcturus at last. Yes, there's no doubt about it, that's the one: "the *arc* of a circle from the Great Bear leads to *Arc*turus".'

'And I ... I think I have actually found the Spica of Virgo ... pass me the book ... yes, that's Spica. Look, Bernard: you extend the arc from the Great Bear, pass through Arcturus and continue the arc to arrive at Spica. It's me who's found it!'

Gradually, as the nights passed, we discovered most of the stars used in astro-navigation: first the easier ones, like Capella with her three little goats, then Vega, opposite Capella, recognisable by the small, slightly flattened quadrilateral to the left of it. Of course, we immediately identified the bright stars in the big lozenge of Orion: Sirius, almost as bright as the planet Jupiter, orange-coloured Aldebaran, Rigel and Betelgeuse (not forgetting the rule of reversed initials, for Rigel is *b*lue and *B*etelgeuse is *r*ed. On the other hand, Altair, in the constellation of Aquila, gave us more trouble, for it rose late at that time. But we eventually discovered it, flying like an aeroplane with its wings on fire. As it happens all these stars used in navigation are also the most beautiful in the sky.

Consequently we did not waste our time but were stocking up with weapons for the day when they would not only be useful but necessary, and my weak point, at that time, was astro-navigation. The Atlantic would afford us plenty of opportunity for practising risky landfalls, such as perhaps in the Galapagos, and above all in the Tuamotus. We must practice stellar navigation ... *Joshua* would be in great need of it later. It is not difficult, you just have to get down to it and not be discouraged by the slightly hilarious results of the first few days.

Our noon position on the 14th November showed a day's run of 138 miles. 105 miles on the 15th (heavens … the wind was dropping), then 130 miles on the 16th (no, it was coming back), but only 111 miles on the 17th (I knew it wouldn't last). Our position was now Longitude 27° and Latitude 17° 40′, some hundred miles north-west of the most northerly of the Cape Verde Islands and outside the shipping lanes: no more night watches.

But the Trade wind had dropped to a mere breath from the east, force 2 and steady, I judged by the calm and relaxed look of the small cumulus clouds and the bow wave, which seemed to murmur in chorus: 'Fabulous weather, children, take it easy …'

The sea, almost completely smooth, had become wonderfully tepid. Moving a few hundred miles south had been enough to get out of the cold current from Portugal (which flows round the Canaries) into the warm equatorial current of deep blue water.

A trial run with the twin staysails up (total sail area 430 sq. ft) proved disappointing: *Joshua* logged 2·5 knots, whereas with the small genoa, the main and the mizzen up (914 sq. ft) she logged 4·5 knots as long as we steered a course 15° off a dead run so that the mizzen would not blanket the mainsail and genoa.

At first sight I thought that this deviation of 15° from the direct course would increase the distance quite considerably. But by drawing a diagram of all the different points of sailing open to a boat that is sailing before the wind without twin jibs, on a sheet of graph paper, I realised immediately that it more than pays to go off course, *for the increase in distance is small compared with the considerable gain in speed with the sails drawing well.*

So, unless we had twin jibs offering a *very large* sail area it paid us to use our normal sails and keep them drawing by going 15° off the direct route (which resulted in an increase of distance of 3½ per cent to 4 per cent) thereby gaining several knots in speed.

On a sloop (mainsail and jib only), on the other hand, things

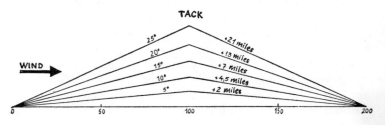

could be different: during trials before setting out on his first
Transatlantic Race, Sir Francis Chichester came to the conclusion
that *Gipsy-Moth II* was no faster with the wind over the quarter
than with the wind from dead aft and the genoa winged out on the
opposite side to the mainsail.

He was dismayed at this discovery, confirmed by a very accurate speedometer, for he had hoped to make better speed and
save himself some of the complications and discomfort (rolling
and having to wing the genoa out before the wind) by sailing
with the wind from over the quarter. But in the case of *Joshua*,
who is ketch rigged, there is no question: we would have to make
long boards with the wind over the quarter until the day when we
could present her with much larger twin staysails, say 340 to
370 sq. ft each, with reef points, if possible!

The wind agreed with us by easing off a little more, but we were
leading a peaceful life, without any worries whatever, and for
Françoise everything was a source of wonderment: this scarcely
rippled sea breathing slowly; the little genius inside the self-
steering vane, which did its job without any help from us as
though it was quite normal to steer a perfect course with so little
wind; this clear, clear sky and this incredibly blue sea! And the
dorado we caught this morning!

'I am so happy, Bernard ...'

'So am I!'

And life continued, the days pushing each other along gently.
Joshua logged 2 knots, 3 knots at her very best, and we were
heading south-west to find more wind, but almost hoping not
to find it, so happy were we posed between sea and sky, outside
the shipping lanes, far from everything ... and yet so near.

We covered 240 miles between the 17th and 20th November,
which amounted to an average speed of a little more than 3 knots,
then 300 miles from the 20th to the 23rd, thanks to a little breeze
from the east-south-east, which was unusual but refreshing in
this zone of north-easterly Trades. And all the time the weather
was simply out of this world.

Nothing ever happened, and yet we felt that we were living
as we had not done for a long, long time. We were truly having
a grand holiday in the sun, living with the same intensity as a

mussel anchored to its rock. But it would take too long to explain. And why explain everything? That flat calm, for example, that lasted for four days and four nights with the sea completely calm and yet alive with that slow and peaceful breathing of water that is sleeping. We took down all the sails to let *Joshua* sleep, too. That was contrary to all the principles, for a boat lies best with her mainsail sheeted in hard to stop her rolling. But on that occasion it was not necessary. *Joshua* slumbered bare of all sail in the most beautiful calm I had ever seen in the whole of my life at sea, under a sky that was perfectly transparent in the day and spangled with stars right down to the horizon in the warm, soft nights which are so typical of the tropics.

Nothing happened. But plenty of things happened around us and inside us. Françoise discovered Antares, set like a ruby in the heart of Scorpio, and I found Regulus. And that was something!

I also felt that I was becoming an expert on taking star sights since I discovered that it can be done without the telescope, keeping both eyes open. In this way a star can be brought down to the horizon with a single movement, without losing it on the way, and it is very easy to place it accurately on the horizon because the latter can be seen quite clearly with both eyes open. It is impossible to do this properly when looking through the telescope where the horizon always looks hopelessly blurred. In my innocence I thought I was the first to discover this method, but upon mentioning it to people I found that this little known trick is used by at least two fishermen, two naval officers, by a captain of the Merchant Navy, and by Dr. Stern-Veyrin.

My sight lines of four or five stars (three altitudes for each and then the average taken) were now crossing in a circle 2 or 3 mm in diameter. But I was practising, practising, practising, for I had to be ready for the Tuamotu archipelago with its reefs, that are only just submerged, its currents that are sometimes strong and often irregular. The Atlantic is a perfect training ground where navigation is simple: I had to make the best of it.

Nothing happened, time was standing still, but we discovered and became conscious of so many things. For instance, we learnt that dolphins emit ultra-sonic noises which were perfectly audible to Youki: when she started to jump about like mad, begging to be let loose (she could not climb the ladder) there were always dolphins around the boat. Then, one night, we realised that they weren't ultra-sonic noises at all but a proper concert of faint cries like those made by young mice in their nest. Little cries and modulated whistling noises.

And now that our ears had become atuned to their wave-length we could hear the dolphins coming almost at the same time as Youki did. We could hear them even on deck, *very clearly*, without having to strain our ears.

During all the years I had sailed the oceans I had seen thousands of dolphins, I had even played with them, but I had to wait till I was nearly forty before I discovered that they talked.

Another 300 miles were covered between 27th and 30th November, as we were still pushed along by a light east-south-easterly breeze, running along the 15th parallel on the port tack. The north-easterly Trade had definitely moved to higher latitudes that year.

Then the calm returned, but it was not quite as beautiful as the first one. It lasted a bare 24 hours during which we left the mainsail and mizzen up and sheeted in to damp down what little rolling the sea caused. We still logged 170 miles in three days (noon position on the 3rd December), then another 350 miles up to the 6th December, when our position was Longitude 50° 47' and Latitude 15° 26'. The wind was still coming from the east-north-east. So much for the Trade wind. Still, we had retired from the race three weeks ago!

Joshua's bottom had again become fouled with barnacles, in spite of the scraping I had done, by diving under it, during the great calm between the 23rd and 27th November. I had scraped the hull in Las Palmas harbour before we had left, but perhaps I should have scrubbed it very carefully afterwards to remove all traces of marine life which encourages the growth of this extremely prolific pest.

As a result *Joshua* was just crawling along, but we had plenty of time, for once. Nevertheless, I would not forget the barnacles before the next passage: *it meant careening or at least going to work with a stiff nylon scrubber.* (*Joshua*'s bottom is painted with zinc silicate, which can only be used on steel hulls and stands vigorous scrubbing without suffering.)

Four days later, on the 10th December, *Joshua* had only covered another 370 miles (at an average of 4 knots) while the north-easterly Trade was gaining strength again. Then, suddenly, it was blowing freshly and we logged 142 miles on the 11th. Our position was then very close to Martinique, which we entered the following morning, 33 days after our departure. Three thousand miles in thirty-three days ... that gave us an average daily run of 90 miles, a little less than 4 knots. That was slow for *Joshua*. But how quickly the time had passed. Françoise felt we could have spent another month at sea without being bored for a single minute. I felt the same.

Yet we were pleased to arrive: Françoise because of all that greenery, the coconut palms which were a novelty to her, the luxuriant vegetation of a country that smelt hotly of the sugar plantations. I was pleased for the same reason, but also because all our friends were there: Henry and Ann, Bluche, René Blondeau, Philippe Puisais (who had arrived a year earlier in his *Cap-Horn*).

Néo Vent and *Venus* had not yet arrived. A pity, for we should have liked to see them before setting sail again. We had decided to leave in a week, immediately after careening. Everything was arranged with Mr Grant, the owner of the shipyard where I had careened *Marie-Thérèse II*. Just a good scrubbing down, two coats of antifouling and we would be off. It sounds a bit stupid, but there it was: one cannot explore the Antilles and the Pacific at the same time. We had chosen the Pacific right from the start, and we would return quickly by way of the Red Sea. Everything was settled.

The Great Turning Point

It really would have been too stupid, for the sake of a few days.
So we stayed, thank goodness, to celebrate Christmas on board
Pheb. We were all in high spirits, everybody was there: Bluche,
Blondeau, Puisais, and even Paul Johnson who moored two
hours before our midnight supper on Christmas Eve, welcomed
by our howls of joy.

'Come on, Paul, we haven't started to attack the turkey yet!'

Henry sent a dinghy with a mooring line out to him, and Paul
moored his little *Venus* to the stern of *Pheb*. She looked almost
like a dinghy amid all our tenders bunched behind big *Pheb*.
Paul came on board, dropping with fatigue, his eyes red from
lack of sleep: he had spent forty-eight hours at the helm to be
able to spend Christmas with his friends ... it was touching! But
Auboiroux was missing ... poor chap ... we hoped he would at
least catch a big dorado in place of the turkey stuffed with chest-
nuts which he would have to do without in the middle of the
Atlantic.[1] I also thought of my old pal of the *Snark*, who would be
celebrating with Cathy in Dakar. They were sure to have found
friends ... But it wasn't the same ... we were missing them in
Martinique.

We also missed our children. Nobody could ever take their
place. I noticed that Françoise was momentarily absent-minded,
despite the Martinique punch, the gaiety all around us and the
many plans that are always hatched in the warm and happy
atmosphere of friends getting together.

I was getting to know Françoise rather well and knew when
her thoughts were wandering: she held my hand and pressed

---

[1] *Venus* crossed in 39 days without meeting many calms. *Néo Vent*
took 49 days after having been becalmed, *Chimère* 32 days, *Pheb* 31 or
32 days, I don't remember. Two British yachts who sailed a more
northerly route took only 22 and 25 days respectively. On the other
hand, another well-canvassed yacht took no less than 63 days! She was
becalmed for the best part of three weeks on the 13th parallel. That
year the Trade wind was well established round about the 18th
parallel.

herself lightly against me with a sort of inward smile I had come to know and – hop – she had gone off to join our children who were spending Christmas with their grandparents.

'Françoise ... Françoise! We'll be back home soon ... we could even return from Tahiti via Cape Horn!'

Suddenly she was wide awake.

'You're joking! ...'

'Of course!' (I was).

Henry and Bluche who were listening also knew that I was joking, but they were looking at me in an odd way. And then Bluche told us about the Smeetons, whom he had met: the Smeetons and another crew member were in New Zealand on board their 38 ft ketch *Tzu-Hang* and wanted to get back to their daughter in England as quickly as possible, by the shortest possible route. But the gods were unwilling. Twice they tried. The first time *Tzu-Hang* was running under bare poles on the 50th parallel about a thousand miles from Cape Horn when she was pitch-poled[1], losing both her masts *and the dog-house*. She was able to reach Chile under jury rig and with all her crew. Several months later she set out a second time and was once again knocked down before she reached Cape Horn: Rolled over athwartships, again under bare poles. With both masts by the board but her cabin still in place *Tzu-Hang* once again reached Chile under jury rig. Twice she failed, and so Miles Smeeton called his book *Once is enough*.

Françoise only listened with half an ear, with that absent-minded, inward smile of hers. Yet what Bluche was telling us was fascinating. Take the first accident, for example:

---

[1] Pitch-poled: when a boat buries her bow while running before the wind and is tipped 'stern over stem'. This happened to *Sandefjord* in the North Atlantic.

I quote Torlief, Tambs' crew who was helming *Sandefjord*:

' ... The boat buried her bow in the sea several times. The last time, just as the bow was engulfed by a wave, an enormous roller came up from behind and turned the boat stern over stem ... '

With her deck swept clean, her mizzen by the board, her life raft, compass, sails, anchors and roof of the wheelhouse gone, her bulwarks torn off completely, one topside plank missing, her rigging loose, her hull full of water and looking altogether like a wreck, *Sandefjord* reached land where Tambs learned that the race he had come for was not taking place ... because his boat was the only entry.

Beryl Smeeton (the wife) was at the helm when *Tzu-Hang* capsized and the 10 mm thick line of her safety harness snapped like a thread without breaking her ribs. Smeeton explained why to Bluche. It was like breaking the string round a parcel: if you take two turns round your hand and give a sharp pull it snaps clean off. But if you pull gently you cut your hand without breaking the string.

I had committed a grave tactical error in not leaving immediately after Christmas (we had already careened the boat at Mr Grant's). The previous long stops had been justified because we had been able to spend two and a half months with our children this way.

But it was now the 13th February and we were still moored in the bay of Fort-de-France, and this time there was no excuse for having lingered so long. On arriving in Martinique we had intended to collect the mail, post our own letters, scrub the bottom at top speed and to be off without delay so that we would have time to enjoy the Pacific before returning via Torres Straits and the Red Sea. As for the Antilles, they would have to wait until 'the next time' when we would do them thoroughly, like Le Toumelin or Bluche, but without staying away for over a year. Bluche, in fact, was back in France by way of the North Atlantic within four months (just before the cyclone season) after having visited the whole chain of the Antilles without hurry or fixed schedule.

This is what we would be doing one day, but not that year. After all, we had come from France *to get to know the Pacific* and realise our long-cherished dream. And now we had spent two months on Martinique ... without having seen anything of the Antilles except for some nice walks with Henry and Ann. Ports of call were our weak point, we never managed to leave on the intended date.

Now we would have to make up for the delay, for the two months by which we had shortened our planned stay in the Pacific. It was no good crying over spilt milk, so we decided to leave the following day and try to catch up with Auboiroux who had left for Panama two days before.

Joshua set sail on the 14th February at 8 o'clock in the morning in a beautiful Trade wind full of promise and logged 180 miles in the first 28 hours. Another 180 miles was knocked off by the 16th: she had obviously decided to make up for the delay.

What a splendid breeze ... The sea was quite rough, but the bow was slamming through it, and it was wonderful to listen to the sound of the boat racing along on the white crests, almost surfing at times to show us what she could do.

Another 171 miles were logged by the 17th. The wind had eased a bit to force 4 to 5. *Joshua* was sailing a course of 10 to 15° off

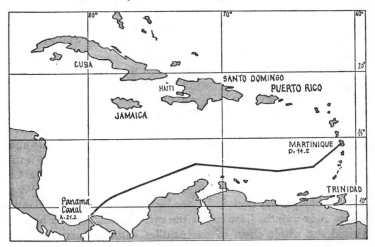

a dead run, with the staysail lowered in order not to blanket the small 323 sq. ft genoa. I went up on deck frequently to ease a sheet, take another turn round a cleat or sweat up on a halyard, for *Joshua* was going splendidly and it was my job to urge her on and see that she was making the best possible use of this fine breeze.

Hurry, *Joshua* ... hurry!

And *Joshua* hurtled along through the middle of the flying fish, making them drop on deck during the night where they got caught under the booms of the twin staysails sheeted right down to the bulwarks. We collected heaps of them every morning, much smaller than those in the Atlantic, but many more of them. I noticed with surprise that half of all the flying fish we picked up had four wings instead of two. They were slightly more rounded than the 'traditional' flying fish and the additional two wings near the tail were only half as long but wider than the main wings. And I had not known this before!

Strange, these four-winged flying fish. I must have seen dozens in my life yet never really noticed them ... And the dolphins, whom I had never before heard talking ... Now I could hear them as plainly as you can hear the birds sing in the wood. Why had it taken me so long?

And now I could suddenly hear a new note in the singing of the bow, another sound underneath the song of a happy boat: '... *give me wind and I shall give you miles* ...'

I could hear it more and more clearly: '... *you want to get home quickly ... give me wind* ...' I could hear it on deck, I could hear it coming from the end of the bowsprit as I was sitting on the pulpit, sometimes for hours, watching the bow throwing out the spray. I could hear it as I lay on my bunk, holding in my hands the little globe of the world which the children had sent me for Christmas. It was the voice of the bow wave, and I could hear it as plainly as I could hear the dolphins, I could feel it in my bones: '... *there are several routes home ... I am a fine boat ... but don't choose the wrong one ... give me wind and I shall give you miles* ...'

'Bernard! ... Bernard! ... Wake up! What are you staring at on the globe?'

'I was looking at something ...'

'But why are you looking down there? ... Bernard ... you aren't thinking of going home that way? ... Bernard ... look at me ... you don't want to go home that way? ...'

I didn't want to argue about it for the moment. In any case, I didn't know yet, it was too soon, you cannot rush into an undertaking of that magnitude. '... *give me wind ... I shall give you miles* ...' But I mustn't choose the wrong route either, and being certain of something does not necessarily mean being right. '... *there are no reefs down there ... only wind ... I am a fine boat ... give me wind* ...' If we went home by the westward route, as we had planned from the beginning, we would have to tear through the Pacific in order to get through the Torres Straits before the start of the bad season, and we might come to hate the Pacific as much as I had hated the Caribbean Sea eight years ago.

'Bernard ... look at me ... you aren't going home that way ...!'

'Listen to me, Françoise, and remember this: I have already lost two boats, I don't want to lose this one. Now, *we* will take *Joshua* by the route which *I* consider the safest, the most logical. I am your husband ... but on board *Joshua* I am *first of all* the skippe.!'

Hurry, *Joshua* ... hurry! ... It was a joy to see the boat sailing before the wind, steered by the little goblin hidden in the steering vane who had enabled us to do an average of 7 knots since our departure, in a force 4 wind with plenty of push behind it. On the 18th February our day's run was 162 miles, 160 miles on the 19th, 168 miles on the 20th, 160 on the 21st. *Joshua* was now twenty miles north of Punta Manzanillo and 43 miles from the moles of Colon which mark the entrance of the Panama Canal ... providing the wind held out ... please, God, make it hold a little bit longer ...

Joshua entered Limon Bay at 10 p.m. on the 21st February and anchored in the shelter of the big outer mole which lies across the bay, after having covered 1,224 miles in 7 days 14 hours.

We were very tired after this crossing which had turned into a bit of a race. I think we were practically exhausted. But we sat for a long time in the cockpit side by side, gazing in the direction of 'our' Pacific. There it was, a few miles away, at the other end of the canal. We felt very close to each other and I sensed that Françoise, too, had heard the voice of the bow wave as *Joshua* was speeding along. '... *I am a fine boat ... give me wind and I shall give you miles ... you are in hurry ... you want to get back to your children ... give me wind ... I am a fine boat ...*'

Now *Joshua* was asleep at the end of her anchor chain. A well deserved sleep after having worked hard. She had done a fine piece of work, all hand-made. And I felt that I was seeing her for the first time as she *really* was: splendid, utterly beautiful, with the right amount of freeboard that let the sea flow by smoothly, with her uncluttered, curved decks surrounded by very low bulwarks only 2 inches high, so that the water would never weigh her down and worry her when she had to really defend herself. And then there was her central cockpit protected by two cabins, and the inside steering wheel. Certain things would have to be added before she could go down there with an easy mind: a dome on top of the hatch, a seat from which she could be steered from inside for more than 24 hours, if necessary, runners ... but they were all do-it-yourself jobs for which I would have plenty of time before the start of the southern summer. We still had *eight months* of the Pacific ahead of us.

What a fine boat she was ... by God, she was *beautiful*. Knocker achieved a miracle when he designed her ... racy ... built of steel ... without unnecessary frills.

It was strange, but this was the first time I understood my boat properly. Perhaps because it takes time to feel certain things.

'Françoise ... darling ... you will always have to have confidence in me.'

'If I had not always had confidence in you I would not be here now.'

'Françoise ... *Joshua* is a *Cape Bird* ... and I didn't know it.'

'I think I have always known it ... and I have still come as far as this. That means that I shall stay with you ... and with *Joshua*.'

12

Panama – Galapagos

I shall spare the reader a detailed account of our passage through the Panama Canal. It is of no interest, since our sole aim was to arrive without incident and as quickly as possible at the other end of that beastly canal ... We had heard enough about it and knew that many bowsprits and cross-trees had been left at the bottom of the locks.

But everything went well with *Joshua*: the pilot came on board early on 26th February and we were having supper in the Pacific in the evening of the same day, moored to a buoy at the yacht club at Balboa. What a relief!

We went through the canal under sail, sometimes using the engine to help. Nothing happened to arouse our emotions, not even while we were going through the Pedro Miguel locks which we entered under jib, taking the way off her by zig-zagging. Unless there is a complete calm, the wind is either from dead ahead or from dead aft for the whole length of the canal. In our case it was from deaf aft (the Trade wind).

A friend who was planning to go through the canal several months later wrote to me: '... are the locks *really* as dangerous as some authors make out in their books? ...' I replied: '... Yes. You can get a *real* bashing unless you take careful precautions.' The most important things to have are four nylon warps with a minimum circumference of 2 inches for a 10-tonner. These must be at least 28 fathoms long and coiled to perfection so they can run out smoothly without the slightest hitch. *Joshua*'s warps were on 55-fathom drums and that was no luxury. Nor were our four strong mooring bitts, (two forward and two aft), especially in the rising locks that lead to Lake Gatun, for the eddies in this first group of locks are impressive and *really* dangerous, and the slack has to be taken in at the same speed as the water rises. This means that there has to be a nimble person to each warp, that is to say four seamen besides the pilot and the helmsman. The Canal Company provides professional seamen (15 dollars per person) to supplement crews if necessary. We had one member of the yacht club at Cristobal, who came along out of kindness, and two men from the Company. It was cheaper than a new bowsprit, and, in any case, the Company insists that there be five on board besides the pilot. (The Company also hires out warps if required).

We have to compliment the Company on the pilot and on the strict orderliness with which everything is managed throughout the length of the canal. Accidents are rare, but they can be rather serious for small yachts, and I did not hesitate to dive into the lock at Miraflores to retrieve a mooring line which had been badly thrown, for everything has to be done quickly and without fuss.

We arrived at Balboa on the 26th February and had intended to leave this fairly clammy place without too much delay and be on our way to the Galapagos. Two weeks later we were still there, with Auboiroux, watching the pelicans fish. But we had time. To think that at Martinique we had both decided, sick at heart, to give the Galapagos a miss so as not to run the risk of missing the season for getting through the Torres Straits ...

Now there were no more timetables, no more rush, no Torres Straits. Instead we had the chart of Tierra del Fuego, provided by the American Hydrographic Service at Panama. It was so much simpler, so much more logical ...

We also had our visa for the Galapagos.[1] But, above all, we now had *the time* to go to the Galapagos, leisurely, without hurrying. And the time to stay there several months if we wanted to. A member of the yacht club at Balboa who knows that archipelago well showed us on our chart the ideal place at Santa-Cruz de Galapagos to careen between two tides. He showed us where to find the best lobsters, on which island the drinking water is really drinkable, which are the best anchorages and where we could catch the largest turtles!

---

[1] We paid 30 dollars for this visa (covering both boat and crew.) Another yacht, larger than *Joshua*, also paid 30 dollars. Another paid only 6 dollars and the members of the yacht club at Balboa assured me that this visa was no longer needed for yachts. But this was not what the Equador Consul at Panama (a conscientious man) thought. Later I learned that the Ecuador Consul at Colon (Atlantic side) asked Pierre Deshumeurs for only 3 dollars. 'Nobody can make head or tail of this,' said Auboiroux to me ... and he left without a visa to cut short any further argument.

And to have gone past all that without stopping ... the thought of it would have made us ill ... But we were no longer in a hurry since we had decided to return home via Cape Horn, after having enjoyed the Pacific, in our own good time. This return via Cape Horn was not a snap decision: After careful consideration it had become more and more obvious that this was the logical route for *Joshua*. Here is why:

The usual route that yachts take from Tahiti to France leads via the Torres Straits and the Cape of Good Hope. Or via Torres and the Red Sea. This is the classical route for small yachts.

But when one thinks of it, this classical route is strewn with snags: the weather can be vicious in the reef-infested waters between Tahiti and Torres. Also, (and above all), it is imperative to choose the right time of year for Torres and the Cape of Good Hope. The same goes for the Red Sea. A look at the Pilot Chart brings this home very quickly.!

In other words, the westward route not only calls for thorough *planning,* but its full of very obvious risks for anyone who is in a hurry. *For it is not enough to want to hurry, we would also have to find the time to get the sails and rigging into perfect shape* for this long voyage.

By returning via Torres and the Red Sea we could have arrived at Suez in December 1966 and been back in the Mediterranean in the winter for the last lap back home. Not so funny! However, only by leaving Tahiti as soon as we got there could we have got through Torres before the onset of the monsoon season, and without finding the time to overhaul the sails and rigging thoroughly. In other words, if we had wanted to return by way of Torres Straits we would have had one long rush, without time to breath or enjoy our ports of call. The same problems would have arisen if we had gone back via the Panama Canal: we would have had to pick the right time of year and make a very long detour via Hawaii to find favourable winds. And all that in order to arrive in France by July or August 1966.

One look at the globe, though, will reveal that the distance is the same via Cape Horn, with one important difference: one can be home in four or five months.

So the return via Cape Horn would be much quicker. It might be very rough at times, but at least everything would be straightforward: no reefs. And we would have many months to prepare

Joshua thoroughly before the onset of the austral summer, which is the favourable period (December/January). In this way we might be able to be back with the children for the Easter holidays, six months or a year ahead of schedule, and after having *really* enjoyed the Pacific.

I read Miles Smeeton's *Once is enough* which a friend at the yacht club gave me. It is a first class-book. In it Smeeton analyses *Tzu-Hang*'s accident in a very thorough manner: what he saw, what he did not see, what he thinks happened, so that other yachtsmen might benefit from it.

I also planned to see Robinson who was then at Tahiti and who had weathered a hurricane with unimaginable seas on the route we would be taking. He had written a book about it which I would get at Papeete. According to a friend who told me about it Robinson's conclusions coincided more or less with Smeeton's: slow the boat down as much as possible in a following sea and take the seas from astern. Since Durban I had felt that this was the way to deal with the kind of super-heavy weather which I had not yet met with, and this was one of the reasons why *Joshua* was given a central cockpit and two cabins.

At Tahiti we would build a look-out dome and bolt it on top of the main hatch, so that we would be able to survey the whole horizon, and install a seat next to the inside wheel under the dome. This would make a proper steering position sheltered from the cold and the sea, which would multiply our safety factor by ten, by a hundred, or perhaps indefinitely if we should happen to meet with the same disaster as *Tzu-Hang*.

We would leave Tahiti with several cards in our favour: *Joshua* was indestructible because she was built of steel, she would have an inside steering position, all the spare clothing stowed in the lockers would remain completely dry (long live steel) and, finally, we would be able to remain at sea for five months by filling only two of our four water tanks. And even if we should meet with big trouble in the Atlantic after passing the Horn, we would not die of thirst because we were equipped to catch rain water. These were already four great advantages.

There remained a fifth advantage, which was a tremendous one: *we would benefit from the experience of others.* All those who have rounded the Cape help others who come after them. But those who failed often help more; it is a bit like mountaineering. So we stood a very good chance of succeeding all along the line ... not forgetting that we were not alone: without Knocker and without Fricaud there would have been no *Joshua* and without Smeeton and his book we would, perhaps, have lacked that certain extra know-how which sometimes helps you to master a difficult situation.

True, it would not be all roses 'down there', but I preferred that solution by far to the idea of returning via the Torres Straits, which would take much longer and be more risky. But one thing was certain: with *Joshua* we could take the logical route without risking our lives. And if we lost our masts there would be no problem: we could always make a port in Chile under jury rig as *Tzu-Hang* had done and go via Panama after repairs!

'All right then, we'll take the logical route. Do you agree, Françoise?'

'Yes, I agree. I trust you!'

Joshua dropped her mooring on Sunday the 14th March and anchored two hours later 7 miles from the Balboa Yacht Club in a bay sheltered by the small island of Tobago. This was a peaceful spot where we scrubbed the bottom by skin diving before setting out on the next lap: the 900 miles which separate Panama from the Galapagos Islands. We had chosen what was considered to be a bad time for this passage: little wind or head winds, little-known currents and dead calms, sometimes of long duration. So we had to get as many of the chips as possible stacked in our favour and start with a completely clean hull which would offer the least resistance to the feeble winds prophesied by our Pilot Chart.[1]

There was also the question of season, which can make all the difference on that lap: thus, most yachts coming from Europe arrive at Barbados (Antilles) during December, visit the chain of the lesser Antilles during the good season and then continue

---

[1] Pilot Charts: American charts which give, for every month of the year, a wealth of useful information for mariners, such as winds, percentage of calms, direction and strength of general currents, percentage of gales, season and paths of cyclones, etc. These Pilot Charts give an overall idea of conditions, which is indispensable for long voyages. Their price is reasonable: in 1963 a set of 16 charts covering the whole of the South Pacific and the Indian Ocean cost $3.50. The Harbourmaster's Office at Panama stocks every chart in the world.

on their way to Panama before the return of the cyclone season which, according to the Pilot Chart for the Caribbean, is between May and June. They get through the canal, stop in Balbao for a breather, to careen and watch the pelicans fish, then set sail for the Galapagos. Unfortunately, the season, which is never really favourable on that lap, had deteriorated even further: the Pilot for June, July and August forecast mainly headwinds, force 4 on average, for a good part of the way, with calms likely at any time of the year. But what was more serious was the adverse current from June to September (the icy Humboldt current).

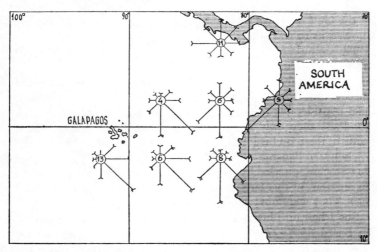

Pilot Chart for March, April and May. The figures indicate the percentages of calms. The arrows indicate the frequency, direction and force of winds.

Many interminably long passages from Panama to the Galapagos have *partly* been due to the fact that the season has no longer been favourable. I say *partly*, for conditions in this sea area, which has been cursed by so many large and small sailing yachts, are never *really* favourable.

Nevertheless, by crossing during the good season one can 'help things along a bit'. Thus Jean Bluche's *Chimère* knocked off this stretch in only ten days, without using her engine. Other yachts have made the correct crossing between December and February, which are considered the best months because of the fair currents all the way. It is also during those three months that

95

the easterly trade is strongest in the Caribbean Sea and can cross the Isthmus of Panama to blow as far out as the Malpelo Rock, from where a yacht stands a chance of catching the south-easterly Trade which will blow her straight to the Galapagos. But all this is theory

Late in the afternoon on the 16th March *Joshua*'s bottom was spotlessly clean and there was not a trace of plankton left on it which might have encouraged barnacles to cling to the hull. But it had taken the two of us two and a half days to complete the job which I usually managed in one day on my own. The cold water of the Gulf of Panama (Humboldt or Peruvian Current) had not allowed us to stay in it for more than ten minutes at a time.

The uninitiated might be surprised to learn that even if a hull is barely fouled by algae this will be enough to slow it down very appreciably in light winds. But once barnacles get a hold the effect is catastrophic, for these crustacea, which grow on a stalk, offer considerable resistance to speed through the water. Thank goodness they only live in the open sea. Le Toumelin found loads of them on his log line despite the fact that it had been turn-ing between Panama and the Galapagos. And I seem to remember that Slocum, puzzled by the erratic readings of his log, found to his amazement that large barnacles were clustered round the *brass rotor*. They were obviously not subject to dizziness!

But I had no illusions in this direction. In the Indian Ocean, on board *Marie-Thérèse*, I had always made use of calm spells, or of lying hove-to, by pulling the barnacles off one by one be-tween my finger and thumb in order not to spoil the paint on the bottom. Between Panama and the Galapagos I would at least be able to use the scraper if the crossing took long enough for them to get a hold.

For dead flat calms were certainly no myth on this stretch which we were about to tackle during the period of the vernal equinox.

But at least there were no gales to be expected in these latitudes during the equinox: zero per cent of gales according to the Pilot Charts.

Equinoctial gales may be typical of high and moderate latitudes, although venerable, white-bearded scholars have, it seems, thrown ink-pots at each other arguing about this point. I am still too young to have an opinion, but prefer to remain in harbour during the equinox ... it's the herd instinct! (in high and moderate latitudes, not where we were then)!

Yet, if for some reason beyond my control I should ever happen to be at sea during the equinox, I should be careful not to make any mistakes in my latitude calculations, for the sun's declination changes to 'minus nought'. For instance, it changes from 0° 08' South to 0° 15' North between the 20th and 21st March. And if you go on subtracting the declination (as you have rightly done up to and including the 20th March) instead of adding it to the latitude calculation for the 21st March, you may well find yourself on some rock which you thought you were wisely leaving some twenty miles to leeward ...

Another thing is that, on the equator during the equinox, only one sight can be taken of the sun in 24 hours because the azimuth is the same all through the day: due east in the morning, due west in the afternoon. Thus, *all the positions of the sun are orientated north-south at that time of the year (near the equator).*

This meant we would have to navigate very carefully by the stars so as not to be too far out as we approached the Galapagos. 'The bewitched archipelago', the ancients used to call it because of the freak currents that are to be found in this sea area: you may see an island late in the afternoon, set course for it during the night in a light breeze and find nothing but unbroken horizon at daybreak ... the island has floated away with the current to play hide-and-seek and you might as well toss a coin to decide whether it has disappeared to the left or to the right. This game is enough to give you heart failure.

But on board *Joshua* we were a hundred per cent prepared. We now managed to ascertain our position within a circle not exceeding 2 mm in diameter by taking four star sights. I am not writing this to boast but because I was amazed at how I could have been sailing for so many years without ever having taken a star sight. It made navigating so much safer, so much easier ... and it had been child's play to learn how to do it.

Joshua set sail on the 17th March at 8 o'clock in the morning and with a steady nor'westerly breeze she made Cape Mala at a rate of six knots, while we prayed that it would last!

It lasted and *Joshua* headed towards Malpelo Rock, the first stepping stone on the route to the Galapagos. The wind remained a steady force 3 to 4 and the sea, a beautiful sea, promised a favourable wind for at least the next forty-eight hours, for there was no sign of any swell from the south. By midday the following day we had covered 159 miles in 28 hours since leaving Tobago, and the sea was beginning to warm up. It seemed almost incredible!

Everything pointed to the weather lasting. To start with, the wind was plainly the north-east Trade. Secondly, the sky was crystal clear. Finally, I was keeping a careful lookout to the south, and there was no secondary swell coming from Malpelo or elsewhere.

And the miracle actually happened: 128 miles covered by the 19th and 85 miles by the 20th, which put us 63 miles south of Malpelo, only three days after setting off, in what is theoretically the zone of south-easterly Trades, *without having run into any calms on the way*!

The sky remained as blue as ever, the sea stayed calm and had now turned beautifully warm: this was the Equatorial Counter Current which comes from Cape Mala and branches off towards the west. It had helped us to find the south-east Trade, for here it was: first a light breeze from the east, force 2 ... then a light south-easterly, force 3.

Joshua must have found favour in the eyes of both the Gods of Europe and Asia: 117 miles on the 21st March, 125 on the 22nd, with a steady south-easterly breeze averaging force 3, sometimes only force 2, and a fair, wonderfully warm current to help us along. We had covered as much as two-thirds of the way in five days and were sailing in what was a veritable playground for turtles. We saw seven in one day, sunbathing on the surface of the water. Unfortunately our harpoon was seconds late every time, but I think that if we could have brought ourselves to use the engine we could have had plenty of fresh meat on board. One turtle, when touched by the harpoon shaft, simply lifted its head and went back to sleep This reminded me of a turtle hunt Mico Sauzier once undertook in a flat calm in the Atlantic, off Ascension Island: since his engine had broken down, Mico launched the dinghy to harpoon a turtle ... successfully.

But being so incredibly lucky with the weather in this renowned 'rotten' sea area we did not dare incur the wrath of the gods by

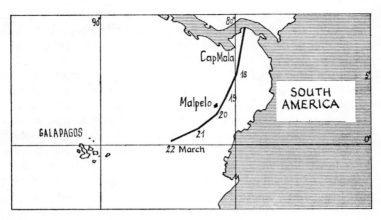

spending half an hour trying to catch a turtle. Anyway, there would be plenty at the Galapagos!

While we were a bit sorry at having to do without fresh meat, fish was nevertheless served at every meal. In the days of my two *Marie-Thérèses* fishing had always been poor. I had only once caught the head of a barracuda in the Indian Ocean (a shark had had the rest) and nothing ever in the Atlantic. I used to trail only a single line behind the boat which could never have given the illusion of a whole *shoal* of small fish. This was undoubtedly one of the main reasons why dorado and bonito ignored my bait. Never having caught anything I had lost faith and just left the hook to rust without baiting it, and the vicious circle closed. Otherwise I might have caught a famished dorado one day.

Since I had had *Joshua* I had regained confidence, and we were trailing four choice pieces of bait. It paid! Three bonito and one dorado between Casablanca and the Canaries, eleven fish between the Canaries and Martinique (7 dorado, 2 bonito and 2 large tunnies, about 30 lbs in weight), but nothing between Martinique and Christobal, except for four broken lines.

Except in the case of very large fish our lines were no longer in the habit of breaking: they were now made of nylon, 3 mm in diameter, and sprung with two strong rubber shock absorbers, cut from the inner tube of a lorry tyre. In this way the fish did not strain the line when fighting. The dorado we caught, weighing between 10 and 20 lbs, were extremely powerful and perfectly capable of breaking a very strong line. And if a dorado turned its

99

nose up because it considered the line was too plainly visible, very well, let it chase flying fish, but if it succumbed to the temptation in the end, which was often the case, it found itself invited to dinner, whether it liked it or not.

On the other hand, if a large fish battled at the end of the line for the best part of the night (we did not spend all our time on deck) it would finish up by tearing its mouth. This happened with tunny, in particular, who have very delicate mouths. It seldom happened since we had taken to using the large double hooks without barbs which professional fishermen use. A slip knot in the line would tell us when a fish had bitten. The bait consisted of a small tuft of nylon taken from a new piece of rope, nice and white, knotted onto the double hook. The log, of course, was not used in the open sea, but was put back into service as we approached land.

The wind dropped right off during the night, backing east-nor'-east, with short spells of calm from time to time ... hm! ... it had been too good to last. I consoled myself by diving under the hull: it was as clean as when we had left, which was a bit of luck in these light airs. For, in the Atlantic the barnacles that had accumulated *within several days*, because we had not cleaned the hull properly before setting out, must have doubled the wetted surface and killed the boat stone dead in light airs between the Cape Verde Islands and Martinique. Now *Joshua* was slipping along nicely towards the Galapagos, responding to the slightest

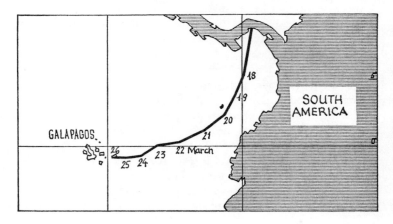

puff of the gentle force 1–2 breeze. When racing helmsmen polish their hulls it is not 'to make them look good' ... It had taken me time to realise that on this point racing and cruising are very closely related.

Another 94 miles covered on the 23rd March. This put us within 180 miles of Chatham and Wreck Bay, which is the obligatory port of entry for visiting yachts. We had thus covered 700 miles in six days, and the gods were not yet tired of seeing us sailing with an awning up as protection against the sun and to catch a bit of breeze at the same time ... for our luck lasted to the end, and two star observations at 5 a.m. on the 26th March put us 20 miles to the east-southeast of Chatham Island and 38 miles off the anchorage of Wreck Bay.

So we had almost arrived, less than nine days after leaving... This was extraordinary good luck, and we would have to burn incense on the bowsprit and in the cabin, for *some boats have taken up to sixty days to cross from Panama to the Galapagos*, in roll-neck sweaters, in rotten weather, against a foul and icy current, impeded by never-ending calms, under a leaden sky, beating against head-winds, followed by blazing sunshine which turned the sea into molten lead.

Yes, we would have to burn incense, for instead of all this *Joshua* had had *the most marvellous weather of her life*: a magnificent sky with stars almost down to the horizon, a warm current providing us with fish for every meal, and a smooth, smooth sea on which our boat had glided along like a happy dolphin at peace with the universe.

Alas, at midday we were becalmed for good, five miles off the coast. What a pity we couldn't finish under sail ... I had to get the starting handle out. It is in such circumstances that one realises what an immense service a very small motor can render: *Joshua*'s 7 hp motor seemed ridiculously small for pushing a boat of 12 or 13 tons ... but it pushed us towards the anchorage at a rate of 2·3 knots. That was its cruising speed – I could have reached 3·3 knots by driving it, but it vexed me to have to get the whip out.

The instructions to navigators recommend great prudence on approaching the bay, particularly when approaching it from the west, which is what we did, and hordes of sea birds support this advice by dropping out of the sky onto the fish which inhabit the dangerous projecting reef which Alain Gerbault mentions. This long reef (less than 3 ft under water at its shallowest point) was not clearly marked on our general chart of the archipelago. We studied it through the magnifying glass, but there was not much to be seen.

At last ... we cleared the reef towards 3 p.m., thanks partly to the nautical instructions, but chiefly to the gannets who indicated the shallows by their cries of welcome, and a little later we dropped anchor in the peaceful anchorage of Wreck Bay.

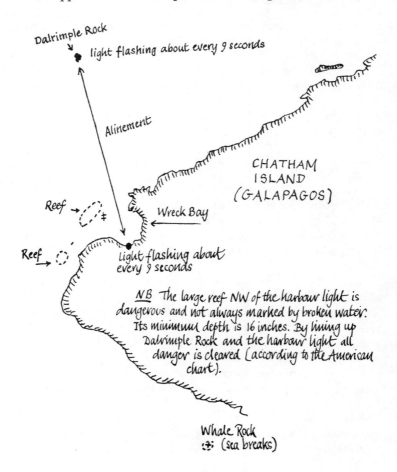

Dalrimple Rock

light flashing about every 9 seconds

Alinement

CHATHAM ISLAND (GALAPAGOS)

Reef

Wreck Bay

Reef

Light flashing about every 9 seconds

NB The large reef NW of the harbour light is dangerous and not always marked by broken water. Its minimum depth is 16 inches. By lining up Dalrimple Rock and the harbour light all danger is cleared (according to the American chart).

Whale Rock
(sea breaks)

13

A World which Fear has Spared

We anchored *Joshua* some thirty feet off the long beach of very fine, very white sand which borders Wreck Bay. Just behind it is the village of Porto Chico, the capital of the Galapagos. It consists of ten or so small, low houses built of boards and stone, with corrugated iron roofs. Over all broods the sun and the shimmering heat, and nothing moves in the heat of the day.

All round the village there is desert. A desert of lava and stone, with its tall, spiky cacti standing like sentinels, its meagre scrub, its appalling aridity. It reminded me a bit of Ascension Island where dozens of little craters cover the coast, making it look like a lunar landscape. There are about 2,000 craters in the Galapagos Islands, which extend from one side of the equator to the other across nearly 120 sea miles. The individual islands bear a great similarity to each other, for they are all of volcanic origin. But the cold current which bathes their shores tempers the climate of the archipelago and makes it the healthiest spot in the equatorial zone.

In the dry season, which lasts from September to January, rain is rare on the coasts, whereas the heights remain green because they are bathed in cloud during more or less the whole of the year. On the other hand, during the rainy season the coastal strips are watered by heavy tropical downpours, while the weather on the heights becomes positively filthy and the road almost impassable so deep is the mud. This year it was late, thank goodness!

But it can also happen that the rainy season misses one year altogether and perhaps another one. Then the goats die on all the low-lying islands which do not benefit from the cloud humidity on the heights. Barrington, Española, Marchina and Pinta are hard hit in dry years as far as the goats are concerned. These were imported by the first settlers and live wild. As for the local fauna and flora (iguanas, turtles, lizards, birds, cacti, etc) they have been so designed by the Creator that they withstand all the droughts in the world: they are indestructible in the desert.

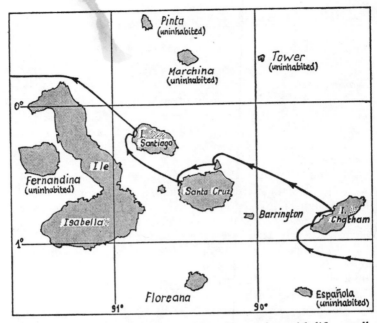

For, far from being dead this desert is teeming with life: small, red-throated lizards fled from beneath our feet and Youki never got tired of chasing them without ever catching one. Birds the size of large sparrows, with light grey, white-flecked plumage, long, fragile legs and the typical beak of insect-eaters approached us with complete confidence and then followed us curiously, without the slightest fear. With a little patience we could have got them to eat out of our hands. And on the smooth rocks at the end of the bay we met our first sea iguana, the famous black lizard which exists only in the Galapagos. It grows up to 4 feet long and has a crest like a dragon on its head. Not at all fierce, it will allow you to approach within several feet before retreating quite unhurriedly. But it will nevertheless, keep its distance.

Back on board *Joshua* we found a pelican installed on the pulpit and another on the staysail boom, which even Youki's fury did not manage to dislodge. Then a third took possession of the dinghy and others swam within several feet of the boat eyeing us expectantly and without the slightest fear. I was to learn later how far this absence of fear can go in the pelicans of Galapagos.

It was time for midday lunch and I had gone for a swim towards the great reef where the gannets were fishing. The first fish caught was a fairly sizeable grey mullet ... which a pelican promptly took off my spear! While I was looking at him, unable to believe my eyes, there were already four more pelicans quite close to me, waiting for me to be so kind as to get their dinner for them. One of them clapped his beak, without malice, as if to say that he would like a bite to eat and would I please hurry up ...

In the end two out of every three fish I caught that day finished up in the stomachs of my pelicans, despite my efforts to take them back and present them to Françoise! Unfortunately, there were no good catches left in the bay (too large to be swallowed by a pelican) because of the proximity of the village, and we had to suffer the disgrace of having to fish for small fish alongside the boat for our evening meal. The pelicans were waiting again, but they were less cheeky because we could at least throw buckets of water at them ... if only to calm down Youki who had become nearly demented with rage at seeing these amiable birds swimming beside *her* boat.

We did not stay in Wreck Bay for long. Not because it was an unpleasant spot, quite the contrary. But we wanted to track down a nice little corner far from possible visitors where we could get down to painting the hull and deck and at the same time enjoy our stay. Barrington, a small, deserted island, 'inspired' us, and Luis, the skipper of a lobster boat from Guayaquil which was moored alongside *Joshua*, described it as the best-sheltered spot in the Galapagos, confirming what we had read in Bluche and Le Toumelin.

'Come on board and copy my American charts,' Luis suggested, 'they are very detailed, and if you have a day to spare I'll take you lobster fishing with me tomorrow. The sea is warm.'

This last remark was not unwelcome. The sea temperature in the Galapagos varies between 26° and 15° centigrade, depending on the time of year, on account of the changing geographical position of the Humboldt Current, and lobsters are caught by skin diving. There can also be differences in the water temperature of some ten degrees on one and the same day and in spots not far apart from each other, when the icy current from the depth rises to the surface for some unknown reason. But at the time the sea was warm in all parts of the archipelago, and Luis promised us another *two months* of it before the return of the cold current.

Luis' lobster boat was a nice big wooden tub, very high in the water, fifty years old, and solid like most fishing boats, built with generous scantlings to resist the weather. She was about 65 ft long, 19 ft in the beam and had a diesel motor and a refrigeration plant that could hold six tons of lobsters. Ten dories completed the fishing equipment. They were stacked in two piles on the upper deck, like plates, to save space during the crossings from the Galapagos to America where the lobsters were sold. The ship was nevertheless fearfully congested: forty men to fish, plus two mechanics, an enormous cook assisted by a young negro and Luis the skipper ... That made forty-five persons who had to live on a boat 65 feet long!

To our question as to how all these people managed to sleep at sea and when the boat was moored, Luis replied very casually: 'I should like to know that myself!'

All these equatorial fishermen were young, 22 on average. They were paid by the kilo of lobsters caught and still managed to make a living, though the catches had dropped considerably for three years. Previously Luis had managed to fill the refrigerator with the help of only twenty men, now he needed forty and even then it took longer.

Having left Wreck Bay at 4 o'clock in the morning we arrived at the chosen spot to the east of Chatham in a beautiful flat calm which promised a sunny day. The dories, each manned by four men, were launched, one after the other, every half mile or so along the coast. That was the start of a hard day, even if the sea was warm in theory ... We went into the water, equipped with flippers, mask and a glove on the right hand and swam along the rocks in the same direction, while one man stayed behind in each dory (fitted with a 3 hp outboard) and ran back and forth collecting the lobsters which were caught by hand in rock crevasses at a depth of between 10 and 20 feet. From time to time we had to relieve each other on board the dory, for after a quarter of an hour's diving the water seemed less warm ... I felt sorry for my companions who were doing this work all the year round, resorting to a pullover only when the sea became really cold under the influence of the Humboldt Current!

We collected mainly red lobsters because the green ones, which are rarer, struggled furiously, dealing out terrible blows with their tails, whereas the red ones allowed themselves to be picked up gracefully by the head without making too much fuss.

In any case, I was grateful for the strong glove which reached above the wrist!

Certain rock escarpments were covered with lobsters. At least that was my impression, but my companions complained: 'You should have been here four years ago! ... I gathered one hundred and twenty-two just by myself, in a cave about six feet down. And now I am thankful if I find fifteen together in one spot. There are no more lobsters left in the Galapagos ...'

What it must have been like, in the good old days! On the other hand, fish are not in danger of extinction here, far from it. I reckoned that some shoals of a certain pearly-grey species, large and flat like plates and with small mouths made for nibbling algae, must have been made up of some three to four hundred fish, each weighing between four and seven pounds.

What I found surprising with such a profusion of fish was that I had only seen a single shark, and a small one at that. I was told that sometimes they were numerous, it quite depended on the day, but there had never been an accident in the Galapagos, the divers insisted.

Hm! ... I could not help thinking of the way a shark had bitten my right foot ten years ago, off the island of Mauritius, when I was 20 or 25 feet down with my legs in the air, swimming past a crevasse in exactly the same position as my companions that day, as they were extracting lobsters from their holes ... True, we were wearing flippers, which had not been the case on the day of my accident.

Yet ... three months later I had narrowly missed being attacked by a small shark (about 5 feet long), which shot out suddenly from behind a clump of corals while I was retrieving a harpoon I had lost in twelve or fifteen feet of water in the Cargados Carajos in the Indian Ocean. On that occasion I had wisely been wearing flippers, but I thought that all was up with me when the shark started to tremble in the way I assume all sharks do when they are about to charge, and I had only had time to simulate a gesture of attack with my arrowless gun, while Christian Couacaud had beaten the water with all his strength above me to stop that shark trembling.

Twelve years had passed without erasing from my memory this nervous trembling of a shark about to attack. I only collected seven lobsters that day, watching my big toe in its flipper all the while, while my companions caught one hundred and eighty-five between four of them without flicking an eyelid. I must say that at their age I had calmly dived into the muddy and shark-infested waters of the Straits of Malacca to collect, at a depth of 20 feet, the mud I needed to stop the leaks in my junk *Marie-Thérèse*.[1] I could have achieved the same result by dropping the anchor several times and hauling it up covered in mud, but it had been so much simpler to shout to the sharks: 'Shoo, you rabble, I'm in a hurry!', for everybody knows sharks only attack humans in exceptional cases, and that accidents only happen to other imbeciles ... Still, to a lad of 25 ignorance is bliss.

Barrington, Island of Seals

At 6 o'clock in the morning on the 31st March, five days after our arrival on Chatham, *Joshua* set sail for Barrington, 25 miles away. An hour later the outline of Chatham vanished in the fine-weather haze, despite a gentle north-easterly breeze which moved us at less than 3 knots ... and *Joshua* would have passed south of Barrington, which was hidden behind the mist, if we had not taken a sun sight at 10 o'clock and calculated our latitude at midday!

It seems surprising to have to resort to astro-navigation on such a short trip and in splendid weather, but without this

---

[1] The Indonesians make up a filler, which is applied and which hardens under water, by mixing equal parts of mud and ordinary cement. When the leaks are numerous and difficult to locate the Asian mariners dive under the hull with a box full of sawdust which they turn out some 6 feet below the keel: the sawdust rises in a cloud and is sucked into the leaks where it swells in less than a minute. The result is very satisfactory on the mooring but less durable at sea. I have often resorted to this quick and simple remedy on board my junk *Marie-Thérèse* in the Indian Ocean, and the repairs have remained effective for anything from a few hours to over a week.

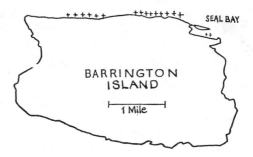

precaution we would quite simply have missed the island, because the current which was flowing north-westerly at the start (we checked this by taking a series of bearings when leaving Chatham) later turned almost due south, and there was no landmark in sight that would have made us notice the change. There was splendid sunshine, but the fine-weather haze which enveloped us like a veil made it impossible for us to make out any land that was further than a few miles away. Bewitched islands ...

At last, towards 2 p.m., Barrington suddenly appeared only four miles away to our left, after we had changed course by 40° on our original course at the outset ... How many treasures, I wondered, were still hidden in these islands which the ancient buccaneers had difficulty in finding again because they lacked good chronometers by which to calculate their position!

Our problems were over. Using the chart we had traced on board the lobster boat we made our way along the east coast, which is free of dangers, and soon found the entrance to the small bay marked by an islet (the only one off Barrington) just past the north-east corner of the island. In a light, following breeze we entered under sail without difficulty. And even in a headwind the entrance would have been wide enough to tack into in this calm sea.

We had arrived. *Joshua* was swinging to her anchor which we had let go in 10 feet of water over a sandy bottom, in a green transparent lagoon, wonderfully peaceful and one hundred per cent safe.

On the left, the rocky islet, about 500 feet long and covered with a sparse vegetation of giant cacti and green thicket, would protect *Joshua* from the ocean swell. Besides, there was a wide causeway of black lava linking the islet with the island, so that the lagoon was completely closed off to the north.

On the south side about 150 feet away we were protected by the mass of Barrington. There were some convenient slabs of flat lava onto which we could haul the dinghy out of reach of the tide when we wanted to visit that part of the island. Ahead of the bowsprit, some 500 feet to the east, was the entrance to the lagoon, just wide enough to allow us to tack out in a headwind, but too narrow to cause us any worry in the anchorage if, by chance, it should ever blow fresh from due east.

Some 300 feet behind us, at the far end of the lagoon, we recognised, as though we had seen them before, the two white sandy beaches separated by a round of rocks, where Le Toumelin had landed in his pram while *Kurun* had stayed here. The one on the right, the larger one, was just then covered with large seals.

And all round the boat we could watch a ballet of nature: seals, pelicans, gannets, fish! They were all there, full of curiosity and without mistrust, and the seals intrigued us most of all. The large males only swam past, surfacing like dolphins, and shooting a glance in our direction as they lifted their heads out of the water to take a gulp of air. But the young ones, with extreme grace, swam all round *Joshua* and kept their little round heads out of the water for a long time, with an almost human expression in their very large eyes. One could sense an immense curiosity in them, a need to play with everybody, much more so than in the dolphins.

There was a turtle ... no, two of them ... their rounded shells looking very much like the back so the young seals. We had not noticed them immediately. Good heavens ... this lagoon was full of turtles, at least five, perhaps seven or eight of them.

They spent very little time on the surface: just long enough to lift their heads out, each no bigger than a fist, breathe for a few seconds with the top of their shells out of the water ... and in the blink of an eye there was no turtle ... It would be very difficult to harpoon them under these conditions.

We watched them for a long, long time ... It had been so long since we had eaten fresh meat, and turtle meat is delicious: every bit of it is tender. I admit that we could not bring ourselves to kill one of these trusting seals, except as a last resort. But the turtles and the fish were not part of the typical, sacred fauna of the Galapagos: turtles can be found in all the oceans of the world.

In the coral archipelago of Cargados Carajos in the Indian Ocean, where I had once been employed by a fishing company, turtles were hunted with a special harpoon called a *clou*. It was a kind of spike of octagonal section about 2 inches long and ⅝ inch in diameter, terminating in a large disc where it fitted into the shaft, like the detachable heads of certain harpoons used for large fish. (The disc prevented the *clou* from penetrating the lung, the turtles having to be delivered alive, once a month, to the market at Mauritius).

But how could this smooth *clou* hold a turtle weighing 200 pounds? The answer is quite simple, although scarcely credible: *as soon as a turtle is hit it tightens and hardens its shell by a defensive reflex* and the steel, embedded only 2 inches deep, can no longer be pulled out.

This technique was only used for the males who did their courting on the surface. As for the females, the fishermen of Cargados waited for them to come on land on dark moonless nights to lay their eggs, and turned them over on their backs. But here at Barrington it was most unlikely that the females would come out on the beach inhabited by seals ...

'Bernard ... did you see that one ... It stayed up for at least ten seconds without diving, and it had its head out of the water nearly all the time?'

We watched ... with watering mouths: not only did some turtles stay up a bit longer than was safe, but nearly always they surfaced near a patch of submerged rock, clearly visible from the deck, where presumably there were some delicious algae growing.

Quick into the dinghy ... with all due respect for the peace of the place, but just then my greatest desire was to be able to present Françoise with a turtle before sunset!

The harpoon we used for dorado (and turtles!) consisted of an arrow from an underwater gun lashed securely to a bamboo-cane with a maximum diameter of 2 inches. The whole thing was 7 feet long, very light and manageable. The arrow protruded by a little more than 2 feet which made sure that it would go right through any fish without the shaft stopping it before the barb had completely opened out.[1] For turtle hunting I tried five fathoms of nylon line to a 4-gallon jerrycan which was to serve as a 'shock-absorber'.

To throw a harpoon with speed and accuracy while standing upright in a *Bardiaux* (a folding dinghy) may seem a bit risky. In fact, this folding dinghy is almost as stable as a good pram and I found that it was the ideal tender for turtle hunting. With it, I could row *very fast*, facing forward (without losing sight of the turtle) and get up easily when the moment came to throw the harpoon, thanks to its good stability ... and to prove it ... whack ...!

Thrown from ten or twelve feet the harpoon went in as though it was cutting butter, going right through shell and plastron. I was crazy with joy and started to yell: 'Françoise! ... Françoise! ...'

I had been watching the spot for almost two hours and had missed two turtles, one of them at point blank range – I could have cried – and three times I had got there too late to throw the harpoon.

But now I could see the jerrycan race across the water, in great circles, and my heart swelled with the same kind of intense joy which I had felt as a kid when I had struck a green pigeon with my sling after having sat from dawn till ten o'clock in the morning crouched on the branch of a tree in the Indo-Chinese forest, where the birds were attracted by wild fruit.

The poor turtle struggled for over half an hour and it hardly weighed 90 pounds. After that I abandoned the jerrycan: as soon as my harpoon had struck home I took in the slack line, careful not to get myself entangled and capsize, and then finished the turtle off with hammer blows ... may sensitive souls forgive me ... In this way I presented Françoise with four more turtles during our stay on Barrington (not more than one a week).

To begin with, Françoise was slightly put off by the delicate,

---

[1]This type of dorado harpoon is, in my opinion, much superior to the best among the pronged harpoons, which I have always used with disappointing results: The dorado is a powerful fish and manages to free itself in one twist despite the four prongs of the harpoon. The harpoon from Capetown, on the other hand, which is of the type of an underwater harpoon, never lost me a single dorado during the whole of my Atlantic crossing in *Marie-Thérèse II*.

pink meat with a slightly green tinge. But after the second turtle she discovered a recipe for 'blanquette de veau' and then amused herself by bottling it successfully in Nescafé jars fitted with seals cut from an inner tube, simply following the instructions in the booklet which had come with our SEB pressure cooker, a large model (10 litres = 17½ pints, I believe).

Our largest turtles weighed around two hundred pounds, and since we had started painting the boat we towed them to the islet to break them up on the rocks. This was much like opening a tin with a knife: by slicing all round between the shell and the plastron. We used to call this 'Father Christmas Day' because a crowd would gather round us to help us celebrate ... The Pelicans were always first, beak outstretched, asking for their bit. When it came to gluttony they took the biscuit, swallowing without exception *anything* which would go down their gullet: guts, fat, bones, in short everything, absolutely everything. They even fought over the most improbable pieces! But they became really amusing when one of them tried to gulp down a piece which was too large, a turtle's foot, for example. The eyes of the poor chap condemned to suffer the torment of Tantalus then assumed an expression of despair as his companions stood round him in a circle waiting for him to abandon the choice morsel.

Meanwhile, the rocks all round us would become covered with red patches: jumping crabs who had come to join in the general hand-out ... a little bit here ... a little bit there ... a bit of jostling, naturally ... some real brawls (put yourself in their place) ... then everybody was happy and filling his stomach on a piece of meat that had obviously fallen from heaven as if by a miracle. We spent hours sitting on a rock watching the red crabs eat. The largest among them were the size of a hand and all of them contracted to jump from rock to rock, not unlike spiders. The record jump we noted was about twenty inches. At first we wondered why nature should have taught them to jump so well. They gave us the answer themselves one 'Father Christmas Day'.

It was in the middle of the feast, everybody was enjoying their bit, when suddenly I saw something like a whip-lash at the foot of a rock and in a flash there was one crab less ... The others jumped to safety. A moray had caught a crab that had not been quick enough three feet from the water's edge! Afterwards we learnt that the morays in the Galapagos manage to move over the rocks for as much as fifteen to twenty feet to seize a prey that is asleep.

As for these jumping crabs, we collected half a bucket full of them, by throwing stones at them, before they became our friends, praising the Lord for such abundant and free food. But these crabs with their fragile shells turned out to be inedible on account of some bitter substance which came out in the cooking juice. But we discovered another succulent variety of crab, one with a greyish-green, very hard shell, which lived tucked away under the stones on the beach. There was no respite for those, especially since they grew as large as a fist. Yet a feeling of respect for this domain of nature stopped us from taking all the crabs indiscriminately, and we left the small ones in peace.

Our first major conquest in this world which seems to know no fear was a small wader with pearly grey plumage, all legs and beak, who had been a solitary fisher. Soon he came running as soon as we landed, asking for his shelled winkles ...

It happened bit by bit, as is always the case in nature: Françoise first threw him a piece of turtle which nearly choked him, and I myself (may heaven forgive me) fed him jumping crabs cut up into tiny pieces. After some ten days of patient approaches he ate out of our hands. After that he never left us as we toured the rocks in search of green crabs and winkles for dinner. And when I went hunting with my underwater gun he waited wisely on a rock, beside Françoise.

We came across numerous sea iguanas in groups of three to fifteen in the course of these foraging expeditions. Those on Barrington did not seem to get bigger than 30 inches long, with flat tails like crocodiles', and they never let us get closer than six or eight feet. They were matt black with a small crest and bathed only at certain hours. In the heat of the day they loathed the water: sitting on a rock overhanging the sea they did their utmost not to get wet. All the same, they live on algae, which they fetch from the water.

Land iguanas were very much rarer on Barrington and we only saw seven or eight in all, always on their own. They were large and suspicious, although in the long run those on the islet became a bit more familiar. One of them, an enormous specimen and doubtless very old, always slept in the same place near a thicket and let us come close on condition that we did not take the slightest noise ... for he was a very light sleeper. He must have weighed a good forty pounds, and we often sat for a long time by the side of this almost prehistoric animal whose sleep we respected by taking infinite and religious precautions not to wake him.

We were fascinated contemplating this green dragon, all creased and crumpled, who seemed to have been asleep for thousands and thousands of years under the giant cacti of the islet. In the presence of this fantastic creature we almost felt we had travelled backwards in time.

In the amazing world of Barrington all the animals with whom we lived in daily contact became more like humans every day ... unless it was us who became more like them! ... But it did not matter in this community where everyone is everyone else's friend (with the exception of the turtles ... and I felt sorry for them).

Our most extraordinary friends were the seals. We played with the young ones in the water, at the edge of the beach. They were amazingly friendly: they allowed us to touch them, even stroke them. Only in the water, though, on land we inspired them with real terror if we came too close.

Many of these little seals suffered from a kind of purulent conjunctivitis which did not affect the old ones. One of them, the smallest, was nearly blind. As he swam, following the rocks of the islet, he did so with extreme care so as not to knock himself on the stones. But he always recognised us and he was the most affectionate and the happiest to play with. But we did not succeed in treating him, or any of the others, with our Argyrol eye-lotion.

There was one thing which baffled us: in six weeks of daily contact with the seals we never managed to stroke a single one of them on the rocks. Towards the end of our stay they suffered us to approach quite closely, but as soon as our hands touched their soft, silky fur a look of terror came into their eyes and they suddenly panicked. It was a fearful panic which wrung our hearts and against which we could do nothing.

Even the young that lay hidden in the grottos of the lagoon to recover from their terrible half-moon shaped wounds inflicted on them by sharks would not let us touch them when we brought them fish. All animals whom one feeds regularly when they are suffering will eventually accept man's caresses, but not the seals. At least not on land. Or maybe not at that particular time of the year. There is so much we don't know about animals.

Five of the seals in the lagoon had been wounded by sharks. They were all young ones between 3 ft 6 inches and 4 ft in length. One of the bites, a very deep one, was more than 10 inches in diameter ... This gives you an idea of the size of the shark: a good six feet!

But the young seals displayed an incredible ignorance: one night I heard something go 'flip ... flap' about fifty yards from the boat and I hurriedly got into the dinghy where the harpoon was always left handy with its line coiled, ready to run out smoothly.

'Françoise ... with any luck I'll bring you a ray!'

'Be careful ... I'd rather you left him alone.'

Françoise is very fond of ray with butter, but the last time I had harpooned one it had very nearly smashed everything up and I had struggled for over three-quarters-of-an-hour before hauling him on the rocks, after unrepeatable adventures! A 60 lb leopard ray has much more pull than three turtles weighing twenty pounds each!

But instead of a ray I found a young seal playing with a fish in the moonlight. He had it by the head and 'slap' ... he slapped it on the water. I picked up the fish which he had let go and then gave it back to him, and he went on playing with it without letting my presence disturb him in the slightest. Heavens ... to think that sharks feed at night and after sunset often penetrate into channels and other fairly shallow spots where they are rarely seen in the day!

During the day a large solitary male seal swam back and forth along the rocks which border the lagoon alongside the islet, and we were almost certain that the old males took turns from morning to night in supervising the area reserved for the young and sounded the alarm as soon as a shark came into the lagoon. We only saw a single shark during our stay, but a Galapagos settler whom we met later had seen the largest sharks of his whole life on Barrington ... perhaps it all depends on the season ... or unknown factors.

In any case, the large male on watch (it was not always the

same one) hated to see us play with the young seals in the water. If he caught us in the act during his round he grunted furiously, beating the water with his hind flippers ... and we leapt for the beach while the little ones fled, knowing very well that they were not allowed to fraternise with bipeds. Then they came back as soon as their guardian had gone off on his round! Their behaviour had a striking resemblance to that of human children: if a thing is forbidden ... they wait for the parents to turn their backs. They knew that we were waiting for them close to the beach, up to our waists in water, so that we could make a quick get-away as soon as the old cross-patch arrived. They always came back as quickly as possible to be stroked, rubbing their silky fur against us, knowing very well that we were not sharks ...

It also sometimes happened that a female weighing between 300 and 400 pounds would appear suddenly while we were playing with the young. She would shoot back and forth four or five times, very close, and then go away, obviously reassured. But why were they so afraid of us on land?

We wondered whether the large males could be dangerous to a swimmer. Luis and his fishermen said no, but then Luis did not play with the young seals ...

When I was swimming by the islet (where the water was deep) to spear fish with my underwater gun, Françoise kept a look-out on the rocks and threw a stone in the water above me so that I could get out quickly before the guardian arrived.

But then you can see the back of a seal emerge idly some 100 yards away and suddenly find it on top of you, the seal having swum under water at amazing speed. Thus, I often found myself face to face with this massive creature weighing, perhaps, 650 pounds, before Françoise could warn me. And each time the big male came straight at me, then veered off at right angles and continued his way along the rocks without having shown the slightest hostility towards me. He had simply wanted to find out who I was. But I could never suppress the feeling of panic which came over me when I saw this big, round mass less than three feet away from me ...

Did sharks dare attack an animal that size? As far as we could see they did not, for none of the adult seals of Barrington had any sign of bites along their flanks. In any case, God has thought things out too well: a seal's flippers are almost black (while their pelt is generally light grey) and this black colour puts sharks off. This was fortunate for the young, for if a seal has his flipper bitten this deprives him immediately of his sole asset: the speed with which he can catch fish or escape sharks.

We noticed an interesting fact about the young seals: they stayed 'young' (adolescent) for a very long time, for we could see seals weighing some two hundred pounds still being suckled by their mothers! (The teats are internal, nothing protrudes which could slow down their speed in the water).

The time had passed quickly ... *Joshua* had been ready for several, weeks, shining with new paint. Already we must think about leaving our seals, our little tame wader who would have to learn to fish on his own again, our gannets, our pelicans and our jumping crabs; as well as all the little birds on land whom we knew so well and who had followed us around on our long walks across the heights of Barrington. But all the goats of the island were dead ... The last drought had been too long and left in its wake blanched skeletons. They lay in the grottos where these immigrants from foreign shores had waited for the heavens to relent and had died of thirst, while our fat green iguana had slept peacefully on the islet, by the side of his thicket.

We had come to Barrington with the intention of staying ten days at the most, just long enough to put on two coats of paint, and point our bows towards another island in the archipelago.

But we stayed six weeks in the anchorage without feeling for a single moment that we would like to go elsewhere, or that time was dragging.

For on this island, which one might think is a God-forsaken desert, life burst forth with a primitive richness, intensity and innocence that seem to come straight from the bowels of the earth.

And everything which surrounded us had slowly, very slowly, revealed itself, and its essential truth had become more and more transparent. The truth of the apparent cactus desert and of these animals that seemed to have come from another world. A world so very old, and yet so young.

On the evening of our arrival, Barrington had reminded me a bit of my first impression of the Cargados Carajos archipelago in the Indian Ocean, where I had spent one of the most rewarding times of my life, after having wondered at the beginning how anyone could live in such a spot which had nothing to offer but sand, sun-bleached corals and sea birds. And now that we were weighing anchor to leave the bay of seals Barrington still reminded me of the Cargados, only very much more so.

We did not think of what the return trip via Cape Horn might have in store for us. It would be long, without any doubt. We might also have a very tough time down there.

But one thing was already certain: Cape Horn had given us a very big present in advance: the time to get to know Barrington and to savour it to the full, with a primitive, *total* intensity such as our jumping crabs must have felt on eating a piece of turtle that had dropped from the sky.

Santa Cruz, Island of Men

Late in the afternoon on the 11th May our anchor went down in 3 fathoms of water in Academy Bay (Santa Cruz Island), five hours after we had left Barrington. This anchorage was rather open but seemed safe enough, for there were five boats in it all the year round: the big *Beagle* from Darwin Station, about 58 ft long, and four others between 19 and 29 ft, built on the spot by the settlers by incredibly hard work and a good deal of ingenuity.

All around us we saw the same giant cacti, the same desert-like landscape so typical of the Galapagos.

On the low cliffs, to the left of the anchorage, were the two stone houses built by Gusch and Karl Angermeyer, Germans who had been on the island for some twenty years. A little higher, on the same side, was the small wooden hut of a new German settler. New, because he had been there for less than ten years … and ten years is the minimum for the Galapagos. After that you call yourself a resident.

Further along on the left and not visible from where we were anchored was the wooden house of Fritz Angermeyer. He, too, was an old settler.

A bit further still, on the same side of the bay, were four more houses. One belonged to the De Roys, who had been on the island about ten years. They were Belgians and had two children, one of whom had been born on the island. We met and immediately liked each other. The other was the house of a German family who had come to retire here. The third was abandoned. It had belonged to a German dentist who had been attracted by the mirage of the Galapagos but who had eventually left for good. Finally, the last house, a magnificent building, belonged to an American who had come here in his yacht on a cruise with his wife and son and decided to stay. The boy, who was 12-years old, went to school in the dinghy.

The equatorial village of seventy inhabitants was at the deepest part of the bay. A dozen shacks of boards and corrugated iron hid the solid house of the old Alsacien Kubler who had come here forty or fifty years ago when the spot really had been a desert ...

To the right of the village there were some more roofs almost hidden by the dark green foliage of mangroves. These were the settlers of the 'right bank': a Swiss, a Belgian, and American. Another Swiss lived in the village.

Even further to the right there was Darwin Station: two modern buildings, smart but without luxury, that housed scientists who came here to study the fauna and flora of the archipelago. The *Beagle* (a sailing yacht with an auxiliary motor) was there to take them from island to island under the command of Karl Angermeyer.

That was it. We made our round and said hello to everybody, trying to understand a little of their lives. But what attracted our attention more than anything else, at least initially, was the tiny cove hidden behind a dense clump of mangrove between the village and a steep cliff. It was accessible through a narrow channel at high tide. It was here that we wanted to careen *Joshua* during the three days of spring tides at full moon.

Careening went off without a hitch on the small hard sandy beach behind the mangroves: a line forward, made fast to a big tree stump, an anchor aft, two mooring lines on either side leading from the mast-tops and anchored as far as possible from the boat to ensure that she would stand upright on her keel, according to the universally approved method. But it is always frightening to see one's boat in this position ... and we led a few more ropes from the masts to some large rocks. We decided we would rather take ridiculous precautions than see *Joshua* fall heavily on her side. (We had not brought props with us, they were too cumbersome).

We scrubbed the bottom while the tide ebbed, and gave it two coats of anti-fouling while it was rising ... and *Joshua* was back on her mooring near *Beagle*, in front of Gusch Angermeyer's house, at high tide.

Phew! ... We were worn out. 39 ft of boat is an awful lot for two people to careen between two tides. Even then we would not have managed it the same day if André and Jacqueline De Roy had not had the bright idea of giving us a hand with the scrubbing.

The De Roys had arrived at Santa Cruz ten years ago: first André, to 'see whether it was possible'. Jacqueline had followed six months later with Tui, their year-old baby, burning their bridges behind them. He had been 28, she was 24. What had they done before? Art and pottery, also a lot of canoe-camping round Corsica.

Their beginnings at Santa Cruz had been terrible: entirely without money they had lived in the tent, in the fog of the plateau, where their main concern had been to survive, to plant something to eat and wait for it to grow ... and then to protect their potatoes from the wild cattle and pigs. For a time they suffered *real* hunger up there.

But they had rounded the cape. They had come down to the sun, built a 20 ft hard-chine boat for fishing baccalao (a kind of cod, we were told), and were now working for two months of the year, during the season when salt fish could be sold at a good price at Guayaquil (in Ecuador).

Soon they could leave the tent for a small house they had built themselves a hundred yards from the sea, with stones, planks and much hard labour. They raised ten goats, chicken, designed three attractive postcards, caught turtles, hunted wild goats and listened to good music in the evenings. There were now four of them: Tui had become an attractive girl of eleven and Gilles, born on the island, was eight. Jacqueline gave them lessons. As for André, he was always doing some useful job, making a bread-oven, a cistern, a fishing net.

At the time we were there André was busy fitting out a 26 ft boat which was designed to carry the whole family and enable them to get about and study the fauna of Galapagos together on behalf of independent research scientists. Basically, this is what fascinates the De Roys: scientific research in the Galapagos.

Many have come here, lured by the mirage of the Galapagos. Many have left again, unable to cope with the reality of life in this hard country which tolerates no half measures.

Only a small percentage have stayed, overcoming the hurdle of physical hardship in the first year, then the five-year hurdle, which seems to be one of the hardest: it is then that they realise what loneliness is. *For in the Galapagos everybody lives on his own, by himself.* This cannot be explained in a few lines, not even in a few pages ...

Then comes the ten-year hurdle, which involves the children: will the children be able to adapt themselves to life elsewhere if one day they wanted to leave? In fact, this problem does not really exist, because man is almost infinitely adaptable.

Some of these settler families live 'up there' on the green plateaux which are shrouded in cloud all the year round. Their primitive life consists of working in isolation. They grow vegetables, raise cattle, come down to the village once in a while to exchange goods, and perhaps also to see the sun. For 'up there' they are in the clouds.

The lowland settlers, on the other hand, get as much sun as they want. Sun, hot, dusty soil, deep lava gullies, and cacti, cacti, cacti ...

But up on the heights as down by the sea there is something that is difficult to find elsewhere: a simple life, primitive in the noble sense of the word, free from all false values. Which does not mean that all true values co-exist harmoniously in this extraordinary community.

Prospective settlers anxious to get to this paradise on earth would be well advised to read first Margaret Wittmer's book *Floreana* before blindly buying a ticket for the Bewitched Archipelago. For Mrs Wittmer has been living in this paradise for thirty or forty years. She knows what she is talking about.

14

At the Gates to Polynesia

We weighed anchor at daybreak on the 1st June and were immensely pleased to pick up the Trade wind again, despite a very rough sea during the first twenty-four hours. A number of currents come into conflict with each other in the vicinity of the Galapagos. We often felt as if we were running on to reefs. But everything sorted itself out, the wind freshened from the southeast and *Joshua* was on her way to the Marquesas.

Nine days after we had set out we were already half-way there, having covered 1,471 miles at an average daily run of 163 miles, including two runs of 187 and 192 miles, during which we had sometimes stayed as long as four or five seconds on the crest of a wave ... was she going, was she not going? ... With a sinking feeling in my stomach I often wondered whether *Joshua* had not surfed for the last time.

Fishing was rewarding in spite of our speed: a ten-pound tunny, a dorado two days later, then four dorados one after the other. And something told us that it wasn't finished yet. All hands on deck to salt fish! ... What a pleasure it was to rush along on the open sea, the sails full, heading for the islands of the Pacific while the Southern Cross rose a little higher in the sky each night.

The stem hummed with pleasure during the uneventful passage: a sun sight towards ten o'clock, a meridian altitude at noon, a pencil line drawn on the chart to ascertain the distance covered since our position on the previous day ... then Françoise asking the same old question:

'How many?'

And myself giving the same old answer:

'Slowing down a bit ... looks like the wind is easing off.'

By complaining for the sake of appearances I attracted the evil eye: the wind really did ease off after the tenth day out and we logged only 131 miles on the 11th June. We ate a small tunny to console ourselves. Then the wind became fickle, force 3 to 4: 155 miles on the 12th, 131 miles on the 13th, 157 miles on the 14th, 144 miles on the 15th, 160 miles on the 16th ... ah, we were off again ... But no, the wind eased for good in the middle of

the night and for the rest of the trip *Joshua* crawled along in force
2 to 3, her daily runs never exceeding 130 miles. On the 19th
June we only did 118 miles.

What did we do all the time on this uneventful passage? Nothing,
absolutely nothing, except live in communion with our boat,
which was sailing happily towards the Marquesas, the Tuamotus,
Tahiti, with plenty of wind, wind, wind. One must have sailed
far away from any land to know how full and rewarding a day
at sea can be without anything happening. It is so different from
coastal sailing where one is always a little apprehensive, tense,
prepared for anything. Out there, in the open sea, we were prepared simply to live.

Françoise spent hours on deck, looking at the white foam
running past the boat and giving names to clouds. She only saw
three rainbows at the bow because the sky, though very clear,
was nearly always dotted with large cumulus cloud. I often sat
beside her, watching the foam run past in an endless string of
bubbles.

But my *favourite* place was on the pulpit where I spent long
moments in a state of semi-hypnosis. It was here that I could
really feel the sheer power of *Joshua*, this harmony of strength
and gentleness which emanated from the bow and enveloped the
whole boat like a halo. A halo of seven colours ... including the
red ...

It was here that I could best hear, with all the fibres of my being,
the song which the bow had been singing ever since Martinque ...
*give me wind ... I shall give you miles ... thousands of miles ... thousands
of miles ...*

And felt utterly at peace with myself, with Françoise, with my
boat: wind ... *Joshua* would have as much of that as she wanted
on her return through the high latitudes, after having thoroughly
enjoyed the Pacific as we had enjoyed Barrington: without a
programme, without a timetable, without leaving a trail of regret
in her wake.

Then the austral summer would come, the favourable season
to round the Horn from west to east with the least possible
fuss (December to January) and return to the children at the
start of the Easter holidays on a boat that had been got ready
without undue haste. *Really ready.*

We would then have won on all three scores and it would all be justified in my eyes: the boat, the Pacific, Cape Horn.

It would all be justified, and besides we would have had the most exciting sailing a mariner could dream of, on the only route which could get us back home in just a few months.

The only one ... but also the most beautiful for a boat like *Joshua*. She would sail close-reefed along the way the old sailing ships used to take when they returned home in a single lap, by the shortest route ... *thousands of miles ... thousands of miles ... prepare my rigging well ... you will pay dearly for every mistake ... thousands of miles ... thousands of miles ...*

The joy of weighing anchor ... the joy of sailing on a limitless ocean ... of feeling the blue speck of an island on the horizon being born and growing within oneself ... of seeing the boat sailing for her anchorage at top speed ... All that explains many things. It also excuses a lot!

Twenty days after leaving the Galapagos our noon sight on the 21st June placed us 60 miles from the anchorage at Taa hu ku (on the island of Hiva Oa) and 35 miles off the island of Fatu Hiva. *Joshua* had covered 2,982 miles at a daily average of 147·8 miles (I apologise for all the figues, but they will interest seagoers).

We were still too far out to be able to arrive in daylight, and a night entry did not tempt us this time: the sky was overcast, almost menacing. Navigation is simple enough in the Marquesas archipelago because the coasts are clear. But the moon, in its last quarter, would not rise till about midnight and would not throw enough light on the high cliffs dropping steeply down into the sea. Besides, there was no lighthouse on the Marquesas. This was a pity because coming in at night has something exhilarating about it, a kind of magic ... But we never took any risks, and that night it would have been risky: no lighthouse, no moon, drizzle. We were also a bit tired ...

The wind got up at dawn and blew from the east-nor'east across a moderately rough sea. *Joshua* was doing 7 knots. Suddenly ... Fatu Hiva appeared in a break in the weather, a little to port, at 2 p.m. ... all blue with a bit of green. Splendid ...

'Bernard ... isn't it beautiful! Wouldn't you rather stop here first? It's simply beautiful!'

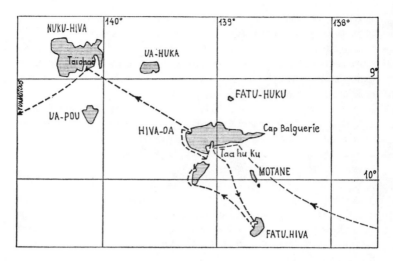

'No. In any case we would get there too late, and according to the pilot there are vicious squalls in the lee of Fatu Hiva when a fresh Trade wind is blowing. We had better stand on for Hiva Oa. We shall be quite close by sunset and can heave-to while we wait.'

At 3 p.m. the islet of Montane could be made out a little to the left of the bowsprit. This is a small island about 4 miles long inhabited only by wild sheep. Soon afterwards some of the outlines of the large island Hiva Oa appeared, but its summits (over 3,000 ft) remained shrouded in cloud.

Our position at 6 p.m. according to compass bearings, was 10 miles from Hiva Oa, 6 miles from Montane, 18 miles from the bay of Taa hu ku. The sun went down at the same time as the wind dropped and the clouds dispersed as though by magic, leaving us with a complete view of the whole of the southern group of the Marquesas.

It looked like being a calm night: the sea had gone down and we were already in the lee of Cape Balgerie. *Joshua* was perfectly hove-to like a gull waiting for the day, waiting for the moon to climb about 30 degrees in the sky, before she would continue on her way to be at the entrance to Taa hu ku by dawn. We watched over her sleep, tacking every hour: one board towards Hiva Oa ... one board towards Montane ... one board towards Hive Oa ... one board towards Montane ... She made no fuss about it, with her mainsail and mizzen sheeted right in, staysail backed and helm down. We had taken the jib down to diminish leeway.

'Françoise ... let's have some coffee.'

'With a 480 sq. ft genoa we would have arrived during the day.'

'We would have arrived last night ... it would have been just the same ... how about that coffee?'

The day finally dawned while we crept along the coast of Hiva Oa, sails winged out in a dying breeze. And all our tiredness disappeared at once when we saw this scenery of fantastic grandeur.

It looked as though whole mountains had been hurled into the sea like gigantic cataracts of stone. Here and there, as though they had been hewn by mighty blows of an axe, ran gullies. There was no sound, not a cricket, not a bird to be heard. We felt that we were listening to the ultimate silence as we sailed along the coast so close that we could almost touch it, fascinated by its awesome beauty.

A detailed description, or even a photograph, could never convey the scene we were contemplating. Something would be missing: a kind of magnetic current flowing in waves from this mass, a little terrifying in the power of its attraction.

A very gifted painter might perhaps be able to convey the message of the Marquesas to a few privileged souls capable of sensing a fluid dimension which can be expressed neither in words nor in pictures. For words and pictures cannot express the formidable green silence of the vegetation, the white and grey silence of the rock of the Marquesas. For ordinary mortals there is only one answer and that is to go and see for themselves. It is worth the voyage.

On the 22nd June, towards 7 a.m., the anchor was dropped in ten feet of water in the cover of Taa hu ku, which is deep and well protected, although the swell from the south comes in as though it were at home here and forced us to lay a second anchor over the stern to keep the boat's head to the sea. Then at last she lay quietly.

To the left of the anchorage a mountain crest sweeping round like an amphitheatre presented to us a pink and mauve cliff face across which the sun, still low in the sky, cast its rays obliquely. On the right there was another, lower, mountain. In front of us, at the deepest point of the cove there lay a beach of pebbles and very black sand on which a perpetual swell broke in lacy white froth. Coconut palms with dark-green foliage overhung the beach, covered the valley, scaled the hillsides. I had never seen coconut palms so high up any hillside. It was as though they wanted to enliven this extremely severe landscape. But it was the clear river which emerged in the middle of the beach which gave this splendid yet somehow frighteningly majestic landscape its only crystalline note, which it would otherwise have lacked.

Three weeks later we were still there, in this anchorage where everything was new each morning: the overpowering, majestic scenery, the limpid river flowing between the pebbles, where we picnicked nearly every day, with a heap of coconut fibre smouldering away to ward off the mosquitoes, the neat village of Atuona with its green roofs in the next valley, scattered along one of the most beautiful beaches in the world. And the Marquesians are such charming people. We knew we were at last at the gates of Polynesia.

At that time of the year the natives were busy getting in the coffee harvest. The coffee, which is of excellent quality, grows wild in most of the valleys, and men, women and children go out on horseback in the first light of day, with sacks hung round their necks. Their work is made difficult by the dew which drops like rain from the plants whenever they are touched, and by the thick jungle through which they have to clear a way with their matchets. One rarely sees a Marquesian without his matchet. It is like a small sabre with a wide blade housed in a hand-sewn sheath of rawhide. A second, smaller sheath sewn against the first one, contains a whetstone. The matchet is used for everything: to clear tracks in the forest, to shape logs for building houses, to strip bark off the bouraou trees for making lashings, to open coconuts, etc.

Apart from the coffee season (about two months) it is copra that keeps the inhabitants of the islands permanently busy: the dry coconuts are gathered at the foot of the trees (with the point of the matchet) thrown together on heaps with something like a sling and shelled on the spot with the help of a stake driven into the earth. The nuts are then opened with the stroke of a matchet, the white pulp peeled out with a very short knife with a wide blade and finally put to dry. This is done in the open air, either on the inclined trunk of a coconut palm in fine weather (the pieces of pulp are then placed one on top of the other, the curved side turned upwards) or on a raised platform adjoining the house, protected by a sliding roof which is pushed over the drying loft at sunset.

All the coconut palms on the island are ringed with a zinc band about 20 inches wide, which is nailed round the trunk at about 15 feet off the ground. This smooth band stops the rats from climbing the tree, providing the tree is kept well trimmed so that they cannot climb the lower branches and by-pass the band. These rodents do terrible damage to palms which are not ringed, biting through the young nuts which then rot under the tree. In the Antilles it is quite common to see the ground strewn with small nuts bitten off near the stem where the fruit is soft. But in the Marquesas, and I believe in the whole of Polynesia, the French Government provides the zinc bands free and also awards a bonus for the use of these bands. A bonus is also paid for every coconut palm planted in the place of an old tree. It is a way of stimulating the proverbially indolent Polynesians to some effort.

But are they really indolent? They build their houses, go fishing, harvest their coffee, dry their copra, look after the coconut palms … in a word, they do their bit and live frugally without making unnecessary needs for themselves. And when they have finished their day's work, well, they watch the coconut palms grow or have forty winks. I call that wisdom.

We spent quite a while with O'Conor and his wife on our way back from our usual picnic on the beach, late in the afternoon when everyone had done his work.

He was about forty, a Marquesian from Fatu Hiva, despite his very light skin, his blue eyes and his Scottish name. He had got round the archipelago and knew a little about the Tuamotus and Tahiti. His French was, nevertheless, very sketchy. His eyes were always laughing, but O'Conor was not talkative. He liked us, one could feel it.

Mrs O'Conor, fifteen years his senior, was a native from Hiva Oa. She was a buxom woman with wonderful hair, and her whole person radiated kindness. It was a pleasure to see her beam at Françoise when the two women chatted. She had been educated at a convent and her French was quite good.

They lived a hundred yards from our beach in a hut about 10 feet square, built of Bouraou logs standing upright, with a roof of palm leaves and a floor of stamped-down earth, slightly raised. There was no ceiling and a number of utensils, an underwater gun, a saddle and harnesses hung from the joists. Nor was there a bed, just a mat.

A horse, a sow, a dog which did not belong to them, but was always around, six chickens, a duck accompanied by four ducklings (the rest had been eaten by the rats), several banana trees behind the house, a hundred-year old mango in front of it, a stone oven built against one of the outside corners of the house, those were all their possessions. No, I forgot the outrigger canoe pulled up under the palm trees on the beach, in which O'Conor occasionally went fishing in the well-known spots. For the fish here, as everywhere in Polynesia, are poisonous or edible depending on the place where they are caught, irrespective of the species of fish.

A parrot-fish caught in one spot is always safe, while the identical parrot-fish caught in another will paralyse you for a month. Only the predator fish (tunny, bonito, scad, etc.) are free from this curse. But it can happen that a tunny has eaten a poisonous fish, which does not affect him, and then a whole family may be writhing on the floor while the dogs howl themselves to death. Dogs are worse affected than humans and often die in terrible pain.

O'Conor and his wife were humble people without riches. They possessed no coconut palms, no land, and worked for others. They were paid in kind: out of two sacks of copra one went to O'Conor, one to the owner of the coconut plantation. Out of three sacks of coffee O'Conor got two, the owner of the valley in which it was harvested the remaining one. For in the Marquesas the smallest valley, the tiniest ravine, though almost inaccessible, belongs to some family or other and has been handed down through the generations.

O'Conor picked coffee in the season, maintained the undergrowth of the coconut plantation off which we were anchored, threw coconuts on heaps with the point of his matchet, went fishing in his pirogue, and hunted frigate birds with a catapult. I had always thought I was pretty well unbeatable with a catapult, but O'Conor shot better than I did and often hit a bird in full flight.

His wife dried the coffee on a sheet of metal over a small fire and shelled it by beating the sack with a stick. She stripped the fibre off the coconuts, cracked the nuts and removed the kernels which make the copra. She looked after the poultry, the sow, and the meals. Except on feast days she no longer cooked food in the oven with heated stones, as was the custom once. Now the *ourou* (the fruit of the bread-tree) was put on the glowing embers, the fish was grilled, boiled or fried and corn-beef heated in its own tin.

Françoise and I went to see them every day late in the afternoon and enjoyed the peace of their hospitable hearth and the affection which radiated from every gesture of these simple people living in harmony with the earth and the forest.

Memories of my native Indo-China were brought back to life by this big mango tree, these coconut palms, this shack at the edge of the bush, the chicken pecking bits of grated coconut from between my toes. The delicious, pungent smell of the coconut fibre, which was kept smoking to chase away the gnats and stung our eyes, took me back to the days when during my holidays in Indo-China I had slept on the beach, in a rush bag, with the fishermen of the Gulf of Siam.

For Françoise the South Sea began here in all its sweetness, on the threshold of this hut with its mango, and the coconut palms, behind the beach of black sand, milky with foam. For me it was all as I had imagined it to be since reading Gerbault when I was a child. Here were all these things in their original purity, and they were real.

'Let me beat the coffee a bit ... you are tired.'

At first she would not let me beat the coffee, now she enjoyed it. She did not want Françoise to grate the coconut. Now she smiled happily when Françoise grated coconut to help her make oil for the lamp which cast its light over the scene after it had turned dark. Here it took twelve nuts to make 1 litre of oil. In Indo-China it took only ten because they were bigger. The grated pulp is pressed in a cloth to extract the milk, which is then boiled. The water evaporates, the oil remains.

At the beginning she was ashamed to talk about her people's past and replied obstinately: 'They were heathens, we are Christians ... I don't know how it was in those days.'

Later, she was still ashamed, but we had gained her confidence

and she told us a little about her people's past. It came out bit by
bit, and there were large gaps in her story, for it had been so long
ago that her grandmother had told her secretly: '... large ovens ...
they could put twenty people inside for the big celebrations ...
large pirogues, three times as large as our boat, with a hundred
warriors in each to attack another island or another valley ... but
they were heathens ... when I was a little girl it was dangerous to
go out at night because of the people from the other valleys ...
the ceremonies ... but the Catholic Fathers had been here a long
time, and the French policeman, too ... but I was never allowed
to go to the beach on my own ... because of the ceremonies ...
there were still many heathens when I was a little girl ... but now
everybody is a Christian.'

She talked and talked, and we could see the big pirogues leaving the bay on the night of a new moon to settle some old quarrel
with the inhabitants of the neighbouring island; the heavy wooden
clubs ... the pikes ... the boatload-full of tattooed bodies that
were brought back after the attack for the huge *Kaï-kaï* (the
ceremonial meal); the flicker of the torches, the war dance and the
love dance, with belts made of human hair that fell in cascades to
below the knee swaying to the rhythm of the wooden tambourines
and the flashes of light that were like the joy of living, the joy
of fighting, the joy of loving the vanquished and loving equally
him who would be the killer one day.

'But they were heathens ... now we are all Christians.'

We could sense her immense distress as she recalled, for our
sake, her people's past. It seemed that her shame was tinged with
fear. Except when she talked about the pirogues: then her eyes
flashed with pride.

These pirogues had been hollowed out of tree trunks with stone
axes. The stone had been a black stone, shaped and polished,
with a double shoulder near the top to lash it to its wooden
handle. One might say it was almost like the European adze,
made of stone instead of iron. Looking at this tool (copies can be
bought in the Marquesas, sometimes with an original stone
blade) one is filled with admiration at the thought of these naked
men carving their huge pirogues.

But above all one gets an idea of the extraordinary mystery
of the Polynesian migrations, during which these people crossed

vast stretches of the Pacific with no more than outrigger pirogues, and a sea sense which we can scarcely imagine: it is four thousand miles from Fiji to the Easter Islands, and as far from the Easter Islands to Hawaii, and they did this in the age of cut (or polished?) stones, with a calabash pierced by three holes and filled with water to observe the altitude of stars: the bubble sextant ... by which they found their way back to the islands. Hm ... Few mariners believe in the calabash of the ancient Polynesians, and nor do I.

Yet these expeditions that set out in pirogues to discover new lands were not suicidal – that would have been unthinkable: if they left they must have done so with the certain knowledge that they would return if they found nothing. But how did they manage to return? How did they manage to find again an island they had discovered several years before?

In any case, a similar language is spoken on all the islands, and if one of the King's vessels with Tahitians on board discovered the Hawaiian Islands the Tahitians could understand the inhabitants of the new archipelago. The same goes for Easter Island, a tiny spot in the midst of the vast Pacific Ocean: more or less the same language is spoken there as on Tahiti, Fiji or the Hawaiian Islands. So they must have found it. But how?

Three weeks flashed by and seemed to us like a single day. Just when we were beginning to grow roots we had to be on the move again.

Joshua left Taa hu ku on the 10th July by the light of a beautiful moon and made for Fatu Hiva (45 miles away), where we anchored two hours before sunset among the extraordinary scenery of Hanavavé (Bay of Virgins).

This is a small cove where the water is as smooth as a millpond. It is open only to the west and dominated by red cliffs about 600 feet high with impressive overhangs punctuated by enormous black rocks stuck to the walls. At the far end of the cove there was a narrow valley, almost a ravine, with its beach, its palm trees, its tropical vegetation and, of course, its river, babbling gaily as it cascaded over the rocks.

I had seen countless attractive spots during my wandering existence, but one like this ... never. I know, I know, one often says that, because anything which is novel always seems more beautiful. But neither Françoise nor I had ever beheld scenery which combined in such a compact way all the elements of utter beauty. Hanavavé is radiant with beauty. Nothing like the severe and colossal majesty of the coasts of Hiva Oa. Hanavavé is a perfect masterpiece. The most beautiful sight we had ever seen.

The small, straggling village is hidden by a cliff which projects and forms a tiny basin to the right of the bay, very convenient for landing. A sloping concrete ramp is used to pull up the pirogues. But none of this could be seen from the anchorage.

At Hiva Oa we had kept ourselves very much to ourselves, apart from the ritual visit to the O'Conors. Here we took a much greater part in village life. People were definitely more handsome here than on any of the other islands in the group. I wonder what the reason for this is. Maybe because the island, due to its rather low production of copra, is relatively isolated and contacts with the outside world are limited.

The inhabitants of Fatu Hiva were particularly pleasant and hospitable. We could not put a basket down without having it filled with oranges, grapefruit and wild roots. And if we did not bring a basket, the oranges were left in the dinghy (Fatu Hiva is the island of oranges).

The village was preparing for a festival on the 14th June: garlands were being wound, skirts made for the dances, and people were training for the *tamouré* competitions in which Hanavavé was to compete with the main place on the island, the large village of Omoa, on the next bay.

The villagers were slightly surprised that we had not gone on to Tahiti to spend the feast days there ... but we preferred the peace of the most beautiful bay in the world!

On the 14th June, well before daybreak, most of the villagers piled into the big, clinker-built whale-boat, while the rest took their seats in pirogues and everybody was off to Omoa (5 miles away) with a great pop-popping of outboards. *Joshua*, too, weighed anchor and went to join the feast (the village chief had officially enrolled me to defend Hanavavé's honour in the 400-meter swimming competition!).

We stayed at Omoa for two days ... but I cannot tell you the story, it would be too long!

16th July

The whale-boat and the pirogues arrived back at Hanavavé. We had lost the dance tournament. The dancers from Hanavavé had been better ... but those from Omoa, though technically inferior, had been quite ravishing, which had impressed the jury (the schoolmaster and the 'weatherman', both Tahitians, and therefore neutral). On the other hand, we had won the pirogue race, the 400-metre swimming competition (well done, Bernard!) and the cross-country run, but lost in the javelin. Since the prizes had been awarded in cash they had wanted to give me fifty francs ... I had refused with dignity in favour of the second (a lad from Omoa), and immediately we had been covered with oranges.

17th July

Out lobster fishing with Té-Ao and his cousin. It is enough to make you shiver; they fish for lobsters at night here,[1] by diving with a waterproof electric torch. Crazy. I flatly refused to go into the water and showed them my right foot:

'Sharks?'

'Yes, a shark.'

There were three of us in the pirogue. Té-Ao and his cousin went into the water, came up with a lobster each (shot with an under-water gun) and climbed back into the pirogue with eyes as large as saucers:

'Bernard ... it was as large as the pirogue ... and its eyes ... as big as this!'

This time they were really scared ... I did not have to show them my foot.

18th July

A great bustle in the village at daybreak. Dogs barked and fought and got beaten with thole pins. Then the big whale-boat was launched from the slip with fifteen men and fifteen dogs. The dogs were calmed down.

'Bernard, are you coming? We're off hunting.'

I seized an oar and rowed with the crew: I wanted to do my

---

[1] In this part of the Pacific lobsters live at inaccessible depths. But they come near the surface during the night and can then be found 10 to 20 ft deep.

share of the work like the others in return for my share of the
hunt. We had been eating corned beef for too long on board
Joshua, for we were as scared of the fish as of the plague ... I
imagined myself paralysed for a month, and Françoise and Youki
immobilised too, incapable of laying a kedge!

We rowed northwards along the cliff. An hour later the dogs
were thrown into the water off a small village. Two men were
put ashore armed with a short, broad-bladed knife each: for wild
boar. The dogs would run it to earth, then it would be finished
off with the knife. The whale-boat would pick up this first group
on the way back.

Two more hours' rowing against a stiff breeze and a sea which
was beginning to build up since we were no longer completely
under the lee of the island, then we rounded the north point and
arrived off a cleft in the mountain. Everybody disembarked by
jumping on a ledge on the cliff face. Two youngsters stayed behind
in the boat to mind the anchor rope, ready for any manœuvre
(coir rope, coral bottom, a fair amount of swell).

Four men (including me) climbed to the top. The others got
busy in the ravine rounding up the goats and driving them up to
the top where we were waiting with stones – no, veritable
boulders!

One hour ... two hours ... the herd was approaching, we could
hear their bleating distinctly ... soon we could hear the gravel
rolling down from under the hoofs of the disturbed goats and the
feet of the men. Up there, we were barring the only exit.

Suddenly, everybody was there and the massacre commenced.
I am not going to shed any tears over telling the story, for I had
my share in it like all the others! But it was, nevertheless, a night-
marish spectacle, a crazy slaughter with stones and matchets ...
goats were taking the shortest way down, bouncing for 300 feet,
their skulls smashed ... others descended in a kind of gliding
flight right down to the sea which we could see far, far below
at the foot of the cliff. Flying goats, indeed! I saw some fly that
day! Well ... let's change the subject. It could not have been very
pretty in those days when these people settled their little debts
on top of some ravine or other that did not belong to anybody ...

It was already late when we got back to the boat with our
nineteen dismembered goats, which were sure to be tender after
a descent like that!

Wind and sea were with us on our way back and we soon arrived at the first valley. Taking the dogs back on board was quite a performance for they reckoned it was too soon to finish the hunt. These dogs loved hunting, but they had thrown themselves on the first young boar that came their way while the big grown-up boar had got away too far to be caught. I could imagine how the two furious men had whacked the dogs for this tactical error. We had to count the pack carefully, whistle for the laggards, and plead with them to come. It took a good hour to get the fifteen dogs on board and count them again in the boat to make sure that none had been forgotten. For any dog left behind would never return to the village but hunt on his own and thus decimate the number of wild goats.

At last we were finished and returned to the village shortly after sunset. I was given my share, which I presented to Françoise: a goat (I only took half because we had no refrigerator) and a nice lump of fat.

20th July

Goodbye, Hanavavé. We weighed anchor towards midnight. The time had come, Françoise had nothing left to do: she had given away her dresses, her perfume, some of my sailmaker's nylon thread. There was not a mirror left on board. But these people were so pleasant, so genuine. As for myself, I gave them all our used sheets for tying up their horses.

One of our friends made me a present of a piece of black stone he had found in a cave, deep inside the mountain. The cave had been full of human skulls.

'But they were heathens ... we are Christians.'

It was impossible to get him to take me there.

'No, I cannot take you there ... it is very dangerous, the rock is rotten ... high up on a mountain ... and you are not allowed to look ... they were heathens ... I only took the axe I have given you, and even that I should not have taken ... they were heathens.'

'Goodbye, Hanavavé ...

21st July

We let go the anchor late in the morning in Resolution Bay (Island of Tahuata). It was an excellent anchorage with a sandy bottom, recommended by our English chart, No. 1640. I prefer

English charts by far, they often give plans of bays and useful details in all the corners that would otherwise be empty. Their paper is of excellent quality and lasts much longer.

Tahuata did not attract us: the people seemed a bit flabby. We certainly missed our friends in Hanavavé who had been so gay and lively. But Resolution Bay is not without beauty, far from it. We made use of our stay here by seriously practising our astro-navigation with a view to the crossing to the Tuamotus. Our sun observations now put us within half a mile of our anchorage. And one night at 8.15 p.m. (no moon) a sight of Spica put us within 1·3 miles of our known position (no telescope, both eyes open).

I found that one had to 'moor' a star when the night was very dark or the horizon not very clear. Mooring a star means placing it slightly lower than the apparent horizon, which is inevitably a bit blurred. I think it is the only way to get a correct altitude after dusk, or when the sea is rough. Bravo, Bernard, you certainly didn't invent anything, but you did find it out all by yourself! But joking apart, we made great progress by working every evening in the anchorage.

26th July

We set sail at 3 o'clock in the morning and were back at Taa hu ku by daybreak. We jumped into the dinghy to take a sack of oranges to the O'Conors.

We also said goodbye to the Fathers of the mission, who led us under a lemon tree and told us to fill two baskets. They also gave us honey from their hives. The good Fathers. On our previous stay they had lent me a copy of the Instructions for Mariners from the year 1894 in which I had found a mass of interesting details on the very tricky navigation in the Tuamotus. A gold mine ... it was good to hold this old book that smelled of the days of sailing ships.

27th July

We got under way late in the morning and anchored before sunset in the bay of Hana Menu, on the north-west coast of Hiva Oa, quite near the beach. It was a peaceful spot, a completely calm anchorage with a beautifully tended coconut plantation. Lucien Rohi, the owner, had worked a real miracle by ingeniously catching the water from a spring and piping it to his house through a series of big bamboo canes pierced at the top of each knot. Over 300 feet long they were, and never a leak. Henry Wakelam would have been delighted to see such an impeccable piece of work: a real pipeline made with a matchet, brains and pride in a job well done.

Needless to say all the coconut palms were ringed and there were no damaged nuts lying on the ground. But what surprised me was the height at which the bands had been put round the tree: very high up (although the plantation was kept perfectly clear, without any undergrowth). Mr Rohi explained to us that the rats were stubborn, intelligent beasts: unless the band was placed as high as possible they were hardly tired when they came to it and sometimes managed to get over it by clinging to the overlap in the zinc band, particularly if the palms were nearly vertical, as these were. But if the band was placed very high up the rats were already tired of climbing when they reached it and had not enough strength left to make their way along the overlap. They preferred to take their custom to a plantation where the trees were banded lower down.

Our intensive practice in the observation of stars continued: I took three sights, noting the time, and took the mean. Françoise did the calculations from Dieumegard (about ten minutes altogether). We were getting closer and closer to our known position in the bay: we were ripe for the Tuamotus. That left only the mail. We had to pick it up at Nuku Hiva – the northern island – where the harbour-master at Tahiti had had it forwarded by the *Calédonien*. The ship was due to arrive on the 5th August.

30th July
Left for Nuku Hiva. We had little wind all the way and took almost forty-eight hours to cover the seventy-five miles that separated us from Taiohae Bay (Nuku Hiva), one of the safest anchorages in the whole of the archipelago. But we were not going to grow old here ... the spot did not appeal to us. It was just one of those things, we could not help it. When I thought of Fatu Hiva ... and of the O'Conors' hut at Hiva Oa, with the wonderful scent given off by the coconut fibre ...

Perhaps there was another reason for our growing dislike of the place: the *nonos*, those small flies no bigger than a pin-head whose bite can become inflamed. In the southern group of islands you only meet the white *nonos*, on the beach. But here, a Nuku Hiva, there was a second kind: the black ones. They are found chiefly away from the beaches (reserved for the white variety). I was not affected by these beasts but Françoise was, and she still showed the marks a year later.

5th July

The *Calédonien* arrived this morning ... eighteen letters: from the children, the family, friends. A heavy envelope was stamped Dakar ... Pierre Deshumeur's handwriting ... hardly credible ... there were at least ten pages!

We hurriedly got down to writing, for the mail boat would be leaving on the next day. Everything had to be posted that night.

Short letters, scribbled down quickly, for our friends, rather more like telegrams: '... just a line, old chap ... we shall write more from Tahiti, the mail goes in an hour ... we shall probably be back early next year ...'

For Deshumeurs, my old friend from the *Snark*, there was a nice long letter with lots of tips, concentrated tips, because he would soon follow in our wake: 'See so-and-so at Cristobal ... see so-and-so at Balboa about tins – half price ... Galapagos ... Barrington ... Futu Hiva ... heathen skulls ...'

Long letters to the children: 'We are almost at Tahiti and shall be able to write to you every week by airmail. We shall leave there at the end of the year and you will be without news from us for several months, but we shall probably be with you for Easter. That's not very long to wait.' We told them about the Marquesas in detail, we gave them good advice (which they would not read ...). We told them all about Youki, after whom they asked in every letter.

There it was, we ran to catch the mail ... bang, bang, on went the rubber stamp ... what fun it was to receive letters, and to write them as well. I pity anyone who lives through life without ever looking forward to the postman.

15
A Dream at a Price

Everything on board was ready, nothing kept us now. In a few days there would be a full moon and we wanted to wait for this before crossing to the Tuamotus, this dangerous archipelago of low atolls which lies scattered between the Marquesas and Tahiti like a barrier. The currents are treacherous and sometimes strong and can take a boat off-course in an unexpected direction. This is why we had to make sure that everything was in our favour when entering these dangerous waters by waiting for the moon. Moonlight is indispensable for getting good star sights at *any moment*.

I quote a passage from the Instructions for Mariners from the year 1894 which I copied down in ink on our chart of the Tuamotus so that I should always have it in front of me:

Visibility of land
Conditions of visibility are the same for all the islands, but for every island conditions are quite different depending on whether it is approached from the wooded side or the side on which the reef is bare. In normal weather the groups and fringes of coconut palms can be seen from 12 to 15 miles from the mast of a schooner (50 ft high) and from 5 to 6 miles from the deck.

The bare reefs are marked by breakers. In calm weather, when the sea does not break, they cannot be seen until one is right on top of them. The same is true if one is blinded by the sun.

The breakers, if the light is good, can be seen from 3 or 4 miles. In a calm or a light land breeze and especially at night when all is calm on board, the roaring of the breakers can sometimes be heard over a long distance if a strong swell is breaking on the reef. This is a valuable indication but must not be relied on too much, since there are numerous reasons for its disappeareance.

Landfalls:
From all these considerations emerge several rules to be borne in mind when making landfalls. The main rules are:

1 Do not try to make a landfall at night except under exceptionally favourable conditions from every point of view.

2 If possible, choose for a landfall an island which is completely wooded, or else the middle of a coast of which a long stretch is wooded. (For *Joshua* it would be Manihi or Takaroa, both wooded).

3 Keep a very thorough look-out by setting up a regular watch when the ship is estimated to be some twenty miles from land.

4 Keep the vessel in a constant state of readiness to change course. If these precautions are taken land may be approached without anxiety (even if visibility is only 1 mile).

5 At night or when the horizon becomes obscured, stand away at once from the island being approached, or which the navigator suspects he is approaching, from the side on which the coast is bare, and keep a distance of at least 10 miles because of the currents. Since the land presents the same appearance everywhere (fringes of coconut palms, groups of coconut palms, or reefs) it is not always easy to know which is the precise spot of the coast one is faced with. If it is only a question of rounding the island, this does not cause great problems. But if one is looking for the navigable channel, one must know to which side to turn.

Where a channel flows into the sea and the current is outgoing, and where a channel flows into a lagoon, and the current is ingoing, a line of eddies is formed. In the former case, these eddies appear convex as seen by an observer approaching from seaward, and concave in the latter case. By climbing up on the mast one can thus find out for certain, before entering the channel, whether the current is flowing in or out, or whether there is no current at all. The eddies produce a choppy sea, which is sometimes very marked, in the middle of the channel. It is therefore necessary, especially with a small vessel, to approach on one side, since by passing through the middle the boat runs the risk of having the waves sweep her decks or even of falling beam on to them and losing steerage way.

Four hundred and twenty miles lay between us and Takaroa, our first stop in the Tuamotus. We weighed anchor on Saturday, 7th August at 2 a.m. and stood out to sea with a steady south-easterly Trade and an almost clear sky. Everything started off well and we logged 7 knots, which put us 72 miles from Nuku Hiva by our noon position.

But on the following day the wind backed to the north-east and dropped, while the sky became overcast: 110 miles covered on the 8th August, 130 miles on the 9th, with the sky clearing. Our astro-navigation exercises bore fruit by enabling us to fix our position within a circle of less than a mile in diameter. Alas, it was too good to last: the sky became overcast again, the wind dropped and a big swell from the sou'west gave warning of foul weather just before the barrier of the Tuamotus. We would have to stand out to sea before tackling this labyrinth if the weather was going to deteriorate in earnest ...

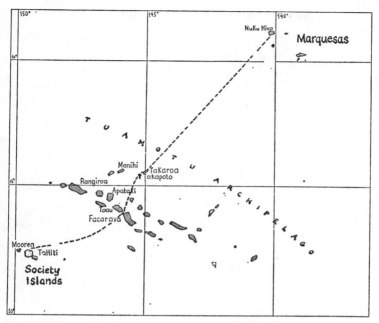

Thank goodness, it cleared nicely at dusk on the 10th August, and we were able to take four reliable star sights. The atoll of Takaroa, which we had chosen for our landfall, was 52 miles in front of our bowsprit ... but the weather was really turning foul now ...

The night was rotten, with frequent squalls, some of them violent enough to make it worth handing the foresail. What a life! And then the wind promptly veered to the sou'west in the squalls, a dead noser. It really was sickening. We hove to at 2 o'clock in the morning with the foresail stowed, the staysail backed and the helm down. Torrential rain fell during the last squall.

Then the wind suddenly backed south-east at 4 o'clock in the morning ... right on the beam! We gave up trying to understand and went on our way, heading for Takaroa. Both Françoise and myself were on deck, alert for the least sign, the least smell, the least noise that was unusual and might suggest the proximity of land. I knew that we were *at least* 20 miles from the coconut palms, but in these tricky parts one can never be quite sure of

one's position, except by a good sight, of which there was no
hope just then.

'Bernard ... the swell from the south-west is less strong ...'

'I meant to tell you ...'

The wind veered back to the sou'west at dawn and we put
Joshua on the starboard tack, close-hauled, while the sky cleared a
little without apparent reason. The swell was definitely going
down, there was no doubt. Someone with a very keen sense of
smell could have picked up the scent of copra ...

'Françoise ... look! ... a hand's breadth to the right of the
foresail ... look hard ...'

'Are you sure?'

'Almost sure ...'

A little later we were sure: a dark line ... land! The sextant
was ready, and a ray of sun towards 7.30 a.m. confirmed that it
was Takaroa. At last we could be certain!

The instructions to Mariners are not encouraging on the subject of entering the lagoon of Takaroa:

... The holding ground is excellent in the lagoon but access is very
difficult because of the strength of the currents and the tortuous nature
of the narrow channel, accessible only to small vessels (8 ft 10 in
draught).

There is a jetty for schooners at the entrance to the channel, near
the village. But we would probably be exposed there to a very
rough sea in this sou'westerly wind. And besides ... I must admit
that to come alongside a jetty broadside on in this fresh wind with
all those coral reefs around did not tempt me much. We either had
to enter the lagoon or heave-to off the Tuamotus to wait for
better weather. The last alternative was not very attractive ...

But Bluche cheered me by the invaluable advice contained in
in his book *Le Voyage de la Chimère*:

'... We entered the inside channel at the slack of the ebb.
Everything was easy until we got to the end, the spot where it
turns to the left at right-angles. The current there is fierce and
causes strong eddies.' Further on, Bluche writes '... The thought
of leaving the lagoon worried me a great deal, particularly in a
northerly wind. My heart beat faster as I took *Chimère* into the
channel at the slack of the ebb. By a miracle it was all very simple
and the strong turbulence which had inconvenienced us on entering was not dangerous ...'

So we had to enter at slack water when the eddies would be almost non-existent and wait in the lagoon, eating coconuts, until a Trade wind would allow us to get through the Tuamotus without tacking, without suffering excessive fatigue, and without being scared to death watching for reefs ...

Towards 9 o'clock *Joshua* was quite close to the north-west coast of the atoll, in front of the wreck of the three-master marked on the chart, perched on top of a barrier reef. The sea had become calm (under the lee of the atoll), the sky was filled with large clusters of cloud with wide spaces of blue between them. The breeze held well, force 4 with 5 in the gusts, and steady from the sou'west. This forced us to tack at first but would enable us to negotiate the channel later on a broad reach in optimum conditions.

Everything was ready at midday, which was, in theory, the time of slack ebb: the anchor was hooked to the bobstay, the chain run out across the deck, the mooring lines coiled in case we should come alongside the quay. And there we were in front of the channel, which I could see in full from the lower crosstrees: first it opened like a funnel in the reef, with the quay on the left near the village. Then it continued *almost straight*, very long (300 yards, perhaps), like a green trench cut through the brown of the reefs just above water level. There was no current ... we had arrived exactly at slack water (My God, was this channel long, and narrow!)

'Go about, Françoise ... I must think ...'

I no longer knew what to do. There could be no question of going alongside the quay under sail, we would come to grief, I could see it just as though it had already happened, and our little motor would be no good in this wind.

I climbed down from the mast, terribly put out.

'Go about again, Françoise.'

The channel acted like a magnet, we had to enter it at once while the tide was slack ... or tear ourselves away quickly and roll about out at sea. But I had seen the crystal-clear lagoon from the mast-top, inviting and luminous.

'Françoise ... here we go ... stand by the mizzen sheet ... look out, here we go ...'

There was a chance that there might still be some cross current, perhaps some dangerous eddies that would make *Joshua* yaw about. If she came up into the wind, Françoise would let the mizzen go. If she fell off, she would have it hard in and ease the sheets again immediately as soon as the boat had come back on course. A mizzen is first-class in eddies.

'Françoise ... we're going in ... make sure you are ready with the mizzen ...'

And woosh ... we entered the channel at 7 knots, our nerves at breaking point, all our senses (including the sixth which had awoken) acutely alert ... I had been sailing since I was a youngster but I had never before felt such complete perfection in the handling of a sailing boat. No night entry into a port, no technically perfect piece of manœuvring while berthing between two boats, nothing I had ever experienced could match the intensity of this burst under sail into my first atoll. On either side of us half-submerged corals rushed past like lightning, scintillating greens, browns, mauves, reds, blacks, all mingled with the surface swirl of a very weak following current. The long defile of light green was studded with brilliant jewels, paved with coloured patches and large pools of brown where the coral rose to the surface, causing eddies through which *Joshua* rushed. I turned the wheel hard down on one tack, then hard down on the other, while Françoise at the mizzen paid off and sheeted in, paid off and sheeted in. We were living through these moments at the speed of light.

'Gybe-o'.

There were another fifty yards to go before we would have to alter course sharply to the left and shoot out into open water. We could clearly see the change in the colour of the water which marked the right-angle turn ... another thirty yards ... here was Bluche's big whirlpool ... nothing vicious about it ... it was slack water ... or almost ... *Joshua* rushed on ... I had never felt so much one with my boat ... and suddenly we were out in the blue lagoon, almost speechless, but talking of spending the rest of our lives in the Tuamotus to savour again and again the magic of these luminous, coral-flanked channels ... where the whole of the atoll becomes crystallised in the ultimate purity of sail. I was perhaps beginning to understand what Gerbault felt: pure sailing ... this light shining round the boat ... these tremendous electrical discharges which surge through your vitals and guide you on

Mistral in the Mediterranean

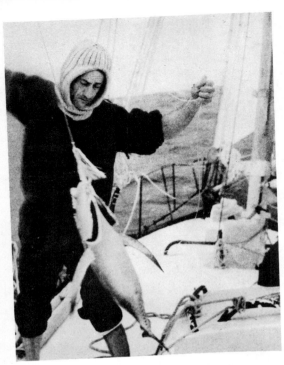

LEFT Tunny fishing

BELOW Dorado

OPPOSITE Gale in the South
Atlantic

without releasing you until you emerge in the blue and green lagoon with this feeling of absolute perfection. It was the finest experience in the whole of my sailing career.

We were now gliding along in the peace of deep water, our nerves relaxed, guided by the inter-play of colours, ranging from deep blue to bright yellow, passing through the whole scale of greens, according to the depth of water. There were frequent patches of brown: enormous corals mushrooming up from the azure depths, or vast reefs of madrepores near the surface. To leeward of them we were in calm water, able to tack on the spot in search of a nice yellow-green patch where we might drop the anchor right close to the coconut palms.

We had put a reef in the mizzen and handed the jib to take way off the boat, at the same time leaving her manœuvrable. We sailed into one inlet looking for the ideal little corner, protected from all winds and as near as possible to the palms. No ... this one would not do for some reason or other. So we would make a quick tack by backing the mizzen and staysail, for there was only just enough water for *Joshua* to turn in, and off we would go again close-hauled, skimming by the corals that were dotted with black sea-urchins and red star-fish to look for another corner that would meet all the conditions of an earthly paradise. It was a real treat to tack back and forth like this in the light and the colour of the smooth water, in the lee of clumps of madrepores put there as a windbreak by the kind Lord himself.

'Bernard ... you are going too close to the yellow ... we'll touch!'

'No ... we'll clear it ... you'll see ...'

We came hard on the wind ... and cleared it, flattening a sea-urchin, perhaps, but without touching! Françoise insisted that we had touched – the telltale.

At last we spotted our paradise: a miniature bay bordered by white corals topped by coconut palms, protected by two reefs of madrepores which closed off this natural harbour and made it as calm as a millpond and safe in all weathers. We anchored in three fathoms over a light green bottom. I put out a second anchor over a patch of yellow and took a warp to a coconut palm. No sharks? No, no sharks as far as I could see through the mask. I dived down to jam the anchors in the coral. It would take a tidal wave to get us out of here. Perhaps the engine, too ... that would depend on the wind.

And, suddenly, the accumulated tension of the past forty-eight hours completely overwhelmed us. Our eyes, red with fatigue, closed and we slept and slept and slept. When we awoke (in the middle of the night) the sou'westerly wind had freshened and howled plaintively through the rigging while the rain beat on the deck. We had nine feet of water under the keel but we might have been aground so little movement was there. How good it was to be here waiting for the Trade wind to return ... praying for the poor devils who were watching out for the half-tide reefs in the Tuamotus with fear in their vitals. How well off we were!

'Françoise ... my dear ...'

'Yes ...'

The wind blew steadily from the south for two days, in squalls, then the fine weather returned. But we were too happy to want to leave here in a hurry. All around us an exuberance of corals spread out. It was the coral which was full of life and gave life to the atoll.

In the calm lagoon it was less vigorous, more delicate. Most beautiful were the Venus's Baskets, wonderful lace-like structures of fragile coral spread out like large water-lily leaves turned up at the edges. We also saw miniature atolls growing on the bottom of the lagoon in small, perfectly carved craters, between three and six feet wide. Yet each element was made up of a unique cell with a life of its own, yet capable of developing into organised colonies.

There also seemed to be signs that epidemics occasionally attack corals, which are, after all, living matter (members of the medusa family), for we came across large patches in the lagoon where entire forests of 'stag's horn' corals had been completely destroyed. Inside these dead forests there was not a fish, not a sea-urchin.

Marine life was evident in prodigious quantities wherever corals were growing, and particularly at the edge of the great outer reef which spread out like a ring, from fifty to two hundred yards wide, on the periphery of the atoll between the palm trees and the ocean. Here the coming and going of the sea provided the corals with all the oxygen they needed to flourish and which they, in turn, passed on to the whole of the abundant fauna of the reef.

We spent our days exploring this outer reef where dense shoals of fish sometimes swam lying on their sides when there was not enough water at low tide. Giant clams encrusted with coral parted their purple lips, nearly every hole was inhabited by small morays, tiny fish lived in nurseries in the 'cheese coral' which was riddled with small caverns where they could grow up in peace in this underwater world where everything eats everything else: even the starfish prise open shells, I don't know how they go about it, but they do it! As for the jumping crabs, they must have been world champions: similar in every respect to those on Barrington, except that they were green instead of red, they were capable of tremendous muscular feats and could jump nearly three feet. It could not have been easy to escape from the morays on level ground ... and the ground was almost level on this reef.

Along the very edge, just washed by the waves, we discovered a variety of enormous sea-urchins with rough, rounded spikes the size of pencils. We opened them by tapping them on the top with a piece of dead coral: three sea urchins for Françoise, seven or eight for me, and we had lunched amply (poor old Youki did not like them).

As for the fish, alas, we only looked at them with watering mouths, for fear of paralysis. It would have been stupid to run the risk.

'Come quickly, Bernard ... this hole is full of lobsters.'

'That's quite impossible'.

'I'm telling you ... I've seen a feeler ... come quickly!'

And it was true. Normally lobsters live at considerable depth in this part of the Pacific and come up along the reefs only at night. But while looking for shells for the children, Françoise had spotted a small cave lined with green lobsters in only 2 feet of water. Groping about, I extracted two of them without too much difficulty, even without a mask, and Françoise grilled them in the shade of the palm trees while I climbed up to cut some nuts. This was the life! The following day we went back with the mask and put the nine remaining lobsters into our fish-tank: a sack hung into the water from the stern of the boat.

The weather had become settled fair and the small Trade wind clouds told us that we ought to think of leaving. We would have liked to stay longer on this atoll, to sail in the lagoon, to look for other anchorages and get to know more about the life on the reef. It was very short, one week, when we could have stayed here another year without getting bored. Yes, another year, I am not exaggerating. Perhaps much longer. We decided we would talk about it again seriously when the children were grown up. There is nothing in an atoll. But there are coconut palms and corals. Especially corals. Well ... we would see it all again, thoroughly, later.

We weighed anchor on the 17th August, one hour before high water,[1] and tacked about in front of the entrance to the channel to wait for the big whirlpool to calm down a bit ...

A light following breeze, force 3, pushed us into the bend when the whirlpool had subsided ... then we came on the wind ... and woosh ... the corals were rushing past at 5 knots, which was quite fast enough and gave us time to say goodbye to Takaroa.

There were no more problems from then on: Tahiti was 340 miles away, the sky crystal-clear, the breeze steady from the east-north-east. The moon rose a little late that night, but it was still fairly full, so conditions were as favourable as we could have wished for.

We left the wooded atoll of Takapoto behind us several hours later and headed for Aratika. We fixed our position by taking star sights at dusk, again at 10 p.m. and once more at 1 a.m. and without more ado we left the atoll of Aratika behind us and in the course of the morning passed between Toau and the big atoll of Fakarava. It was certainly easier in fine weather. Twenty-six hours after leaving Takaroa the way ahead was clear – goodbye, Taumotus. And on the 20th August at 3 p.m. *Joshua* entered the channel at Papeete, tacked twice all standing and moored alongside Fred Debels' *Tereva*.

Hello, Tahiti!

---

[1] The Instructions to Mariners for 1894 say about the Toamotus: high water coincides with the rising and setting of the moon, low water with the meridian passage (superior and inferior) or the moon. This is accurate for Takoroa.

Part II   The Logical Route

I

Preparations

We spent our first week with old friends fifteen miles from the
harbour while *Joshua* rested quietly, moored stern on to the quay.
We had to admit that it was nice to sleep under a real roof from
time to time, to have a garden round the house and the forest
close by, only two steps from the lake. But we were mourning
the loss of Youki, who had been run over by a car. It was a hard
blow, for we had loved this insufferable, yet affectionate, little
bitch dearly.

Soon we were absorbed in a whirl of preparations, despite our
many new friends. Fancy coming to Tahiti to work! Yet we had a
great deal to do to make sure that both *Joshua* and her crew were
thoroughly prepared for the return voyage.

Françoise got several pounds of wool, unobtainable in Tahiti,
by airmail so that she could knit mittens, hats, Balaclava helmets
and socks. She started knitting before we left and continued to
knit once we were at sea, according to our needs. We also received (by airmail) some valuable presents: two oilskins, brushed
flannel pants and vests and underwear. All this was sent by
friends in Paris. The cold had been our worst fear, but now we
were prepared for it. At least there was one important worry less!

Joshua now began to look like a miniature submarine: I had
cut a hole some twenty inches in diameter in the main hatch and
bolted a metal dome on top to make an inside steering position.
This dome was a simple household basin which I had bought in
the market and in which I had cut five rectangular openings
($2\frac{1}{2}$ in $\times$ 5 in) and covered them with Perspex, so that they gave
a view over the entire horizon: a proper gun turret with eyes that
could see in all directions.

A large folding seat (30 in $\times$ 20 in) was then installed at the
right height (mine!) and bolted to the bulkhead with two hinges.
There we were ... now we could steer in safety and even in
relative comfort[1] (especially Françoise, who would have to sit
on a cushion!)

---

[1] *Joshua* has two steering wheels, one outside in the cockpit, the other
inside, against the after bulkhead of the cabin.

Things were taking shape ... things were taking shape!

But the runners were worrying me: no stainless steel cable was to be had at the market, except some that was either too thick or too thin. A friend helped me out with a length of six-stranded stainless steel cable out of which I made two three-stranded runners, following the example of Henry, who rigged *Shafhai* from enormous shrouds he had salvaged somewhere. Instead of wire splicing I used rigging clamps, which is so much quicker. This done, I felt happier about the main mast, admiring those two runners, each of them shackled to a four-fold purchase to counter the pull of the staysail in heavy weather.

With the help of a friend who had the necessary welding equipment I added three more stanchions on either side in order to raise the life-line near the rudder (which gave me greater safety when adjusting the self-steering vane). At the same time I strengthened the small bowsprit pulpit with two welded angle-pieces and linked the pulpit to the life-line on either side with ¼ in chain. This would make handling the foresails safer.

All this took weeks of work ... and several weekends with friends to change the rhythm and get some relaxation. It was funny, but Tahiti was to be the place where we worked hardest!

Robinson[1] came on board during his visit in *Varua* and we found we had a lot in common. I think I shall always remember him by the way he said, in his level voice: ' ... you see, it was from here to about over there (80 to 100 yards) and the bow was completely under water ... I had never imagined that a 70-ton boat could surf like a cork over that kind of distance. Still, I think *Joshua* would have weathered that sea ...' (This was during a hurricane on the 50th parallel south).

Françoise and I worked really hard to get everything ready in time, but it was incredible how much there was to be done. I kept thinking of a truly nautical saying of Henry Wakelam: 'A boat once perished because the box of matches had not been put in its place ...'

It was true, just one small detail can lead to catastrophe.

Two and a half months passed and we were completely worn out,

---

[1] W. A. Robinson is well known to yachtsmen by the story of his cruise round the world in *Svaap*.

nervous, tired. But *Joshua* was ready. She had been put into the floating dock by the kindness of the Navy who, I am sure, had better things to do at the time. This was an enormous weight off our minds. But even then we did not know where to turn next ... remembering Henry's box of matches!

'Françoise, we had better go to Moorea (10 miles) and finish the work off there, in peace!'

All the essentials had been taken care of: the tins had been stowed, and judging by the bill Françoise must have made a good job of it ...

Two out of four tanks had been filled with fresh water (180 gallons), and we had a reserve of another 22 gallons in canisters.

The two other tanks would serve as watertight lockers and were filled with some of the tins, spare clothing, a small emergency radio receiver for the time signals, tobacco and cigarette paper (whatever you do, Françoise, don't forget my tobacco!) and innumerable indispensable bits and pieces which, in this way, would stay dry if we should have an accident.

'Françoise, did you get any batteries?'

'Yes, twelve'

'And matches?'

'I am not quite daft, you know! Did you think of the spare cable for the steering wheel?'

'Of course!'

We spent our last weekend with our good old friend Mico Sauzier whom I had known since I was in Mauritius. How glad we were to be able to spread out our toes by the side of the green lagoon, thinking of nothing, just eating, sleeping, swimming, eating, sleeping, swimming. Thanks, Mico and Touria, our batteries were recharged.

2

A Start ... Like any Other

We spent ten days at Moorea attending to the final details: check-ing the sails, putting a mosaic of Terylene patches and reinforce-ments over the weak spots in the leeches and where the shrouds were chafing. We could work carefully and without haste there on the small wooden jetty used only one hour a day for loading fruit and copra that was sent from Moorea to Tahiti. For the rest of the time the jetty was practically *Joshua*'s private property. It was calm and peaceful there in the splendid tropical setting of Cook Bay, which is deep and well protected from the Trade wind.

For eight months now we had been living in the Pacific with-out tiring of it, far from it. We had enjoyed every stop-over to the full: the Galapagos, where for six weeks we had relaxed like Robinson Crusoes; the Marquesas with their austere peace and benevolent rivers; the atoll of Takoroa with its crystal-clear water where corals blossomed like flowers inside the coastal reef, teem-ing with marine life; Tahiti the beautiful, where we had divided our time wisely between friends and the painstaking preparation of *Joshua*.

And now Moorea, Tahiti's unobtrusive sister, much quieter but no less beautiful.

We should have liked to spend another month or two vaga-bonding in this smiling Pacific before setting sail for France. But the austral summer would not wait. Unfortunately, or perhaps fortunately, for the memory would be the more vivid if we left with some regrets.

Everything was now ready, *Joshua* could go 'down there' with a clear conscience. The water we had on board would last us for five months, the food for much longer. I tried to remove the propeller by diving down equipped with a sledge hammer, for it seemed illogical to drag a brake like this behind us during the 14,000 or 15,000 miles from Moorea to Gibraltar. Unfortunately I broke a blade hammering about, because I did not possess a spanner to fit the boss, which was a mistake. To make it worse, I then could not get that cursed propeller to budge and come off its shaft. In the end I broke another blade and still could not get the stump off, which at least would have enabled me to dive down on a calm day in the Mediterranean and fix the spare prop without losing time.

Françoise sulked a bit.

'Don't worry, Françoise, where we are going there won't be any calms!'

I plugged the water intake to the engine. If all the pipe-work were to burst in a heavy blow at least no water would enter the hull.

The day before I had dived down and scrubbed the bottom to remove even the slightest trace of marine growth which might have accumulated since we last scrubbed a month before.

An old Polynesian had made friends with us. He liked me well enough, but I think he was particularly impressed with Françoise, whom he showered with lemons.

'Here, Madam, take them, they are all for you.'

Françoise was pleased, for we needed lemons for our supplies, and I believe the lemon is the only fuit which stays fresh and juicy during a long passage if it has been carefully picked. But the old boy did not want to accept anything in payment: he had a lemon tree and it gave him pleasure to present the lemons to Françoise, who beamed with joy every time. We filled a whole box in a week.

'Take this, old chap, take it, it's mine, now it is yours. Take the pump, too. Take it, I tell you, or I'll leave it on the jetty!'

This was my bicycle, which I had bought at the flea market during our stay in Casablanca. It had been very useful. But we could not be lumbered with a dismantled bicycle in the forecastle on a voyage for which everything which was useless or a hindrance would have to be jettisoned.

It was good to see an old Polynesian happy, for in his smile the Pacific sparkled, from the Marquesas to Moorea. And we would not see the Pacific again for a long, long time.

'The weather is fine, Françoise.'

'Yes, it's fine. Ready when you are. Everything is stowed.'

'Well then, let's go.'

On the 23rd November 1965, a little after midday, *Joshua* glided out of Cook Bay. The whistle had been blown, the first round had begun. We were in splendid form, boat and crew alike. But this first round, as far as Cape Horn, would have to be fought economically: economy in the use of the rigging as well as the crew. It would be a long battle until we reached Gibraltar, and it would not do to tire either ourselves or the boat in the first stages. Besides, *Joshua* was heavily laden and did not seem in any haste to reach the high latitudes, especially when the Trade wind went suddenly to the south-east and forced us to leave the island Rurutu to weather. The weather was fine enough on the whole and the wind moderate, which is all the better at the start of any cruise, and gave us a chance to fiddle with some details and get our sea legs back.

We trailed fishing lines, one on either side, and hauled our first fish (a tunny) on board on our fourth day out. Françoise prepared it in the Polynesian manner, uncooked: a fillet is cut into finger-thick slices, put into a salad bowl with finely chopped onion and sprinkled with a little salt and the juice of five to six lemons per pound of fish. This is left to marinade for one to two hours, depending on individual taste. It is absolutely delicious eaten with rice, potatoes or bread, and most Europeans living in Polynesia like fish prepared in this way.

On the 30th November, seven days after leaving Tahiti, *Joshua* had only covered 669 miles between our respective noon positions, heading south-sou'west in a southeasterly Trade, force 2 to 4. Our best day's run had been no more than 123 miles, the worst scarcely 60 miles, the sea being quite rough and making it impossible to go too close to the wind.

The force 2 to 4 Trade wind, varying from south-east to south-south-east, stayed with us until the 6th December, broken by a short period of calm. The worst day's run during that time was 105 miles, the best 130 miles. But on the 7th we ran into a flat calm, with the barometer high (1021 mb) and not a cloud in the sky. During the previous seven days we had covered 726 miles. Everything had found its place on board *Joshua*, and I had taken advantage of the fine weather to change the mainsheet blocks, replace the steel wire of the wheel, and reeve two spare halyards for the jib and the staysail. This may seem surprising, but on board *Joshua* we often attend to many small details while we are under way and can work in peace and quiet. And besides, if one was always to wait till everything was completely ship-shape before setting sail ...

On the 8th December a faint breeze came up from the west-nor'west and we were able to put *Joshua* on a favourable course. During the night there was a flat calm, but the long swell from the sou'west seemed to indicate that the Trade no longer felt quite at home here. And not before time, for we were already far to the west of the normal route recommended by our Pilot Chart for sailing vessels passing from Tahiti to Cape Horn at that time of the year. The temperature had dropped appreciably since Tahiti: 15°C in the morning, 20°C at noon.

Our noon position on the 8th December was longitude 155° 40', latitude 39° 08'.

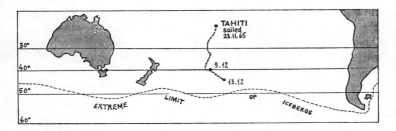

On the following day it seemed that we had struck lucky: the wind remained westerly, still light and broken by calms, but fair. About time, too, for I had started to wonder whether perhaps the Trade wind intended to follow us down to the 50th parallel south just as it followed Robinson in *Varua*. I was hoping it wouldn't, but we nevertheless headed southeast under every stitch of canvas to try and catch the true westerlies, which were still far too hesitant for our liking.

Our noon position on the 10th December placed us at 40° 32' south and 152° 50' west. The south-flowing current seemed strong in this area, for *Joshua* had covered 107 miles in the previous 24 hours despite a night of almost flat calm. This might have been due to shallow water accelerating the general current, for our chart indicated shallows of uncertain position eastward of our route. I would have liked to leave them all to westward of us, which would have shortened our route quite considerably, but the unexpectedly stubborn Trade wind had prevented us from following the customary route for sailing vessels.

Albatrosses had put in an appearance for several days, and we noticed a new variety of porpoise: small and nervous, beautifully streamlined, they were black with a white front, just as though they were wearing evening dress. Porpoises of the cold seas ...

We used that week to work out a system for changing the jib on the bowsprit: a thick iron wire (4 mm diameter) was stretched between the rigging screw of the jib stay and a main mast shroud. The jib that was to go up could then be hanked on to this false, horizontal, stay (to work quietly on deck), and the whole lot pushed right out to the end of the bowsprit on its horizontal stay without any danger of the wind taking hold of it. All that was now left to do was to hank the new jib to the forestay, take down the other one and get it back to the foredeck by the same route. This was a very simple answer to the problem of sail handling at the end of our bowsprit, which protrudes over 7 feet from the bow.

3

A Whole Gale

We had our westerly wind at last, but the barometer was dropping: 1019 mb in the morning, 1015 at sunset. The wind increased from force 2–4 in the day to 5–6 at night. We had close-reefed all sails before sunset and replaced the No. 2 jib (150 sq. ft) by the small jib (86 sq. ft) for I had a feeling that there was some dirty weather brewing in the vicinity and it would not be wise to carry too much sail. Economise, economise, we were still a long way from Gibraltar.

12th December
140 miles covered since our noon position the day before. *Joshua* had got as far as 43° 38′ south, and the glass was falling: 1013 in the morning, then 1011. We handed the mainsail around 6 p.m., then the mizzen and the staysail at 10 p.m., carrying on under the small jib alone in a very strong westerly. The barometer was now at 1005 and still dropping.

13th December
The wind dropped right away, and we re-hoisted the mainsail and the mizzen. The weather was continually changing: overcast with drizzle during the morning, bright sun in the afternoon with cirrus and cumulus in the sky. But the barometer continued its steady fall: 1003 in the morning, 996 at 8 p.m. We had all sail off before nightfall, except for the small jib, for the fun was beginning, heralded by ever increasing squalls.

Towards midnight it was blowing a whole nor'westerly gale. But we were ready for it. We had been ready for a long time. Or so I thought. I had read *Once is enough*, read and re-read it and studied it as though I were studying for an examination. I had read *To the Great Southern Sea* and had studied it in the same way. I had been to see Robinson. He had treated me like a seaman and talked to me with precision about technical matters. Robinson is a true mariner, a great mariner, a genuine blackbelt with no conceit about him. And I knew my lesson by heart.

All the warps we would need if we met with the same seas as

Tzu-Hang and Robinson were tidily coiled in the after cabin. I had broken up pigs of iron pierced with a hole at either end through which I had rove a strop. These handy pigs, each weighing about 40 lbs, were stowed under the after cabin sole against the foot of the mizzen mast, where they were immediately accessible. I had even painted them so that they would stay clean and not spoil the boat, for it is wrong for a boat to be neglected under the pretext of bad weather. These pigs would be used as weights at the end of hawsers trailed from *Joshua*'s stern to slow her down as much as possible in heavy weather. Francis Coen, who had been a member of the Tahiti Nui Expedition with Eric de Bishop, had given me one of those heavy nets used to load ships. A thing like that trailed at the end of a rope is better than any sea anchor, in my opinion.

Smeeton reckoned that *Tzu-Hang* had not been slowed down sufficiently when she met with her first accident. *Joshua* would be slowed down in time, thanks to Smeeton and Robinson.

The deck was cleared of everything except the net which was lashed down on the roof of the after cabin, against the mizzen mast. Having seen Erling Tambs' *Sandefjord* in Capetown, read Smeeton, seen Robinson and been on board his *Varua* I was only too well aware that nobody could really know the sea or imagine the magnitude of its fury in high latitudes. Françoise and I had left nothing to chance during our preparations. We might have committed errors but not mistakes in the moral sense which we attach to this word. Before our departure I had written to a friend: '... Françoise and I have done everything which is humanly possible to make sure that *Joshua* will present herself down there in a state which will not embarrass him, whose name she bears.' (Joshua Slocum) This was, perhaps, a bit grandiloquent, like the love letters one writes when one is very young. But it was true.

Now I was watching the sea rising in fury. But we were ready, in the truest sense of the word, and without any grand words. Or so I thought. At around 6 a.m., on the 14th December we were running before a whole gale under bare poles. We had stowed the small jib in the after cabin and shackled the forehatch down to prevent it opening in the case of an accident. The staysail, mainsail and mizzen had been rolled up tightly and furled against their spars so that they would offer the minimum resistance to the wind and the seas.

I disconnected the automatic self-steering gear and unshipped the vane while Françoise was steering from inside, with the hatch closed, sitting on our special helmsman's seat and facing aft (i.e. facing the waves).

I put hawsers out over the stern, working quite calmly on deck because Françoise had the boat well in hand, and ten minutes later *Joshua* was trailing:

– 22 fathoms of 4½ in. hemp rope weighed down by three pigs of iron of about 40 lbs each.;

– 16 fathoms of 3⅛ in. hemp rope weighed down by two pigs of iron of about 40 lbs each;

– 27 fathoms of 1¾ in. nylon rope weighed down by two pigs of iron of about 40 lbs each;

– 32 fathoms of 1¾ in. nylon rope towing the large net as a sea anchor;

– 55 fathoms of 1¾ in. nylon rope trailing freely with nothing attached to it.

I had tied a large, firm knot into the trailing end of each rope so that the pigs of iron, if they slid along the ropes on their bowlines with which I had fastened them on, could not slip off the ends. Why all these pigs of iron? Because, by virtue of their weight, they would make the ropes trail obliquely to some extent instead of horizontally. They would offer thus more resistance and slow the boat down more effectively, preventing it from rushing forward at great speed and burying its nose in the sea like *Tzu-Hang* had done. It was impossible to judge our speed, since the sea was white with foam which was running over the foredeck, giving the impression that *Joshua* was moving backwards instead of forward.

The white crests drew closer together, and despite the force of the wind we could hear their muffled rumblings. Those seas made us think of some large animal asleep in the undergrowth, and the little hunter listening as it stretched and yawned and all the time not knowing what it was – because the hunter had never seen a gorilla.

I had been at the helm for some ten hours, eyes level with the small windows in the dome over the helmsman's seat. It was night, but even with an overcast sky and no moon it was a bright night, because the sea was phosphorescent and made it possible to see the rollers approach from far away, as though they were lit from inside. This made it much easier to steer before the seas, not only approximately but *dead* before, roller after roller, as I had learnt it in my lesson. The helm demanded the utmost attention, because the ballasted warps exerted a pull of their own, and whenever *Joshua* yawed even slightly she was sluggish in coming back stern to sea. On the other hand the warps were slowing her down very nicely, which had become rather necessary, for every fourth or fifth breaker covered the boat, sweeping the deck from end to end. The central self-draining cockpit was never empty for long; no sooner was it empty than it was once again full to the brim, but without weighing *Joshua* down, for she had only to roll twice for three-quarters of the water to be thrown out on deck.

'Françoise ... are you asleep?'

'No ...'

'How's the barometer?'

'... 987. It looks as though it had stopped falling. You must be dead-beat, Bernard.'

'No, I'm alright, this is thrilling. I think the seas must be quite enormous, I can hardly wait to see them in daylight.'

'Wouldn't you like me to take over from you?'

'No, the helm is really quite a handful, I can only just manage it myself. If you could make me something tasty to eat, that would be great ...'

'I'll get you something hot and filling.'

'You must be kidding ...'

'Wait and see!'

It is often said that women on board bring bad luck to a boat. This may be true in everybody else's case, but my Françoise is the miracle of miracles. Five minutes later she was feeding me on my perch with lentils and sausages. She had heated the tin by pouring meths into a saucepan wedged between cushions on the cabin floor.

It was becoming more and more difficult to hold *Joshua* before the seas because the trailing hawsers made her less and less manœuvrable as the seas got bigger. She was yawing more, even with the helm right down, and what I had vaguely feared eventually happened. But it was my fault, for my attention must have momentarily wandered after fifteen hours at the helm. Carried by a wave *Joshua* suddenly came beam on to the seas and when the breaker arrived it was too late. A rush of icy water hit me in the neck and the next moment *Joshua* was heeled rapidly over. The angle of heel increased steadily but not abruptly while all the external noise became dim. Then the silence was suddenly broken by the unholy din of a cascade of objects flying across the cabin ... three or four seconds ... then *Joshua* righted herself.

'Bernard! ...'

'What's the matter? ... Are you hurt?'

'No ... I though the hatch had opened and you were no longer there ... Are you hurt? ...'

'No ... a bit wet, but alright otherwise. *Joshua*'s back on course. Clear up that mess ... How's the barometer?'

'985. It has fallen again, only just now it said 987 ... You know, I thought we had capsized, but the tins are still under the floorboards.'

'We must have had the masts in the water, but not much more than that. That's really woken me up!'

The night was beginning to get lighter, but day was not breaking yet, and it was in this transitory period between night and day that *Joshua*'s fate took a turn for the worse.

The boat was running exactly stern on to a fast approaching wave, nicely curved but not excessively large, on the point of breaking ... or maybe not breaking. Waves that show this kind of hesitation are fairly frequent. I was wide awake, I think I was even extra-lucid at that moment.

The stern lifted as always, and then, accelerating suddenly but without heeling in the slightest, *Joshua* buried her forward part in the seas at an angle of about 30 degrees, as far as the forward edge of the coachroof. Half the boat was under water. Almost immediately she emerged again ... We had almost been pitch-poled by a slightly hesitant wave – I would not have believed it possible.

The hideous truth struck me like a thunderbolt, and then a cold shiver ran up my back and gripped me by the nape of my neck. I don't think it was fear, for there has to be reason for fear. We would always get somewhere alive, thanks to our steel hull. What I felt at that moment was worse than fear: I suddenly realised, in a flash of enlightenment, that *Joshua* was simply a very good Trade wind boat but was entirely out of place where she was at that moment. She was out of place in the high latitudes of the South Pacific, where only *real boats* have the right to be.

But then ... how had Vito Dumas[1] done it? He claimed that he had crowded on sail running before the wind in all weathers ... I bet he never saw seas like these ...

'Françoise ...'

I was on the point of saying to her: 'I am sorry, I've been wrong, we'll have to return via Panama, *Joshua* hasn't got it in her.'

'Yes ...'

'How's the barometer?'

'... Bernard ... it looks as though it's rising ... I'm sure it was touching 985 last time I looked and now it's no longer touching. Watch where you're going, you'll put her beam on, you're due east instead of southeast ...'

'Due east ... are you sure? ... At last! ... The wind has gone round to the west, that means the depression is moving away and the glass will rise today. Try to make me some coffee; very strong!'

My brain resumed its normal rhythm as daylight returned. It made me think of that well-known surgeon's phrase: 'If he holds on till morning, he'll pull through.'

But what was the secret, Vito Dumas? For it's true, you crossed the three oceans by the southern route single-handed, in a wooden boat half as big as mine. You claim to have had sail up in all weather – I know that's impossible, and yet, there must be some truth in it. But how did you do it? ... You are dead now and cannot answer me ... I have seen Sandefjord *at Capetown ... a lot of people maintain that it's bunkum, that she was never pitch-poled at all but simply rolled over ... but I know she was pitch-poled alright. So, how did you do it ... in your little* Legh II, *one sixth the size of* Sandefjord *and half the size of* Tzu-Hang *and* Joshua *... for you did it, no doubt ... but how? ...*

'Françoise ... I'm sorry, but it's important. Can you find the book by Merrien and look up "Vito Dumas"?'

... If I could just grasp a tiny bit of your secret ... without some sort of knack you would never have got across three oceans without at least one serious accident ...

'Here we are ... what do you want me to read out?'

---

[1] Vito Dumas completed a remarkable voyage round the world, single-handed, from west to east by way of the Cape of Good Hope, Tasmania and Cape Horn in his yacht *Legh II.*

'Start at the beginning of the chapter and read out everything in italics, I'm sure there was something important.'

'Wait ... here's something: *"Fortunately the staysail was strong. It was left up from beginning to end and all the sails arrived in Argentina undamaged."* '

'See what else there is in italics.'

'Let's see ... *"If you want to become a seasoned mariner ..."* '

'Yes, I know, turn the page.'

'There's something here which isn't in italics, but it looks important to me. Listen "Whenever the wind strengthened he left all his sail up and had the boat what one might call planing on the waves at a speed exceeding fifteen knots for short moments. To start with, he says, it is an impressive experience, but one gets used to it. With the boat moving at the same speed as the wave, the wave is no longer dangerous".'

'Ha! ... if we had followed that method we would have done ten Catherine-wheels by now! ... Still, read on.'

'... This is what the famous pilot Bohlin from Gloucester says: "With a following sea and a gale like this (1905 Transatlantic Race) the waves lifted up our stern and then ... we simply slid away from them, we escaped them. They tried to break on board but the boat would not let them, escaping them every time just as it looked as though they had caught her. This is why I left all that canvas set; our mainsail pulled us from under the waves. Many say that carrying sail in heavy weather is sheer folly; maybe it is foolish the way some people do it; but sometimes it is equally stupid not to carry enough. Boats have been lost precisely because they shortened sail too much on this particular point of sailing".'

'This does not apply to boats our size. I seem to remember that this man had quite a large boat. Doesn't it say?'

'... yes, a 92-ton schooner?'

... And still, you did it ... and Legh II *was a small boat. But* Sandefjord *was a large boat, she reminded me of a big bull when I saw her at Cape- town ... and she was pitch-poled ... and you weren't ... yet you carried sail, I believe you ... but you couldn't have carried any sail in this kind of seas, don't spin me that yarn, for if you had carried any sail in these seas you would have been pitchpoled like* Tzu-Hang *... and like* Joshua, *almost ... and in your little* Legh II, *without an inside steering wheel, all on your own, you would have been swept off the face of the earth in two seconds flat*

and nothing more would have been heard of you ... And yet, you covered the three oceans, including the Indian Ocean, the worst of all, and not at the best time of year, either ... if you could just tell me a little about this business of carrying sail ... for I believe you, maybe not one hundred per cent, but I know that there must be something in this business of carrying sail ...

'Françoise! ... there's a nasty looking wave coming up, wedge yourself against the forward bulkhead ...'

It wasn't all that big, but I recognised its kind: it had been a wave just like this that had nearly pitchpoled us a little while ago. *Joshua* was almost dead stern-on to the seas, maybe some ten degrees off, but I still had time to line her up.

I don't believe in ghosts and I don't like to look ridiculous ... but I could have sworn that I heard ... : '*Look, I'll show you ...*'

When the wave, coming up behind us at an angle of ten degrees, started to lift our stern, *Joshua* heeled a little, which is perfectly normal. Then this hesitant wave, which did not even bother to break, threw her forward at a fantastic speed, despite all the hawsers she was trailing. *Joshua* heeled over further without burying her bows, which was to be expected because in heeling her leeward bow was resting on the water like a ski. When she came out of that plane, after about thirty yards, I had Vito Dumas' answer. And ever since that day I thank Vito Dumas for having shown me, and also Jean Merrien for having introduced me to Vito Dumas and *Sandefjord*.

'Françoise! ... Quick, I want you to take the helm for two seconds, I'll explain. Pass me that knife ... no, not that one, the Opinel!' The seas were breaking in big, powerful rollers but that did not stop me from making a quick trip on deck to do what needed doing. Just as long as I was quick and kept a wary eye on the breakers.

I opened the hatch, undid the end of the safety line[1] from the

---

[1] Three $1\frac{1}{4}$ in. nylon lines had been made fast some days ago to fixed points welded on deck – a very reliable arrangement. These were our safety lines which allowed us to move about the boat, including the bowsprit, like dogs on a lead. There were two for forward, the ends of which were made facts near the mainmast, and one for working aft or in the cockpit, the end of which was made fast near the mizzen mast. These three lines were long enough to allow us to tie ourselves to them by a bowline *before leaving the cabin.*

jib-sheet cleat, took it inside and closed the hatch again. I tied it round me with a bowline, watching the course all the while, steadying the wheel with my knee. The seas seemed less irregular than the night before for I had the impression that it was easier to hold *Joshua* on course. Perhaps it was the first light of day that gave me that impression.

Françoise was crouching on the chart table. When the right moment came, I left by the hatch and closed it behind me while Françoise took over the helm. One ... two ... three ... four ... and five. With a few blows I cut all the hawsers with my Opinel jack-knife which cuts like a razor and which no-one is allowed to touch, not even Françoise. Then I regained the cockpit, opened the hatch and quickly resumed my position on the helmsman's seat which Françoise had vacated by climbing down on the galley side so that she would not have to let go of the wheel.

We could notice an enormous change in *Joshua*. She had no longer anything in common with the wretched boat of the night before which had made me think of the little hunter trying to parry the blows of a gorilla, with his feet caught in the undergrowth. We would surely have come to a sticky end then ...

Now *Joshua* was running along unimpeded, under bare poles. As each wave came up at an angle of 15 to 20 degrees she heeled over, and took off on a plane, resting her bow against the trough. She responded to the helm without hesitation in coming back before the wind. And those enormous breakers that looked as though they were about to smash everything to pieces? They became harmless when taken on the quarter.

It is amazing how things can change ... The wind had not abated, the seas were every bit as big as they had been an hour ago. I should have been worn out after twenty hours at the helm when every other wave presented a problem, twenty hours during which my hands, my back, my shoulders had started to ache. Yet every-thing had changed because a dead seaman had replied to my insis-tent question. Five blows with my knife had freed *Joshua* of the chains she had been dragging. A small gesture, but what a difference! ...

To be sure, even before that, *Joshua* had not been in dire peril: a steel boat built like her could shoot the Niagara Falls. But the masts were in danger, for we had been on the point of sticking our nose in like *Tzu-Hang*, maybe sooner, maybe later, but it would have happened as surely as one and one make two, as sunshine follows rain. And not tomorrow, either, but today.

But that small action had changed everything and I knew that it would not happen, not if we kept a ceaseless vigil and were extremely careful. I thought of Vito Dumas, sailing three oceans single-handed, without an inside steering position! ... Compared with a man like him I was just a miserable landlubber, a shocking amateur with no guts, sitting there on my steering seat that was only just short of a back-rest and a leather cushion to make me thoroughly comfortable. And there was Françoise telling me, with great relief, that the glass was rising.

'Forget the barometer, Françoise, you *must* get some sleep!'

'And what about you? You haven't come down from your perch for twenty hours!'

'Go to sleep, I'm fine. You should see this fantastic sea! And how happy *Joshua* is ... Sleep, the depression is moving away. I promise you that afterwards I'll sleep for twenty-four hours at a stretch.' I, too, was happy despite feeling very tired. Everything was alright now, I could sense that we were no longer in danger even though green seas were sweeping the deck as far as the look-out dome over my seat. I wondered whether I would still be there if it had not been for the inside steering position. Being attached to a safety line does not necessarily afford complete protection in the cockpit. A man can die of fatigue and cold like Ann Davison's husband. But above all one can be killed by the breakers in a sea like this if one stays out in the cockpit for too long. They were like the blows of a gorilla. Yet the noise of the sea was not horrifying, far from it. It was rather like a deep grumbling, regular and rather muffled like the sound of a water-fall not very far away. From time to time there was a louder booming when a roller broke close by. And when a breaker covered the boat completely there was nothing to be heard at all for several seconds. Then the muffled, regular grumbling of the sea could be heard again. This dull grumbling sound was with us as far as Cape Horn, more or less muffled, more or less powerful, more or less disquieting, depending on the weather. It was the breathing of the sea in the Roaring Forties.

It was broad daylight on the 15th December, when, after 26 hours at the helm, I was finally able to leave my seat, connect up the self-steering vane and set the staysail with a reef in it (97 sq. ft). The glass had fairly shot up: 985 mb at 2 a.m., 1007 at 8 a.m. The wind had swung round to the sou'west, which, together with the quick rise in barometric pressure, was a sure sign that the depression was moving away. The wind was still fresh, a good force 8, which is a fresh gale,[1] but the seas left behind by the very strong gale of the previous 24 hours were so long that despite their considerable height the waves rarely broke and were certainly no longer dangerous when taken on the quarter, which had become our golden rule.

The sky cleared before daybreak and the sun was so bright that it was positively *unbearable*. *Never before in my life* had I seen such bright sunshine. I cannot stare straight at the sun like eagles do, of course not, but even then a normal person can look straight at it for half a second between 9 and 10 in the morning. Not that day: it would have burnt straight through my pupils, and it was not due to tiredness, of that I am sure. There was an *extraordinary* violence in that sun such as I had never witnessed before.

Nor had I ever seen a sea like this in my life. To describe it I have to use comparisons: dunes, hills, mountains in the distance ... but that does not describe it adequately. To think of height and shape and form is not sufficient, either. To speak of 'chaos' would not convey the right meaning, I have never associated chaos with manifestations of nature. True, I was not at Agadir on the day of the earthquake, but then an earthquake cannot be compared to a gale in the South Pacific. The former is a disaster (a natural disaster, I admit) which has nothing in common with the scene Françoise and I were looking at that morning, sitting side by side on the coach-roof, spiritually fused with each other, fascinated, hypnotised by this sea from which radiated a colossal power, a complete, *absolute* beauty.

'Come on, Bernard, you must get some sleep. I'll cook you some ham and eggs and make some Ovaltine. Please ... and then you must get some sleep.'

'Hand me the sextant first.'

---

[1] We had no anemometer and the wind forces given in this book are estimated.

'No, you *must* get some rest. Besides, there's no horizon!'

That was true, there was no horizon left, except maybe for a fraction of a second. Standing on the coach-roof, with the sextant in my hand, steadying myself against the main boom, all I could see was waves. Even when *Joshua* was lifted to the highest crest of the highest waves there was always another wave still higher which covered the horizon, wherever I looked.

'Bernard! It's ready. Give me the sextant and come and eat. What good will it do you if you know exactly where we are? I can tell you: about 3,000 miles from Cape Horn and 12,000 miles from home. And don't worry, there are no rocks ahead of us, we are exactly on the right course. So come and eat, and then we'll sleep.'

'Yes, for twenty-four hours!'

I had already forgotten that south of the 40th parallel you never sleep for longer than a few hours at one stretch. But what I did not suspect at that moment was that Françoise and I had not seen anything yet.

Dead tired, we fell sound asleep around 10 o'clock in the morning, after having checked the rising curve of the barometer: 1007 since 8 o'clock. If anything, the wind had decreased a little, say force 7, and it was still blowing sou'westerly. It could stay there as long as it liked, for both our and *Joshua*'s sake!

Françoise fell asleep first, while I scrambled out of my blankets again to make sure that the chronometer had been properly wound. Then I contemplated that quiet little face, muffled up in a woolly cap, while she slept wedged in between cushions, curled up like a child. And I felt an immense gratitude towards the fate which had made our paths cross. Gratitude mixed with amazement at this small, fragile woman who would have felt as equally at home at a fashionable party in a cocktail dress as she did here on board *Joshua*, with her vagabond husband, wrapped up in the kind of fur-lined clothing that polar expeditions use, in boots and balaclava helmet, on the way to Cape Horn.

'Bernard ... Bernard! ...'

I thought I was dreaming ... but Françoise went on shaking me.

'Humm? ... What? ... What day is it?'

'It's the same day, poor darling. You've slept for three hours. The glass has fallen since we went to sleep ... it's at 1004 now ...

the wind has hardly increased at all but the seas are becoming nasty. You must take a look outside.'

Dear God! ... Dear God ... What have I done to deserve it ... Quick, quick, put on your boots, get into your oilskins and climb on your seat to see what fate has in store for you.

It was not a pretty sight ... a big cloud bank was approaching from the west and would soon cover the sun which was already hazy behind cirrus cloud. It is incredible how quickly the sky can change its appearance in these latitudes, even with the glass steady. Françoise was right: the wind had increased a little, but she had forgotten to tell me that it seemed to be going round to the west. Poor Françoise, we were going to enjoy ourselves if the fun was starting all over again in this sea, which was already enormous ...

At sunset a westerly gale was blowing. Stratus, that miserable shapeless cloud, was chasing across a grey sky. The glass had dropped to 1000 mb. We handed the staysail for I was expecting violent squalls, and its area, although reefed, was still so large that I feared it would be too much. I steered from inside after having shipped the self-steering vane. So we were once again under bare poles. I had made a great mistake in not taking some very small sails which would have kept the boat manœuvrable in all conditions.

Vito Dumas' technique had turned out to be the only one possible for *Joshua*, but with a bit of sail up forward and aft a boat like her, 39 ft long and weighing 13 tons, would have handled better, found it easier to take the breakers and taken less out of the helmsman.

'Bernard, is this another depression approaching?'

'I don't quite understand this. If it is approaching, it should be to the southwest of us now, and the wind should be nor'westerly. Yet it's westerly. It might be a depression forming south of us, but I really don't know any more. In any case, it means gale, that's certain with this sky and this barometer.'

'You ought to let me helm till nightfall so that I can practise while the sea isn't too frightening. If I don't learn now it'll be too late afterwards, and maybe you won't be able to see the gale through to the end.'

'Climb on the chart-table and watch carefully: I'm running

dead before the wind to keep the maximum speed on the boat and make sure that she answers on the helm when she has to. Now watch carefully, you see that wave coming up ... I am still dead before ... and just before the stern lifts I turn the wheel right down ... You see ... she heels over and veers to the right as she ought to ... she is pushed forward and a little sideways ... the moment the stern settles down again, just after the wave has passed I turn the wheel *right over* in the other direction to bring her back again stern on; this is the best moment because the rudder is deep in the water and very effective ... you see ... we are back dead before the wind, and the business starts all over again.

'Watch carefully: you see ... the wave is coming up and we are dead before, going at full speed. You alter course the moment the wave meets the stern, the rudder bites well then, the boat suddenly heels and shoots forwards and sideways. Then you bring her back on course as soon as the stern settles down again.

'But there are two golden rules:

'Wait until the wave is close enough before you alter course. If you do it too soon the boat will lose speed and fail to answer to the helm, and try to broach-to.

'If the helm pulls the other way as the wave is passing underneath her, let it go completely for a second or two. You remember, I explained it all in my first book: if you fail to let go if it sets up resistance as the wave passes underneath you will make her broach-to further as you try to do the opposite, then you will find yourself broadside-on and without way.'

'Let me take the helm now, Bernard, I've understood perfectly.'

'No, not yet. Watch another five minutes while I think aloud so that you can really *feel Joshua* in the seas. You see ... the wave is coming up ... we are dead before and going fast ... now I put the helm down ... we are heeling ... the wheel resists ... I let it go, it turns freely from one side to the other for several seconds and when it stops I turn it right back the other way ... you see ... you see ... and there we are dead before again, without having lost way. And then you start from the beginning, and again, and again, a million times perhaps, and every time the manœuvre must be technically perfect, for it only takes one mistake for both masts to snap clean off and for us to find ourselves in Valparaiso two months later. If we both worked hard there for some weeks I could possibly pay for you to fly to France for Easter. I know we both have a lucky star, but the logical route does not lead via Valparaiso.'

'Alright, let me take the helm, you must get some rest so that you are fresh when I've had enough.'

'No, not yet. Not until you can feel the sea, right inside you. Get me something nice and filling to eat and while you do it try and see *Joshua* as she moves in this sea, try to feel the sea deep inside you, without having to think. Then you can come and sit beside me for another five minutes, and then you lie down on the berth until you can feel *Joshua* as part of the sea, and the sea as part of yourself. When you can, I will let you take the helm, perhaps only for thirty seconds, perhaps for a whole hour, that depends on how I feel about it. You are no longer at the wheel of your little Dauphine but driving a 15-ton lorry without brakes down a winding road at 60 m.p.h. If you don't slow down before each bend by changing gear we are bound for Chile, like *Tzu-Hang*.'

Françoise passed her test for driving the lorry without brakes brilliantly. Not a single mistake nor a second's hesitation during the ten minutes I let her helm under my supervision.

Then she was alone on the steering seat, alone in the face of the most enormous seas I had ever seen, and she continued to steer with absolute accuracy, making the boat heel at the right moment, and come up again as the stern settled down, without going off course more than the necessary 15 to 20 degrees. I could see this from the vertically mounted compass at the foot end of my berth, on which I was at last resting. I could not detect a single wrong note in the concert of sounds, which told me that *Joshua* was not in danger in Françoise's hands.

When I woke up again it was almost 9 p.m. I could hardly make out the small shape of Françoise perched on the steering seat in the gathering darkness (this was the austral summer).

'You should have called me before. It is dangerous to steer in this weather when you're tired.'

'I wasn't tired, but I am just feeling it now. Come and take over the helm, but be careful, the seas are much bigger now.'

Françoise must really have become part of *Joshua* and felt the sea deep inside herself to make that remark ...

The seas were bigger, but in contrast to the night before the waves came from the same direction. They were also less steep because the swell had become even longer. The breakers were less high but much longer.

During the previous night the crests of the waves had broken in massive chunks the size of small houses, and when one of them swept over the boat only the masts remained above water.

Now it was different. Those massive breakers were less frequent, now nearly all the crests carried along breakers thirty to fifty yards long but they were not high enough to cover the boat completely. They frequently swept the deck but rarely as far up as the dome. The central cockpit was not continuously full as it had been the night before. But the glass continued to fall.

We were now almost on the 45th parallel and heading northeast so as not to get closer to the depression.

The wind was less strong than the day before, but the squalls, mixed with hail became more and more violent as the night progressed. During the hours I was at the helm the seas continued to grow, with the breakers becoming longer and higher. *Joshua* was safe running before the seas and I was sure that she could go on like this for a long, long time and never be in danger, for the crew had mastered the situation.

It is impossible to tell the rest of the story, except perhaps by the fire, among close friends, when the right words come easily. The reader wants to know, of course, but there are no printed words to tell the story. And even if there were, they would be inadequate because their meaning would be distorted by the reader's natural desire to understand how it was possible that a boat measuring 39 feet and weighing 13 tons could have got away without major damage, and how the crew held out for almost six times twenty-four hours. And the reader would not realise that beyond a certain point there is nothing to understand.

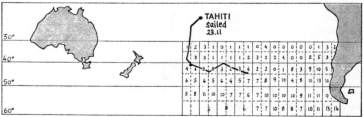

The figures in the squares indicate the percentages of gales in December, January and February (according to the American Pilot Chart).

Neither *Joshua* nor her crew were ever in distress. Françoise was turning into a helmswoman par excellence. The glass continued to drop steadily until it stopped and would not rise again. On the third day it rose again very slowly, hesitantly. In the squalls I estimate that it was blowing at hurricane force and from the 16th December we saw breakers 150 to 200 yards long and up to 20 yards wide, and breaking without interruption for several hundred yards.

How could these waves have continued to break like this without leaving the crest that carried them? Where did these breakers get the stupendous energy by which they continually managed to regenerate themselves?

Usually, when a wave breaks, the breaker becomes detached from and left behind by the crest which may build up a little further on and break again. But at least twenty times in two days we saw a different phenomenon, quite incomprehensible: the roller did not detach itself from its crest but kept being re-born in situ and breaking without interruption. The grumbling of the sea became very loud but we never actually heard it roar. Perhaps because we were sheltered behind 5 mm steel plates.

Joshua was quite safe, taking the waves at an angle of 15 to 20 degrees. The sea had become colossal and supernatural, and the breakers often covered her to above the dome.

If I have tried to describe that gale – as though words could ever suffice – it is only for Françoise's and my sake, so that we should always remember, even when we are old, that for six days a man, a woman and a boat were welded together, totally, absolutely, in and against colossal seas which they at once hated and loved with all their might.

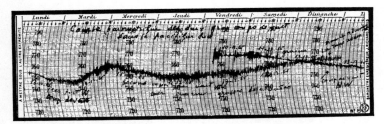

This barograph curve is of relative value only, because the pan was shortened to restrict the amplitude of its oscillations.

4

In the Heavy Seas of the High Latitudes or the Game of the Little Squares

19th December

We reset the small jib at daybreak, rigged the vane and connected the self-steering. Then we slept and slept, while the sea was still running high but no longer breaking despite a very fresh wind, because the swell was huge.

We weren't exhausted, just tired after six days of continual tension, and we decided unanimously that we would let *Joshua* run under no more than her 86 sq. ft even though the glass was steadily rising. Our zig-zag course must have brought us back close to the 40th parallel for the temperature had risen, which was not unwelcome!

Much as a sailor may sometimes be tempted to sleep his fill, his plans are soon spoiled by his boat complaining of too little canvas, and before long I had to console *Joshua* by hoisting the staysail. I made as little noise as possible so as not to wake Françoise. *Joshua* would have liked more sail, but just for once I did not let her have her way and went to rejoin Françoise, who was sleeping like a child and must have been dreaming something pleasant, for she was smiling in her sleep.

'... Bernard ...'

'I thought you were asleep.'

'Now I really do believe we'll see the children for Easter.'

'Do go to sleep, dear.'

'... and not by way of Valparaiso, either.'

One of the many peculiarities a skipper has is his frequently irrational need to know exactly where he is, even if his boat is in mid-ocean, outside the shipping lanes and thousands of miles from the nearest land. He may be tired, and it may be quite unnecessary, but he *must* know his position. So before long I found myself on deck again with the sextant to take a morning sight, although I would have done better to sleep.

The last violent squalls of the night before had moved off to the east and had left behind a very clear sky with some cirrus in it. But the swell was so high that it took me a good ten minutes to get the sun down to a true horizon for half a second.

Since we had reached the high latitudes I had always taken my sights without the telescope and with both eyes open. This method is so much more accurate, giving a reading within one minute on the arc, and in any case it is the only way to use the sextant in these very heavy high-latitude seas, whether the weather was fine or foul. With the telescope I invariably put the sun on the crest of a wave, which of course gives a completely false altitude.

The sight I took that morning placed us ... 85 miles further east than I had estimated, which was a very pleasant surprise. The time by the chronometer was correct,[1] and so were my figures, so we must have covered a much larger distance than expected during the gale. After having taken a meridian altitude at noon, I could fix our position on the chart: longitude: 135° 10′ latitude: 40° 47′.

We had covered 550 miles from noon to noon during the six days of the gale, during which we had had the small jib up for twelve hours, the small jib and staysail for six hours. The rest of the time we had lain a-hull. Allowing for considerable alterations in course and the zig-zag route we had followed I estimated that *Joshua* had actually covered 600 to 650 miles.

In the afternoon swell *Joshua* romped along uncomplaining under the small jib, staysail and reefed mizzen. All the clothing that had become soaked during the past few days was hanging up to dry on wires stretched in all directions above the galley. 'Caroline', the stove, was cheerfully pumping out heat from her two burners, while the hatch was left slightly open to allow air to circulate, otherwise the cabin would have been like a Turkish bath.

All in all the cabin had stayed remarkably dry considering the weather, but a stream of water that had shot down the ventilator

---

[1] We checked the chronometer against the time signals emitted by W.W.V. (Betsville, U.S.A.) every five minutes, giving G.M.T. in morse and local time phonetically (on 5,000, 10,000, 15,000 or 20,000 kilocycles). A metronome beat indicates the seconds. Betsville is a powerful station which nearly all small yachts use. We received it on our Technifrance set throughout the voyage.

when *Joshua* was swamped by a breaker during the first night of the gale, had soaked the foot end of the starboard berth. The lockers stayed as dry as in port; not even condensation had got into them.

While I do not pretend that a steel hull has no disadvantages I now know that even in very heavy weather it is possible for it to stay as dry as a bottle inside as long as the hatches close tightly.

On the 20th December we were running with all sails close-reefed in a nice force 5–6 westerly with a following sea, the glass steady at 1013 and the sky completely overcast. We could have carried more sail but after having survived the last gale without the slightest damage I was more than ever convinced that in this race from Tahiti to Gibraltar it was imperative to allow for two inseparable factors: the rigging and the crew. Both had stood up well for nearly a month because neither had been forced to its limits, and this is how we would have to continue: to make the best possible speed but at the same time to have enough sense never to impose more than half the permissable 'breaking strain'. For we still had a long way to go, even if fatigue should force us to stop at the Falkland Islands after we had rounded Cape Horn and run into heavy weather. Still, we were not thinking of the Falkland Islands just then, we were only thinking of the present, of the sheets and halyards which we had to keep as sound as they were when we left Tahiti. I greased the sheets every day where they went through the blocks, and I did the same to the halyards whenever there was an opportunity (before hoisting the sail). The reefing gear received the same attention: grease, grease and more grease, the sailor's ally, a simple means of reducing wear and keeping all the running gear in order.

The crew had completely recovered from the strains of the previous days, but we were economising our movements, and even our thoughts, and trying to live only for the day. My job consisted in seeing to it that above deck *Joshua* was always kept in the same good order as when we left Tahiti. Françoise busied herself in the cabin, keeping it as spotless as in harbour. She hung gloves and socks up to dry above 'Caroline', cooked, and knitted caps, gloves and socks for a rainy day.

On the 23rd December it was a month since we had left Moorea. We had covered 3,097 miles in thirty days, which is an average of 103 miles a day or 721 miles a week. This was a fairly poor performance for a boat like *Joshua*, who had cheerfully devoured many more miles per week between Martinique and Tahiti. A poor show, but we were still on the right route and not bound for Valparaiso!

We took to playing a game which must be well known to anybody who has ever sailed in these notorious latitudes: the game of the little squares. It consists of keeping the boat on a route where the lowest percentage of gales is to be expected.

These percentages are shown on the small diagram on page 176 divided into small squares 5° each in latitude and longitude. Readers familiar with nautical matters will know that as one gets higher in latitude so the frequency of gales increases. Thus our game was to keep *Joshua* between the 43rd and 45th parallels south as far as 600 miles off the Chilean coast, when we would head straight for a point well to the west of Cape Horn in order not to run the considerable risk of being driven onto the shores of Tierra del Fuego by a gale.

24th December

It is impossible to tell from one hour to the next the mood of the God of the Westwind who rules south of the fortieth parallel. But it seemed that we were going to have a peaceful Christmas. The barograph line had been steady for several days after which the enraged giant seemed at last to have gone to sleep. We could feel his mighty chest rising and falling in long, steady swells from the southwest as he breathed peacefully in his sleep, powerful but calm. He seemed to be well and truly asleep, and his rest was untroubled by that kind of ruffling of the sea which would have come from the northwest had there been another depression on its way, about to wake him up and arouse his fury. It would have taken so little to make him stir in his sleep before rising slowly, grumbling in anger and expanding his immense chest. We had learnt to fear and at the same time to love the Giant Westwind, for he made us live as we had never done before, with an almost painful intensity, as though each hour we lived through gave us a completely new life, as though we were re-born.

25th December

2,200 miles to go to Cape Horn. There was no danger from icebergs yet, for their extreme limit remains south of our route as far as the Horn.

It was our second Christmas at sea on board *Joshua*. The first had been between Alicante and Gibraltar in splendid weather, but then each mile had separated us further from the children. Now each day at sea brought us closer to them.

Since there had been no swell from the northwest for several days we did not change foresails although the glass was falling, thinking that there was probably a small depression forming south of us which would soon go away. We hoped we were right.

The self-steering worked well as always, and we never yawed more than some ten degrees on either side since I had lashed the helm with rubber strips cut from an inner tube to limit its movement. *Joshua*'s vane works on the trim tab principle: the vane, mounted on the stock of a small trim tab, acts directly on the latter, and it is this small trim tab which pushes the main rubber blade whenever the boat alters course in relation to the wind. (See Appendix).

29th December
The barometer continued to fall slowly until 3 a.m., but the wind veered very slightly to west-sou'west from 9 a.m. onwards and the glass started to rise (1008 mb).

We re-hoisted the mainsail, close-reefed, and the staysail around 8 a.m. It was not very cold but gloves were indispensable for working on deck. Although wet, they stopped our fingers from getting numb and small cuts from becoming aggravated. We took great care of our hands, literally plastering them with anti-chilblain cream and massaging the fingers to feed the skin.

It was our intention that not only *Joshua* but her crew, too, should remain in the same good shape they had been in when they left Moorea. So far we were all still sound, except for a chapped patch under the second finger of my right hand with which I had been afflicted for a week. Françoise fussed over it as over a baby's bottom, rubbing it with cream and massaging it at every opportunity, for small causes often have serious effects. We regularly took vitamins in liquid form and Guronsan (with vitamin C) to fight fatigue and chilblains. Our diet was healthy although it consisted mainly of tinned food, for Françoise had stocked a great variety. We also had plenty of lemons, onions and garlic. I think that our health was not only as good as it had been when we set out but better ... thanks to the invigorating climate! Our noon position was longitude 105° 35', latitude 43° 43', and we had covered 183 miles since our noon position the previous day. This was our best day's run since leaving Moorea.

The barometer rose to 1012 mb and the wind eased considerably in the afternoon: sou'westerly force 3–4, while the sky cleared. We were now well placed to start the descent towards the Horn; we just had to try and cross a series of very unpleasant looking little squares as quickly as possible. I stitched another row of reef points into the staysail to reduce its area to 37 sq. ft.

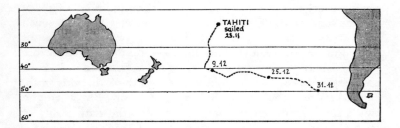

5

Cape Horn to Port

We were now on the second lap of the first stage.

Joshua was running with the wind just over the quarter now, heading south-east towards the Horn, her mizzen well out and the jib sheeted right in because it had a tendency to flap from side to side when it was sheeted as it should have been on that point of sailing. What a pity that our close-reefed mainsail was so often too large for these latitudes with its 200 sq. ft. I thought of the fine runs we could have had, without danger and with much less nervous tension, if only I had stitched two more rows of reef points on the mainsail and one more on the mizzen, before leaving Tahiti. If you set a close-reefed sail in port and stand back on the quay to see how it looks you always think that this small, reduced sail area could take a full gale quite easily. But when you awake from the dream and are plunged into the stark reality of the high latitudes, the truth is quite different: it is not enough for a close-reefed sail to be able to withstand a good blow, but it must also be capable of being lowered easily in all conditions and set again without difficulty, without changing course, as soon as conditions improve.

I also learnt during this voyage that *Joshua* can sail quite fast under greatly reduced canvas even if it is not blowing very hard: off the wind, under a sail area of 950 to 1,000 sq. ft *Joshua* usually covered 130 to 140 miles in a day's run in force 3, 150–160 miles in force 4, and around 180 in force 5.

Under a sail area one-fifth that size (close-reefed mizzen 96 sq. ft, small jib 86 sq. ft) she could manage a day's run of 125–135 miles in a steady force 6–7, and 145 to 155 miles if the 193 sq. ft of the close-reefed mainsail are added, though this is not always easy or wise because of the instability of the weather in these latitudes, where the wind may drop from force 6 to force 5 and a little later increase to 7 or 8 without there being any way of knowing whether it will drop back to 6 or freshen a little more to 9 or 10 ... Thus we were nearly always under-canvassed for lack of small, manageable sails. But if there is a next time I will put this right.

Since then I have discovered another interesting fact: *Joshua*, in common with most ketch-rigged boats, remains balanced off the wind with only the mizzen set! This is incredible, but nevertheless true.

Both Jean Gau, whom I met in Durban, and Wilf, the skipper of *Didikai*, whom I knew in Capetown, tried sailing before the wind under mizzen only, and it worked.

Henry Wakelam tried it in a following Mistral on board *Shafhai* with no problems.

I tried it myself in *Joshua* once, in a strong following Mistral, and then *on a broad reach*, and she remained balanced on the helm. I have also tried it with the self-steering vane, with Loick Fougeron, in a force 3 Trade between Casablanca and the Canaries. The boat remained on course under mizzen alone with the wind over the quarter.

This ability of a ketch to sail under the mizzen only becomes a great asset in high latitudes: the mizzen can be left up all the time, more or less reefed. When the wind decreases the mainsail can be hoisted without altering course. It will go up without difficulty and without jamming itself against the shrouds because it is blanketed by the mizzen. And if the wind freshens it is so much easier to take another reef in the mainsail or to lower it if it is blanketed by the mizzen.

2nd January

Barometer stable at 1011 mb, wind west-nor'westerly force 5 to 6, with the sky fairly clear in the morning but later becoming covered with cirrus and alto-cumulus. 22° solar halo.

Noon position: longitude 95° 35', latitude 48° 05'; day's run 128 miles.

Drizzle during the night.

3rd January

Fine, sunny weather in the morning, wind west-sou'westerly varying all the time between force 4 and 6, barometer normal and stable at 1010 mb. I rehoisted the staysail.

Noon position: longitude 92° 25', latitude 49° 13'; day's run 145 miles.

Cumulus and squalls came in the afternoon, squalls during the nights, but nothing serious. We read a lot of good books during these two weeks. This helped us to stay 'half awake' all the time and eased our nervous tension.

The game of the little squares had become highly exciting, but we were looking forward to playing it in the other direction. At the moment the possible frequency of gales was increasing with every square along our route, and the game was to cross as quickly as possible but without taking any risks by going too fast. We mustn't lose our nerve ...

We were tense, but very close to each other because we felt that we were a crack crew (no kidding) on one of the finest boats, approaching the greatest adventure a seaman can dream of.

4th January

Fine weather but frequent squalls, during which I steered by hand (without disconnecting the self-steering) to check the boat's

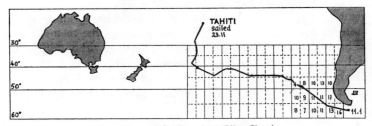

(according to the American Pilot Chart).

tendency to broach-to and to stop the sails from lifting. I took a reef in the staysail and set the reefed mainsail.

The wind was blowing sou'westerly now, force 4 to 5 on average, except in the squalls. The heavy westerly swell which had prevailed during the past few days was going down considerably and the horizon was much easier to pick out with the sextant. The glass was still steady at 1011, which was 4 mb above the average pressure given by our Pilot Chart (1005 to 1007 mb). It meant fine weather all right. We had another 1,000 miles or so to go to Cape Horn.

Noon position: longitude 89° 36', latitude 50° 29'. Day's run 132 miles.

The squalls became more frequent in the afternoon and we lowered the mainsail at nightfall. The wind was then westerly force 5 to 6, 7 to 8 in the squalls.

5th January

The temperature had dropped sharply during the past 5 or 6 days: it was 10°C in the cabin.

Thick weather, with drizzle in the afternoon, glass falling rapidly from 1010 to 1000 mb within a few hours. I was beginning to suspect that another gale was in the offing ...

The wind went round to the north-west, force 5 to 6, but the sea did not get worse. Was there another depression building up near us? It looked very much like it ... We thought it wiser to lower the mainsail and the storm jib, and take a second reef in the staysail. But the wind went back westerly during the night without the glass rising. I couldn't make any sense of it ...

Noon position: longitude 86° 32′, latitude 51° 51′. Day's run 142 miles.

Another 850 miles to go to the Horn. The barometer remained steady at 1000 mb during the night, with the wind west-sou'-westerly, about force 6, the sky clearing from the west. *Joshua* trotted along at 5 knots all night under 37 sq. ft of staysail and the close-reefed mizzen (96 sq. ft). It was infuriating not to have smaller sails!

6th January

The glass rose very slightly to 1001. The sky was covered with stratus and it was drizzling, but I managed to get a sun sight with the sextant, without glass shades, during short breaks in the cloud. We put the storm jib back up at dawn.

Noon position: longitude 83° 40′, latitude 53°; days' run 124 miles.

We were now 320 miles off the entrance to the Magellan Straits and 630 miles from Cape Horn. I altered course slightly so as to remain at a respectable distance from Tierra del Fuego.

Sailing in these parts can be tough going in heavy winds, but on the whole it is simple to make a passage from west to east:

The wind is fair (which makes all the difference) and gales, as a rule, start by blowing from the north-west. Thus they do not make the coast a lee shore if one keeps to the sailing ship route, i.e., well to the west of the coast of Chile. After a spell from the north-west a gale then blows from the west, and it is at this stage that the sailor is particularly grateful for having taken the precaution of keeping well clear of land. Then the wind backs to the sou'west and decreases as the depression moves eastwards, the weather once more becoming manageable. This is the normal cycle of a gale in the high latitudes of the southern hemisphere.

During the southern summer the extreme limit of icebergs is sufficiently far south not to inconvenience a boat sailing from the Pacific to the Atlantic. It is not until it passes into the Atlantic that icebergs become a problem. As for us, we had not got there yet. Everything in good time …

The sky is generally very overcast in these high latitudes, but I nearly always managed to fix our position, thanks to short breaks in the cloud, and by using the sextant without telescope and with both eyes open. Perhaps we had chosen a particularly good year, I don't know. The position given in this log are observed positions, that's to say calculated by the altitude observed with the sextant and the time as read off the chronometer. With few exceptions I had managed to take at least two good sun sights a day ever since we had left Moorea!

7th January

Drizzle in the morning, followed by short breaks and finally a splendid, sunny day. The glass was abnormally high for these parts: 1001–1003 mb, sou'westerly wind force 3 to 4 only. We had re-hoisted the mainsail before daybreak, i.e., at 2.30 a.m.

Noon position: longitude 81° 07', latitude 54° 39'. Day's run 137 miles.

Cape Horn was not more than 500 miles away. I reckoned we had struck lucky and were running into a period of fine weather. We had to make the best of it and crowd on sail, keeping the boat on the most direct route but keeping well to the south of the Horn in order not to get too close to that ill-famed coast, and at the same time not descending too far south and running the risk of colliding with an iceberg. We were still 100 miles from the extreme limit of floating icebergs. All was clear ahead, but I need hardly add that we always kept a weather eye open.

Besides, we had not slept properly for a very long time but both of us had remained constantly in a state of semi-sleep (rather like rabbits). We still did a lot of reading, but our thoughts were blurred. We no longer thought of our friends, nor, I think, of the children, because all our physical and mental resources were centred on a single objective to which we were getting closer each day: Cape Horn.

We wanted to get into the Atlantic with both masts pointing skywards, like respectable seamen, remembering all the big sailing ships that had been lost in those waters, all the dead seamen whose souls lived along the route we were following, and whose benevolent presence I often sensed around *Joshua*.

Above all, there was that of Al Hansen, the Norwegian, who rounded Cape Horn in the impossible direction (for boats of our size), beating single-handed from the Atlantic into the Pacific, well off Tierra del Fuego to avoid the current along the coast. He suffered indescribable hardships and died, smashed by the mighty west wind on the rocks of Chiloé, one thousand miles from the Horn, when he had left the worst behind him and perhaps found what he had come to seek. (This was around the year 1939, if I remember rightly).

What is left to us today of this fine man whom suffering cleansed of all conceit and all folly (if he was ever guilty of them in the first place)? Only a small photograph showing an open, honest face, by the side of his friend Vito Dumas.

8th January

The barometer had risen further in the night and was now at 1005 mb, which was exceptionally high, because the average barometric pressure in these parts (and at that time of the year) is 996 mb.

At dawn the sky was blue with clouds on the horizon. It was fairly cold: 7°C in the cabin. But there was no condensation because, with the sea so beautiful, we left the hatch half open. This really was remarkable weather. We scarcely moved in a light southerly breeze, about force 2!

Then the wind dropped right away and there was a flat calm from 7 to 11 a.m., while the sky clouded over with alto-cumulus so dense that I had difficulty in finding the sun with the sextant. The glass continued to rise: 1008 mb by 9 a.m. ...!

The petrol stove, a present from Fred Debels which he had deposited on the jetty at Tahiti a few days before our departure, was lit for the first time.

Noon position: longitude 79° 24', latitude 55° 16'. Daily run 103 miles.

At 3 p.m., it started to drizzle and the glass began to tumble down, while a fresh nor'westerly was pushing us along with all sails close-reefed ... At 9 p.m., we had to lower the mainsail and, a little later, the mizzen. *Joshua* was now running before a very fresh nor'westerly blow under storm jib and reefed staysail. The barometer had dropped to 1000. I held the boat almost dead before the wind, just within the safety limits, for I considered it wise to gain some more southing and keep plenty of elbow room between us and the Chilean coast, just in case there should be another gale.

Rain or drizzle fell all night long.

9th January

Thick weather, with drizzle and fog all the morning. I managed a rather unrealiable sight by presuming the sun to be in a luminous patch, but I caught it rather more accurately on its meridian passage, and once more shortly afterwards, as a check.

The wind had eased considerably and there was no big swell from the north-west that would have heralded a gale, so at dawn we re-hoisted the mainsail and mizzen, both reefed.

Noon position: longitude 75° 05′, latitude 56° 23′. Daily run 132 miles.

Cape Horn was now 300 miles eastward of us. In the afternoon the sea became really rough and I began to fear that it was the sign of an approaching depression. The glass stood at 995 at 2 p.m., 993 at 4 p.m., 992 at 6 p.m.

But the wind did not increase and I even had the impression that the sea was going down during the night. So the fair weather was holding after all! ... There was no longer any real night but rather a kind of transition from dusk to dawn, since the night proper was extremely short and never completely dark despite the overcast sky.

10th January

The glass had risen: 996 at 3 o'clock in the morning. The sky was thick with cloud, drizzle and fog, but I managed to trap the sun through the thinner patches of stratus and got four good sights between 6 and 10 a.m.

Noon position: longitude 70° 45′, latitude 56° 26′. Daily run 153 miles.

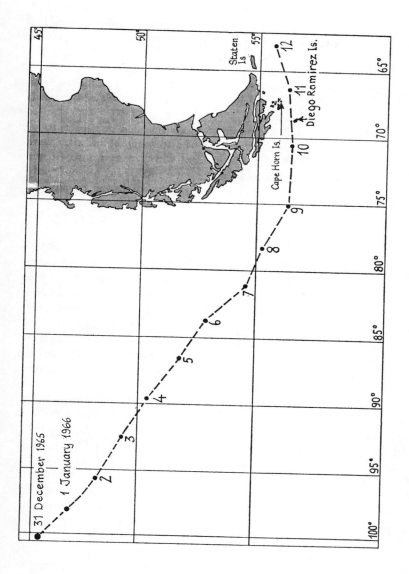

125 more miles to Cape Horn ... and the weather looked like staying fine. The sea was not too rough and there was no sign of an ominous swell. Fair weather ... and with a following wind!

We continued to plot our position all afternoon: I measured the sun's altitude whenever I could make it out through the stratus, while Françoise took down the time when I shouted 'stop'! Then she worked out our position with the help of Dieumegard's tables which we were using for lack of the much handier HO 249 tables.

Our progressive afternoon positions revealed our speed to be 9 to 10 knots (with a fair current of 2 to 3 knots) and they were correct, for ... yes! ... my heart leapt with joy: at 7 p.m., (it was still bright daylight) I could make out a small, bluish spot exactly where I had expected it to be – the Island of Diego Ramirez.

'Françoise! ... come and see ...!'

And Françoise, huddled against me, began to cry softly. We were almost in the Atlantic ...

The stiff breeze which had pushed us along for several hours gradually reached moderate gale force. The barometer did not budge, so there was some hope that it would not come to anything ... But the sea soon became dangerous since we were now in only 50 fathoms of water and high, curving waves were being knocked up despite the fair current and despite the fact that we were already 'under the lee' of Tierra del Fuego (this shallow shelf extends to a considerable distance off Cape Horn and Tierra del Fuego).

Joshua, having reached her maximum speed, tended to yaw as much as 20 degrees under her self-steering gear and seemed to be looking for an opportunity to surf, with a following wave, to show us what she was capable of. Hm! ...

Quick ... down with the mainsail ... that was better: she was easier on the helm, but the wind continued to increase, while the barometer remained completely steady. We were now some thirty miles off Tierra del Fuego, and I was wondering whether this very fresh wind (a good force 8, I reckoned) was not, perhaps, related to the williwaws, those extremely strong local winds that are often met with in the Patagonian Channels and can extend as far down as the mouths of the valleys.

It was certainly not a depression because the barometer remained steady, thank goodness! It was fine weather, after all.

I nevertheless lowered the mizzen before long and let *Joshua* run under storm jib alone, after having adjusted the self-steering vane to stand further out to sea and find deeper water where the seas would be less vicious.

The night passed without incident while we were watching for icebergs (without seeing a single one). The sea was running very high but was no longer dangerous because we had reached deeper water. I was sure I could feel the presence of Al Hansen, it was almost tangible. It was a strange and moving sensation, this benevolent presence ... '*You have a fine boat ... a fine boat ... and your little wife isn't bad, either ... but don't ever try in the other direction ... it is too hard ... too hard ...*'

I also thought with respect of Marcel Bardiaux who had rounded the Horn in the other direction and then continued to beat into the icy spray to round Hermit Island as well, at the onset of the austral winter when the nights are endless.

11th January

The cloudy skies of the South Pacific gave way to rather clearer weather on the 'good side' of South America. The Horn rounded, we had gybed at dawn and were now heading in a north-easterly direction. It was still blowing a gale, but only a moderate one, and the immense swell of the Pacific had given way to a different sea altogether, still running high in the strong wind, but quite different.

A moon sight towards 6 a.m., crossed two hours later by a sun sight, put us in the Atlantic. The barometer fairly shot up: 996 mb at 3 a.m., 1008 towards noon, with an hour's bright sunshine and flat calm in the afternoon, followed by a light breeze from the north-west, force 2! ... The sea had become quite beautiful, and there wasn't an iceberg in sight. What a relief!

Noon position: longitude 66° 22', latitude 56° 19'. Daily run 145 miles.

In forty-nine days we had covered 5,657 miles between our respective noon positions, which amounted to an average daily run of 115·4 miles, without damage or accident. But we still had a long way to go to Gibraltar, and we were already late: when we had set out I had counted on 5,000 miles from Tahiti to Cape Horn, by a reasonable route which would not take us down to the high latitudes too soon.

I had reckoned that if we could be content with an average daily run of a miserable 140 miles, *Joshua* ought to reach the Atlantic in 35 to 38 days, unless she were to end up, against her will, on a nice mooring in Valparaiso.

But really (and without wanting to think too much about it for fear of attracting the Evil Eye) I had hoped with my unfailing optimism that we would reach the Horn in 30 to 33 days, for the simple reason that *Joshua* had easily covered her 150 to 160 miles a day in a force 4 Trade wind. This naturally led me to believe that she would do at least as well in the stiff westerlies, apart from the occasions when she would lie a-hull in gales trailing hawsers.

A bird of the Tropics, I had a lot to learn about the latitudes inhabited by the albatross. The south-easterly Trade wind had followed *Joshua* as far down as the 39th parallel and added another 600 miles to our route. Besides, the lack of really small, manageable sails prevented us from making full use of the fresh following winds which are typical of the high latitudes.

We would now have to get a move on if we were to arrive in France in time for the Easter holidays beginning around the 1st April, for we still had some 10,000 miles to go to Marseille.

6

On the Look-out for Icebergs

We were starting on the second stage, which was bound to be much easier than the first, with only 15 per cent of gales on the Atlantic coast of Patagonia as compared to 25 to 30 per cent on the Pacific coast. The frequency of gales decreased as *Joshua* climbed in latitude towards more inviting-looking little squares.

But we had to keep a look-out for icebergs for more than 1,500 miles, for they extend a long way north, carried along by the Cape Horn Current to warmer waters.

Ocean Passages of the World advises passing between Tierra del Fuego and the Falkland Islands to minimise the risk of melting drift ice. The book also recommends passing to windward of icebergs to avoid the large floes that become detached from the main bergs and drift in their lee. This is what our *Instructions Nautiques* (series J1) say:

In the daytime and in clear weather, icebergs can be seen a long way away. In thick fog, on the other hand, they cannot be seen until they are quite close to the ship (possibly 100 yards), appearing as a dark mass in overcast weather, as a white, luminous mass, magnified by diffusion, in sunny weather.

On a clear night they can be discerned as far as a quarter of a mile away with the naked eye, a mile away with binoculars, 7 to 8 miles away if there is a moon which is behind the observer. Against the moon they are difficult to see. (Since *Joshua* was sailing northwards, the moon was ahead of us and of no help).

In calm weather their characteristic crackling can often be heard or the sound of the waves as they drift. Another indication in the same circumstances is the appearance of a line of brash ice surrounding the berg, with the berg itself to be found in the centre.

Locating icebergs by echo (whistle or siren) is very uncertain. Radar gives satisfactory results in many cases.

As one can see, the problem icebergs pose to a small yacht without radar is not likely to be solved in a hurry.

I had discussed it in detail with a naval officer friend of mine during our stay in Tahiti and had had this little note from him before we left:

There is one clue I give and that is that they have an aura of humidity – you can 'smell' them. An old petty-officer I knew used to sense them before the radar did and that is as much as 5 to 10 miles.

It is quite true that there are 'ice years' and years in which hardly any ice is seen. I hope you will resist the temptation to sail at night if you hit upon an ice year ...

This bit of advice concerning the detective properties of a good nasal appendage had given me heart: I remembered having noticed on several occasions that ice had a special *smell*, without being able to figure out why solidified water should smell any different from ordinary water. Perhaps a change in temperature changes one's sense of smell? ... What I am saying here may be completely stupid, but I cannot help thinking that there is just a bit of truth in it, for this 'smell' of ice had struck me quite distinctly on a number of occasions ... But then, of course, it was equally true that in my first boat *Marie-Thérèse* I had believed in navigating on longitude by watching the sea-gulls and this had enabled me to make a very accurate though permanent landfall when my keel had struck Diego Garcia.[1]

Yet sea-gulls can be a great help at times and so can a 'nose' for ice. I was, therefore, gratified to learn that a petty officer's olfactory organ had got one over radar. Quite seriously, you learn to smell a lot of things about the sea when you have lived with it for a long time. And Françoise and I would very quickly sense the need to heave-to for the night if we saw a single iceberg during the day.

As for 'ice years' and 'ice-free years' there was no doubt as far as *Joshua* and the year 1966 were concerned: after all the hardship we had endured for fifty days and fifty nights (I was starting to complain about everything, like the farmers), the Lord had obviously sent us an ice-free year.

The day after rounding the Horn the wind went from the northwest to the north-north-west, varying between force 2 and force 6 all through the morning. The sea, strangely enough, was so choppy that we had to sheet the sails in hard and batten down the hatch, but nevertheless exceptionally beautiful. This was the current playing up.

---

[1] For lack of navigation instruments, Bernard Moitessier had once run aground in the Indian Ocean in his junk *Marie-Thérèse* (Ed.).

Our position was now latitude 55° 40′ south and the eastbound current must be very strong in these parts, for in a flat calm we saw breaking waves (quite harmless) rising up like pyramids and falling back on the spot. The sea then looked as though it were boiling. Then it became smooth again, and later the whole thing started all over again. This was a completely inexplicable phenomenon since the wind dropped to nothing, or almost nothing, in the course of the afternoon.

I felt a chill in my bones when I imagined what this sea might be like in a gale. But by the end of the afternoon everything had become quite calm, while the glass was still rising: 1008 mb, which was 13 mb above the average pressure in our particular sea area!

The night passed without a breath of air, in a flat calm. We had all sails sheeted home and the sea was absolutely flat, so long was the swell. All the fatigue which had accumulated over the past fifty days suddenly swept over us, encouraged by the incredibly fine weather. For the first time in what seemed like an eternity we slept as children sleep. We slept protected by an abnormally high barometer, for this barrier of high pressure warded off any disturbances which might have come from the polar front.

For the first time in what seemed a lifetime we really slept, with the pale stars overhead watching over *Joshua*'s sleep in a night which was illuminated by an unnatural kind of glow on the horizon, coming from very far south, where the pack ice begins.

And all our tensions, all our anguish, the thousands of small worries of the past few weeks which suddenly crystallised in this immense exhaustion, were wiped away, dispelled by the night of perfect calm that covered us like an eiderdown only 150 miles from Cape Horn and almost on the same latitude, 80 miles from Staten Island, far from land or any danger, without a single iceberg in sight, while Fred's stove warmed our hearts and our bones with the heat of its flame and its red glow flickered beneath the chart table.

And the Lord, who created that night, showed us why the route we had chosen is the most beautiful of all the routes *Joshua* might have taken.

The following day, the 13th January, brought a flat calm and bright sun to complete the beneficial effects of the previous night. The swell was so long that we could hardly feel it. Later, small, almost imperceptible puffs came from the east, so light that it was not worth our while to try and make use of them. In short, it was perfect weather for motor-boating.

Françoise got out her flour and made some bread. It was absolutely delicious, baked in a frying pan on top of Caroline, with an asbestos mat under the pan.

Visibility was excellent and I spent a long time scanning the horizon through my binoculars ... not an iceberg in sight.

Noon position: longitude 61° 50′, latitude 55° 20′. Daily run 45 miles.

A light east to east-nor'easterly breeze came up early in the afternoon, followed by a flat calm from 2 to 6 p.m., with the sky completely overcast with stratus and wisps of mist, then fog.

A breeze from the east finally sprang up around 7 p.m., lasting all night without dispersing the fog, while the glass fell to 991 ... It was too good to last, the game of the little squares was not going to be abandoned so easily. But we were making good headway towards the north-north-west to pass as quickly as possible between Patagonia and the Falkland Islands, leaving Staten Island to port.

Françoise was beginning to think that my instinct had not betrayed me: it was quite conceivable that we had been granted an ice-free year, for we had neither seen nor 'smelt' so much as the tiniest piece of an iceberg. We kept a look-out all night, in turn, straining our ears and trying to penetrate the fog, while *Joshua* slid along slowly on a very calm sea ... the rapid drop of the barometer had obviously been a false alarm, thank goodness. What a diabolical invention the barometer is, enough to give perfectly stable people heart failure. Fortunately Françoise and I had acquired superb equanimity.

14th January

Ultra-light winds for this part of the world, where the trees seem to be all roots and the sheep are wonderfully healthy because they have to work twenty hours a day trying to live by licking stones. We were rather keen to get away from here! ... But we needed a bit more wind.

All morning there was moderately thick fog, then, suddenly,

the sky cleared in one go to give us brilliant sunshine on a long, peaceful swell that seemed to say: 'Don't worry, children, don't worry, there's no gale forecast for this area.' Still no icebergs in sight ...

We had covered 92 miles in the past 24 hours, the Cape Horn current obviously having helped a lot.

Flocks of sea-birds were literally stuffing themselves with minute brown shrimps that formed large, brownish patches some 100 feet in diameter. Those birds were uttering veritable shrieks of joy, and for the first time we saw those adorable little petrels actually sitting on the water. We had come across them everywhere, skimming over the waves and dangling their feet in the water, but never before had we seen them actually sitting on the water.

Large numbers of albatrosses were riding on the water, too. I had read somewhere that this is a sign of imminent bad weather. What a myth, with the barometer rising and the sea so calm! ...

Light breezes broken by flat calms alternated with each other all the afternoon. The barometer shot up like a rocket, from 991 in the small hours to 1003 towards sunset. Well, we were not complaining; it looked as though the weather would hold, and not an iceberg in sight, although a little more wind would have helped us reach those more inviting-looking little squares much faster.

15th January
The barometer went into a spiralling descent around midnight. This time we really were in for a blow, the one that all those albatrosses sitting on the water had been kind enough to annouce the previous afternoon ... just to remind me that old seamen's tales are sometimes true.

First we lowered the mizzen, at 3 a.m., in a stiff north-easter. The mainsail was already close-reefed, but *Joshua* proceeded to smash into the seas close-hauled as though she had suddenly remembered that she had a bone to pick with them, and we hurriedly took the mainsail off her to calm her down a bit.

The stiff breeze rose to a moderate gale, then a whole gale, We decided to hand even the reefed staysail, for we had a long way to go yet, and the sheets would not hold for ever, despite the care I had bestowed on them. The coast was sufficiently far to leeward

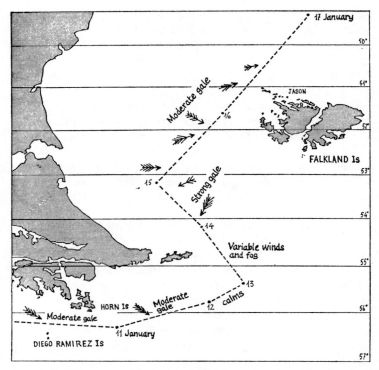

(110 miles) for us to carry on without running the risk of ending up in Magellan Straits, from which 150 miles of open sea separated us. So there was no immediate danger, even though the gale was blowing dead on-shore.

Joshua was now between Patagonia and the Falkland Islands over soundings of 70 to 80 fathoms where the seas can run very high and break dangerously. For one moment I thought of lying quietly hove-to, helm down and staysail a-back, but I soon noticed to my surprise that the breakers were harmless, thanks to our speed and the fact that the boat was heeling and presenting her high top-side to them.

My surprise grew as I watched *Joshua*'s behaviour as the half-rollers struck her between full-and-by and broadside-on.

We were doing 5 knots on a close reach under the 86 sq. ft storm jib, and we were well heeled. From time to time a breaker would strike the heeled hull with full force and explode in a

shower of spray as it hit the bilge, making the boat slip very
slightly sideways but hardly increasing our angle of heel thanks
to our forward motion.

After having watched this for some time, I felt almost certain
that some of those breakers, if taken at the same angle but without speed, would have had us half-way under water.

Sitting on the inside steering seat while the self-steering vane
did the work for me, I watched the sea and tried to understand.
Why did a massive wave-crest striking the boat with full force
almost broadside-on not heel the boat right over if she had a way
on her? Did the fact that her draught was reduced at this angle of
heel have anything to do with it? Or was it on account of her
speed – in the same way that a bicycle going at full speed stays
upright more easily than one which is almost stopped? ...

On second thoughts I did not consider the case of the bicycle
at all comparable: a bicycle remains upright because its wheels,
by turning, act like gyroscopes, as everyone knows.

The draught, then? I felt that the answer lay in that direction.

As a child, when spending my holidays in Indo-China together
with my two brothers, I enjoyed surfing in fine weather in pirogues
on medium-sized rollers, which started to break 100 to 150 yards
from the beach.

Each of us had his pirogue which he sailed single-handed,
running towards the beach on the backs of the rollers, doing his
best to remain stern-on, by helping with a paddle, so as not to
capsize. Those who have played the game know how difficult it
often is to stop the boat from broaching to and being rolled
over.

And I suddenly remembered a detail which seemed of extreme
importance: our pirogues were not always rolled over immediately after having come broadside-on because they were still
going at a fair speed after the first phase of surfing. It even happened frequently that, having lost their forward speed, they ran on
towards the beach without capsizing, although they were pushed
broadside-on by the breakers.

So these light pirogues could side-slip without capsizing in
small rollers which, scaled up to *Joshua*'s size, would have been
enormous. And now the same thing was happening to *Joshua*: her
draught reduced by the angle of heel, she was carried along sideways by some of the big rollers. She carried on without that small,

well-known voice inside me making itself heard, which has always whispered to me in moments of danger: 'Watch out, boy ... watch out ... don't play about ...'

In *Marie-Thérèse* the voice would have spoken to me long ago and I would have been hove-to. But now it was saying nothing, except perhaps that *Joshua* must be a fine boat to be able to carry on safely in this rough beam sea.

At 11 a.m., the glass stood at 984 mb. The seas were breaking massively in the cross current that runs up the Patagonian coast. But we were managing. The sky was overcast and it was raining. I had succeeded in taking a rather laborious sun sight at 10 o'clock. The method of taking sights 'without the telescope and with both eyes open' proves extremely useful under these conditions; there is, after all, a tremendous difference between fixing one's position and having to be content with an estimate ... especially in an onshore gale.

No meridan sight was possible at noon since it had been raining incessantly for two hours, but the glass looked as though it were rising slightly.

At 12.30 the sky suddenly cleared as if by magic, and the wind went to the north-west ... a mere force 5 or 6 ... while the barometer rose by 2 mb. Thank heavens ...!

We went about immediately and headed north-east. *Joshua* was pitching most horribly in a very rough head sea, which went down a little during the next few hours, while we rehoisted the reefed staysail and the close-reefed mizzen.

A second sight taken under favourable conditions gave us our fix:

Noon position: longitude 65°, latitude 53° 07'. Daily run 87 miles.

We were at least 95 miles from the Patagonian coast, and 160 miles off the Falkland Islands. I was glad to know our position with reasonable accuracy for the chart showed the Eagle Reef between us and the Falkland Islands, about 65 miles ahead. Once we had passed that obstacle we would have a free run to Gibraltar.

For the time being Françoise and I took turns in spending quite some time on deck and scanning the horizon through binoculars: no icebergs.

16th January

The wind had dropped to force 4 during the night without the barometer (invention of the devil!) having risen at all, so we thought it wise to leave our mainsail furled as it was.

Our suspicions were proved right, for at daybreak a moderate gale was blowing, this time from the west, i.e. free. The sea remained very manageable and the sky clear. A fix early in the morning showed that we had passed the Eagle Reef, so that was one worry less.

Noon position: longitude 62° 38′, latitude 51° 32′. Daily run 126 miles.

That still left 50 miles to the Falkland Islands and I was vaguely surprised that we had done no better in the last 24 hours considering that we should have benefited from a fair current flowing north-east. We carefully re-read our *Instructions Nautiques*.

At midday we were within 50 miles of the Jason Islands, the last danger to the north-west of the Falkland Islands. *Joshua* was doing 5 knots, and the current seemed negligible, for the log registered 122 miles since the previous day for what was really a run of 126 miles ... Strange that the Cape Horn current should suddenly have gone on strike ... True, yesterday's gale blowing in the opposite direction might have cancelled it out temporarily.

By all appearances we would leave the Falkland Islands to starboard in another ten hours, i.e. at about 10 p.m.

I must mention that we kept a very careful time check by tuning into the time signals sent out by W.W.V. We took three sun sights for the first fix, checked the calculations carefully, and as usual I compared the sun's azimuth (calculated at the same time as the altitude) with the compass reading. This is very important in navigation, especially with a steel boat, where accuracy of the compass readings can be seriously affected by all the metal. I am very meticulous in this respect and calculate a new azimuth for the sun or a star every time I changed course, for the compass variation changes so quickly in these high latitudes.

So we knew *exactly* where we were and where we were going. The sky was cloudless, and all was clear ahead until night-time, for we were, after all, rather good at navigating. When one has crossed the Tuamotus taking star fixes almost every hour it is child's play to avoid the last dangers of the Falkland Islands 30 miles to starboard.

We did not check our position in the afternoon as we had intended because I was tired, the sky was blue, the sea beautiful without an iceberg in sight, and the wind fair. *Joshua* was only doing 5 knots and grumbling at seeing her mainsail still furled, but I was really too tired and Françoise did not insist either, seeing that the barometer could not make up its mind whether to rise or fall.

At 5 p.m. the shape of the Falkland Islands appeared suddenly, clearly visible above a nebulous horizon, almost where they should have been, almost ... but not quite.

Forgetting everything else we gazed at those islands, full of regrets, for of all the places on our route the Falkland Islands attracted us very strongly. All those indentations in the coastline marked on the chart ... all those inlets ... those fjords protected from the winds ... those steep cliffs, with glaciers at the bottom of valleys ... all those penguins on the beaches ... that abundance of fish, just like the Galapagos ...

This was the first land we had set eyes on after 6,000 miles at sea. We had not seen the jagged islands of Cape Horn, nor Staten Island, which we had given a wide berth, and you could not really count Diego Ramirez, which we had glimpsed briefly, with fear in our bones.

And we felt how stupid it was to come so close to that paradise spread out in front of us, without so much as lifting a finger towards the anchor ... just for a few days ... perhaps even a week

But we knew each other well enough to realise that those four days (even with the best of intentions) would have become three months.

At 6.30 p.m., I started to feel uneasy and went below to examine the chart, for something was definitely amiss in the azimuth, and besides the Falklands were growing bigger *much too quickly*; something was abnormal ...

Hand-bearing compass ... binoculars ... The truth dawned on us slowly at first, then struck us like a thunderbolt:

'Bernard! ... those are the Jason Islands! We are quite close! ... The Falkland Islands are hidden by fair-weather haze! ... Look, here ... there were two groups of land a minute ago, now there is only one. That's Steeple Jason covering up Gran Jason. And Jason West Cay must be quite close to us, almost in line with

Steeple Jason; I bet you can see it breaking from here, have a look through the binoculars.'

Françoise possesses many good qualities, among them the ability to read a chart much more quickly than I can. I have often noticed this, it's a kind of natural talent. So, before looking through the binoculars I hurried to the helm to head *Joshua* northwards and get away from that foul spot as quickly as possible. Then we hoisted the mainsail without further ado, forcing *Joshua* along at her maximum speed with her lee deck awash. I had the whole night before me to figure out how I could have made such a monstrous mistake, which not even a beginner would have made. For a beginner would have checked his position by taking a sight at 1 or 2 p.m., and then another one later on, and he would have noticed that *Joshua*, though logging 5 knots, was actually moving over the ground at 7 knots, and that the current, which I had thought was non-existent, had become stronger and was flowing nearly due east, at 2 knots, between the Jason Islands and the Falkland Islands. We would have spent at least a very worried quarter-of-an-hour there in the race, and possibly lost enough feathers to fill an eiderdown.

In his book *Sailing Alone Around the World* Joshua Slocum writes:

In the log for July 18 there is this entry: 'Fine weather, wind south-southwest. Porpoises gambolling all about. The SS *Olympia* passed at 11.30 am, long. w. 34° 50'.'
'It lacks now three minutes of the half-hour,' shouted the captain, as he gave me the longitude and the time. I admired the businesslike air of the *Olympia*, but still have the feeling that the captain was just a little too precise in his reckoning. That may be all very well where there is plenty of sea room. But over-confidence, I believe, was the cause of the disaster to the liner *Atlantic*, and many more like her. The captain knew too well where he was. There were no porpoises at all skipping along with the *Olympia*! Porpoises always prefer sailing ships. The captain was a young man, I observed, and had before him, I hope, a good record.
'Land ho! On the morning of July 19 a mystic dome like a mountain of silver stood alone in the sea ahead ...

The captain was a young man ... and had before him, I hope, a good record!!'

19th January

We were already far from the Falkland Islands, at longitude 54° 40′ and latitude 47° 39′. The weather had been reasonably fine for the past three days, and we had not seen a single piece of ice despite the careful watch we had kept.

But now the weather had broken. The barometer had come tumbling down since the previous day, thick cloud closed in at dawn and it started to drizzle. The glass dropped as low as 977 mb ...

We had had the mainsail close-reefed since midnight, and towards 10 o'clock in the morning it was blowing a gale from the south-west. It rather resembled a *pampero* as described in our *Instructions Nautiques*: sudden drop in pressure, secondary swell from the north, mist in the morning. We took down what sail was left up, even the 86 sq. ft storm jib, and were soon glad we had done so, for the passage of stratus-nimbus was accompanied by heavy squalls. Then the sky cleared, but the wind did not abate.

We lay a-hull and steered from inside with the hatch battened down, running before the gale at first but soon judging it prudent to alter course a little and take the waves on the quarter, for the seas were increasing in size at a surprising speed and would have been dangerous if taken stern-on. While the seas were nothing compared with those in the South Pacific, they nevertheless called for caution.

It needed acrobats to take the morning sight, but I managed it in the end, since the horizon was not obscured the whole time.

Ever since we had sailed in high latitudes I no longer cried 'stop' but banged three times on the roof of the after cabin with the heel of my boot (I was usually leaning against the mizzen mast). At that signal Françoise noted the time from the chronometer, starting with the seconds, as it is done on all ships. For example:

I shouted 'stop' (or banged three times in rapid succession).

Françoise, following the second hand with her eyes, then wrote down: 45s. Then she would look at the minute hand and note down: 15m. Finally she would note the hour: 14h. I would then read the sextant, and Françoise would write down 55° 08′ next to the time.

Most skippers prefer to take the time themselves so as to avoid any argument if there is a wrong fix, and this is what I always did if the weather permitted. I said 'stop' to myself, then moved calmly towards the chronometer (counting the seconds in my head) and read off the time, always starting with the seconds. It is impossible to take in the exact time at a single glance without risk of error, and an error of one minute of time means an error of roughly 15 miles in longitude. On board *Joshua* we have removed the chocks from the sextant case so that the sextant can be stowed without the index bar being returned to zero. In this way, if the calculations turn out slightly haywire, I can re-check the sextant and perhaps find that I have misread it, say 55° 38′ instead of 55° 08′.

From 11 a.m. onwards (977 mb) the barometer started to shoot up and reached 991 at 2 p.m., without the wind easing in the least. I would not say that it was a 'raging storm' just a good blow, but the sea was running high, very high, with massive breakers which I watched thoughtfully from my inside steering position. I doubted very much that a boat of *Joshua*'s size would have been really safe if she had been hove-to in this sea.

The large sailing ships could actually defend themselves against huge breaking seas, for their long hulls, as they made leeway through the water, left a kind of protective turbulence in their wake which extended a fair distance to windward and acted rather like oil, breaking the force of the rollers.

Even a large tunnyman hove-to, could have created a big enough turbulence to windward to protect her against the kind of sea I was looking at, but not *Joshua* nor, I reckoned, any other boat her size. I am dead against heaving-to after *the sea* had reached a certain size and force which is no longer proportional to the wind strength nor the time for which it has been blowing. Ever since yachting has become a sport a lot has been written on the subject of heavy weather, and will continue to be written as long as there are small boats. I doubt whether any of us will ever find the solution to this problem, because I somehow feel that it is linked to the sea area in which a boat sails rather than to the force of a gale and its duration: the size and character of breakers are certainly not the same whether the gale is encountered in the South Pacific, off the coast of Argentina, in the Gulf Stream, near the Azores, off the Moroccan coast or in the English Channel.

The Logical Route

All the photographs of breaking waves in this book were taken during this gale in the South Atlantic. Anyone who is a yachtsman can decide for himself whether in a similar sea he would have chosen to lie hove-to or run before it, under control ...

20th and 21st January
Nothing much to report ... The weather was relatively fine and we even got out the big cotton jib with its 32 sq. ft. But as *Joshua* gained in latitude towards the north-east so the nights became longer and our nervous tension rose. Too many fine clippers had disappeared after having rounded the Horn, struck by icebergs. The fortieth parallel still seemed a long, long way off ... despite the fact that the sun was climbing higher and higher in the sky each day.

22nd January
A stiff sou'westerly breeze, sky covered with cumulo-nimbus. Heavy squalls charged with hail. The seas were getting very big and breaking, but we were running before them under the self-steering, which worked like a charm.

Soon the little voice whispered to me that something ought to be done ... so we lowered the mainsail even though it was close-reefed, for in one squall during which hailstones 'as large as duck's eggs' came pelting down, *Joshua* had almost taken her 13 tons off on a plane, and I was starting to get worried about the rigging. It would have been too stupid to have an accident now!

I promised myself that next time no shroud would be less than 10 mm in diameter so that the boat could be forced along, the way she liked it, in all conditions. I had come to realise that it was a mistake to under-canvas a *steel* cruising yacht off the wind. For this is how things usually go between two large land masses if the weather is unstable:

A squall approaches, the skipper wisely shortens sail to save his mast from being carried away and the sails from being torn to shreds.

The squall passes, the boat crawls along at 4 or 5 knots under its shortened canvas, but more squalls are to be expected. What should he do? Shake out the reefs? Change foresails until the next squall arrives? The cruising man who crosses an ocean is in a race whether he likes it or not. But the race is thousands of miles long and the crew often reduced to one man. That makes all the difference, and yet, if the boat is sensibly rigged for long-distance cruising (or racing, which is probably the same thing) it should make no difference at all.

A cruising boat should be capable of being driven almost continually at the limit of its speed, under the maximum sail area. Even if she is momentarily laid flat by a heavy squall she should come to no harm with strong sails and *utterly reliable* rigging. For in a steel boat, no matter how heavily canvassed, the mast will never be driven through the keel. It is a pity that there are limits to the height of a mast. The triangulation of shrouds and stays must not be taken beyond certain safety limits, Jean Knocker tells me ... Nevertheless, that day I decided that once I was back in Europe I might possibly increase the height of *Joshua*'s mainmast to 55 ft above deck (it was then 49 ft), so that I could drive her at 7 knots in a force 2 beam wind ... even if it meant that I would then have to shorten sail drastically in a blow, particularly when sailing close-hauled. Daily run: a miserable 115 miles!

23rd January
The wind went round to north-westerly during the night and was blowing force 5 on average. We rehoisted the mainsail and the staysail, both with a reef in them, for the wind was still reaching force 6 to 7 in the squalls. The glass was steady at 1007 mb. Although the sky was completely overcast I managed to get two sun sights in the morning.

Noon position: longitude 48°, latitude 43° 28'.

The sea was still running very high but the wind, still from the north-west, settled down to a steady force 4 to 5 from 10 a.m. This abnormally big sea in what was only a moderate blow was probably due to the Brazil current.

At nightfall the glass fell again, reaching 1003 mb at 10 p.m. What a relief it would be to reach the 40th parallel! ... We were tired of playing at small squares, tired of watching for icebergs *where there weren't any*. But it would only have taken one single little piece of ice, sitting in our path quite by chance, to thoroughly spoil our race to the Trade winds. We could not afford to take the slightest risk. And whenever I was about to convince myself that we had *definitely* struck an ice-free year, I remembered the

Falklands, and back I went to look out for icebergs, dreaming of the Trade wind, the flying fish, of fine-weather cumulus and the many, many miles *Joshua* had already left in her wake. She would keep to the rules of the game if we did not break them on our part.

So we continued to spend the nights on watch in turn. It was bad enough for the two of us ... what must it be like for a single-hander? It might even be better if he were to strike an unmistakable 'ice-year', then at least he would feel obliged to heave-to before sunset, having carefully scanned the horizon through his binoculars.

Our two alarm clocks were set to ring every hour-and-a-half during the day and every hour at night (no half-measures for us ...).

But the routine was beginning to fray our nerves ... and we realised that the 'logical route' was, after all, very, very long.

Françoise, sitting on deck in the sun, actually thought she saw an iceberg, quite a small one, with which we were just about to collide ...

I was at the helm in a flash, but there wasn't an iceberg in sight. It was just fatigue. Both Françoise and I had been tired for too long.

It was a danger signal, a sign that our nerves had worn thin

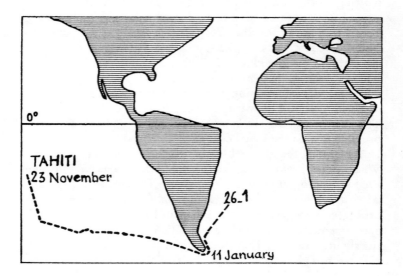

little by little, and had got into a worse state than the main hal-yard, without our noticing it. We had lingered too long in the realm of the mighty west wind.

Logging a daily average of only 115 miles instead of 150 miles has its dangers on a long voyage up to the 40th parallel. Instead of spending 55 days in these ill-famed latitudes we took another six days to cover the same distance. Another six days was six days too many. They were the hardest and most dangerous, and they were quite unnecessary.

Anyone sailing through these latitudes of strong westerly winds must, above all, do so quickly. He must sail at maximum speed so as not to incur those needless extra days at the end, when nerves and rigging are at their worst. It is those few extra days that can be dangerous, much more so than a whole gale.

7

The Horse Latitudes

On the 26th January, at longitude 41° 15' and latitude 40° 23' and after one last, short gale (which had no bite in it), *Joshua* crossed the dividing line between the Westerlies and the Trade winds. She was now in the belt of variable winds which are to be found, as a rule, between latitudes 25° and 40° in the summer (20° to 30° in the winter). The frequency of gales in this belt is very much lower than 'on the other side' of the border.

According to *Ocean Passages for the World* the wind exceeds force 7 on between one and three days each month, the rate rising to 3–4 days at the southern limit of the zone.

This belt of variable winds is commonly called the Horse Latitudes as a reminder of the days of the great sailing ships, which sometimes found themselves delayed here by persistent headwinds and were forced to throw the horses overboard to cut down the consumption of fresh water ... The mutiny on the *Bounty* took place in the Horse Latitudes of the South Pacific, I believe, but in that particular case it was bread-trees brought from Tahiti for the purpose of planting them in the Antilles that consumed the crew's fresh water.

It was not until several days later, at latitude 36° s, that *Joshua* ran into variable winds. If one could call them variable ... for they remained steadily northerly for ten days and *Joshua* only managed 1,097 miles between 28th January and 6th February, heading east-north-easterly, close-hauled, on a course which did not bring us much nearer the Trade winds.

Cruising is one long game of patience, I had said this to all my friends a hundred times over and now I had another opportunity to convince myself.

As for Françoise, she simply declared that I was in one of my 'head-wind moods'. To console her I pointed out that while she did not look exactly ill she had the same kind of misery in her eyes as Tallow, the Van de Wiele's dog, when their yacht *Omoo* approached the Trade winds.

But I remained anxious, remembering that Conor O'Brien had

crossed the three southern oceans past Cape Horn, without meeting with really bad weather (so he says), but had got the worst beating in his life around the 32nd parallel ...

Still, we weren't complaining. As Jean Lacombe says, there are skippers who attract gales, and others who attract calms ... As for us, we always attracted luck, that's how it was, we couldn't help it. So the wind was bound to change. At least that's what I told myself on the 7th February, after ten days of headwinds, when I watched the swell from the east-north-east, which had been slight the day before but was now more pronounced. I did not dare tell Françoise, for she, not having been born in Asia, would have been capable of exclaiming at the top of her voice: 'You really think the wind is going round east-north-easterly? ... That's great! ...'

And immediately the Evil Eye would have been upon us to make sure that instead of the east-north-easter I was expecting we would get a perfect 'noser' for another ten days. So it was better not to tell Françoise, not yet. In Asia, boats have a large eye painted on either side of the bow, to ward off the evil spirits, but Françoise did not realise yet just how much there was in that.

Noon position on 7th February: longitude 18° 55', latitude 32° 05'. Day's run 75 miles.

We had made a mere 25 miles of northing. What a negative way to look at things. Let's be positive and say: we were 25 miles nearer the Trade winds.

Flat calm during the night. *Joshua* waited, her mainsail and mizzen sheeted hard in, jib and staysail lowered to save them chafing unnecessarily against the stays. As for the crew, we read, and then we slept, for the wind would return when it was good and ready, evil spirits or not.

8th February
The wind returned, but still from the north-north-east. Our hopes recovered, though, as the day drew on, for it was no more than a dying breeze, just enough to enable us to make headway against the swell from the east-north-east. If it expired altogether, and there was no doubt that it would, it was sure to be replaced by a flat calm or an easterly breeze. Provided that the evil spirit could not read my thoughts! ...

Our day's run was a mere 36 miles! This was more like drifting than sailing ... But I didn't dare complain for fear of attracting some catastrophe, and even Françoise felt the same.

We decided that during the next calm we would both go into the water and scrub the bottom: the barnacles must have grown thick and fast if the cluster of molluscs by the rudder was anything to go by. But *Joshua* seemed to be moving along normally, even rather well considering how light the wind was. Perhaps the bottom was cleaner than we thought.

Conor O'Brien complained that *Saiorse*'s bottom got so foul between New Zealand and Cape Horn that he had to careen her in the Falkland Islands. Vito Dumas, on the other hand, never slipped *Legh II* between Buenos Aires and Valparaiso, which was a very long trip including two stays in port, at Capetown and Wellington, places where barnacles grow very much faster than in the open sea, even in cold waters. Was it the time of year, or the type of antifouling we used? When we were on the slip in Tahiti I had applied a coat of whale oil to the bottom over the top of the antifouling, for the following reason:

During our Atlantic crossing *Joshua* had been hopelessly slowed down by barnacles which had grown as fast as we could scrape them off (by diving). Watching these cursed molluscs grow

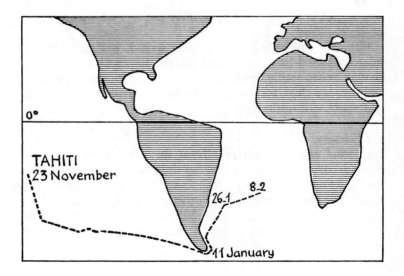

on their stalks I thought of a Spanish fisherman I knew in the Canaries who rubbed his copper-sheeted hull with fish entrails.

'What are you doing that for?'

'It leaves a coat of oil on the copper and makes my boat go better. Everybody does it in the Canaries.'

' ...?'

Well, I thought, this fellow is just kidding himself. His boat may go better for an hour or two, but certainly no longer than half a day.

But between the Canaries and Martinique, faced with those barnacles relentlessly growing, I remembered the naïve explanation of that fisherman and at the same time something else occurred to me: Why is it that there is no marine growth to be found on the backs of fish? Dolphins, too, are completely clean. Why?

Then, during our stay at Martinique, Henry Wakelam had told me that Bluche had given him a can of whale oil. Bluche had taken this oil on board at Madeira, at the start of his first world voyage, thinking that he might perhaps need it some day in heavy weather. But since he had not wanted to turn his deck into a skating rink he had left the oil in its can.

Henry had inherited it and offered me half of what was left when I had told him about my ideas.

'Try it out on *Joshua*, and I'll try it on my boat.'

I applied it gingerly at first (fearing that it might possibly encourage electrolysis – anything is possible) and found the results very encouraging: all the test surfaces which had been treated with whale oil after two coats of antifouling had stayed clean much longer than the rest of the bottom. So we promptly covered the whole of the bottom with whale oil while the boat was on the slip at Tahiti, and I felt we had no reason to regret this step, since the boat was still going well after two and a half months at sea.[1]

---

[1] One month after our arrival at Alicante, that is six months after careening at Tahiti, two patches on the rudder blade that had not been treated with whale oil at Tahiti (as a check) became foul much more quickly in port than the rest of the bottom.

It should be mentioned that the paint used on *Joshua*'s bottom is not a very powerful antifouling: it is a zinc silicate preparation applied in two coats, which is only used on steel, and which gives cathodic

9th February

At last ... the wind finally went from the north to the east-north-east, timidly at first, then becoming stronger and slowly veering easterly. I could hardly believe it ... could it be that we had found the Trade wind 600 miles south of its mean limit, at latitude 32°, when by rights it should not start until around 21°? But there it was, *Joshua* was romping northwards with every stitch of canvas set, and every mile brought us nearer the heart of the Trade wind belt. And for the first time in my sea-going career a flying fish fell on deck in *broad daylight*! Extraordinary! Everybody knows that sailors are superstitious, that's why I could not help taking this occurence as a sign that everything was going to be alright.

Unfortunately, the large 320 sq. ft cotton jib was starting to show signs of bad wear and the wind had increased to force 4, from the same direction. It broke our hearts to have to lower it on deck.

11th February

Wind force 4, sometimes 5 or only 3, but *Joshua* hurried on towards the Equator, with her 1,020 sq. ft of canvas set, under a real Trade wind sky, covered with fine-weather cumulus.

Noon position: longitude 19° 32′, latitude 26° 07′. Day's run 157 miles.

The glass fell slightly, to 1020, which meant that we really were moving away from the South Atlantic High. Like *Omoo*, *Kurun* and *Anahita* we had found the Trade wind much sooner than we expected ...

For the next six days we continued to progress towards the Equator in easterly winds of force 4, sometimes dropping to force 3.

The game of the little squares had started again. But since they were all labelled 'o per cent gales' the game consisted of crossing

---

protection by being corroded away instead of the steel of the hull. Its antifouling properties are secondary, its action being primarily anti-corrosive. But this type of paint is still better than poor quality antifouling, though it is certainly much less effective than a good 'Super Tropical' quality antifouling.

as many as possible in the shortest possible time. Now that the Brazil Current had become favourable and so long as the Trade wind held, *Joshua* could easily polish off one little square (300 miles) every two days, and two in five days if the wind increased. We had some splendid day's runs: 145 miles on the 12th, 178 miles on the 16th. This was more like it!

On the 18th February we celebrated the feast of 'Saint Ten Thousand Miles', 87 days after our departure from Moorea. The first of our fresh water tanks was nearly empty. We had not expected it to last that long. We had used 110 gallons, which left us with another 90 gallons.

Another 165 miles on the 19th, which was to be expected in this plendid breeze. But we now understood why Conor O'Brien said he would have died of boredom if he had had to sail for 5,000 miles in the Trade winds. We felt that we were declining as the days went by, even with *Joshua* covering over 1,000 miles a week since we had found the easterly winds.

As we got out of practice we read a lot, nothing but good books. Life was amazingly peaceful, and we thought of the house we were going to build on the plot of land we had bought before leaving France, but knew that the mighty Westerlies had left their mark on us for ever. We would never forget the powerful, colossally beautiful seas of the high latitudes.

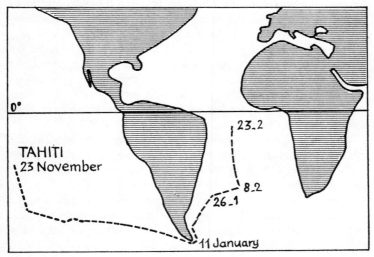

If we ever return to the Pacific we shall certainly come home by the same route again.

But for the time being *Joshua* was speeding towards the Doldrums and the Equator, which we planned to cross somewhere near the 23rd meridian, leaving to starboard a square filled with big black clouds and marked 'ten per cent calms'.

On the 20th February our noon position was longitude 22° 53′, latitude 3° 21′ s, on the 21st, longitude 22° 40′, latitude 0° 53′ s. The breeze was south-easterly now, force 2, sometime freshening to force 3. My kingdom for a genoa!

At last, on the 22nd February, our noon position placed us 50 miles north of the Equator, 91 days after leaving Moorea. I announced the good news to Françoise as I spread the third and last Pilot Chart of our voyage on the chart table: the North Atlantic!

Joshua had covered a round 5,000 miles in 42 days since rounding Cape Horn, an average of 119 miles per day. As for the South Atlantic Trades they had stayed with us for 13 days in which our day's runs had averaged 148 miles, despite a miserable 105 miles on the 22nd February, In all, we had covered 1,934 miles in those 13 days.

On the 24th February we found ourselves in the Doldrums. It had poured with rain all the previous night, with feeble northerly to north-easterly breezes alternating with flat calms.

This was followed by a flat calm from midnight onwards. We lowered the jib and the staysail and sheeted in the mainsail and the mizzen, for the short swell coming from several directions was causing a devilish choppy sea. I felt sorry for the big sailing ships of yore – the crossing of the Doldrums must have been sheer torture for them.

While Françoise was baking bread, complaining that it was too hot, I went into the water with my diving mask on and carrying a scraper, intending to clean the bottom. Greatly to my surprise I found it *perfectly clean*, as clean as it had been when we had left Moorea, three months ago, apart from some very large, localised barnacles on the stern, which I removed in a few minutes.

The reason for this, I assumed, was that we had set out with a *perfectly clean* bottom. Crossing from the warm waters of Tahiti

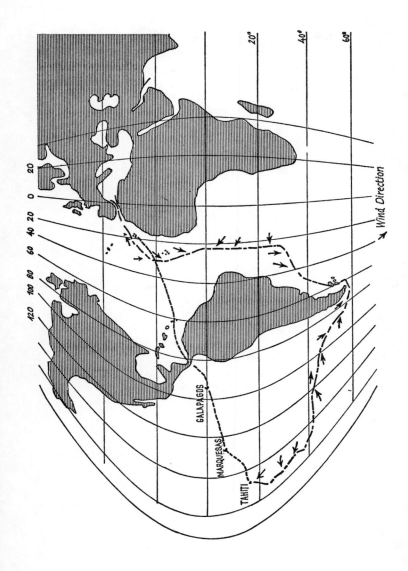

into the cold waters of the high latitudes and back again into the warm waters of the Atlantic had not given the local 'flora' a chance (nor the time) to get a grip on the hull. But I may be completely mistaken. Perhaps the extraordinary cleanness of *Joshua*'s bottom after three months at sea was entirely due to a favourable combination of circumstances connected with the breeding season of barnacles or the rhythm of life of plankton.

8

Trade Winds ... from the West!

On 26th February, 95 days after leaving Moorea, *Joshua* met with the north-easterly Trades in latitude 5° 21′ N, and 24° 02′ W. The Doldrums had let us off lightly, and now we were bowling along full-and-by, course NNW.

We still had a long way to go to Gibraltar: a beat of some 2,000 miles to reach a theoretical spot at 35°N and 40° W, level with the Azores, where we would find free westerly winds, and from there another 1,700 miles to the Straits of Gibraltar. So that left between 3,500 and 3,700 miles yet to be covered (at a generous estimate). Another thirty five-days at sea? I did not dare make any forecasts ... for fear of attracting the evil spirits!

Joshua was now gaining latitude fast. Nine days later she had already covered 1,259 miles, with daily runs of between 130 and 160 miles in a very lively sea. This brought our daily average since the Horn to 120 miles. Our mainsail and staysail made from supple *Cordon noir* Terylene were still in very good condition, but the jib and mizzen, made from stiff material (no trade name) were rather the worse for wear and needed watching on the wind.

By contrast with the South Atlantic there was much more life in the sea now: flying fish were everywhere, and we even caught a dorado, after having nearly forgotten what fresh fish tasted like!

But the few barnacles I had scraped off during the calms in the Doldrums ten days earlier were growing again thick and fast ... Perhaps the Trade wind belt of the North Atlantic favours the growth of barnacles rather more than that of the southern hemisphere. We had been bothered a lot by barnacles during the first stages of our voyage, between the Canaries and Martinique, so much so that *Joshua* would hardly manœuvre when we entered Martinique: we had to back the jib to go about ... All the other boats that had crossed the Atlantic during the same period (November-December) had their bottoms equally covered with barnacles ... I had found this out by going for a swim in the bay of Fort-de-France examining the hulls.

Is it a question of the season, then, or of the sea-area? The whole thing is a mystery, but I suspect that the North Atlantic encourages the growth of barnacles more than any other ocean. Perhaps they prefer the kind of plankton they find there?

Still, at that particular moment they did not seem to bother *Joshua* very much as she sped towards the Azores, her lee rail under and going so fast that she had little pitching or rolling movement.

The previous night had had a little surprise in store for us which gives an insight into the dangers that can sometimes waylay a small yacht: we had passed within two miles of a fishing vessel when, suddenly, a light had appeared quite close, almost under our bows: a lighted buoy ...! I put the helm down in a flash to leave it some thirty yards to weather ... and *Joshua* struck a large float with a long pole and a flag on it. No fishing net had got fouled in the rudder, but one can easily imagine the tangle of knots this little 'incident' might have led to!

On the 8th March, at longitude 29° and latitude 24° the weather deteriorated, the squalls becoming stronger and stronger and the glass dropping. Soon we had to lower all sail in the face of a northerly gale – in the Trade wind belt!

Later the wind backed north-westerly, remaining very fresh throughout the night, and we bowled along under a single-reefed staysail and storm jib, heading straight for Gibraltar ... It is strange how distances can change with the direction of the wind: if we had been close-hauled on starboard tack in a normal north-easterly Trade, Gibraltar would have been very, very far away, about 2,300 miles ... but since the wind had become free we were only 1,430 miles from the Straits. Our morale was correspondingly high!

The next day we were a mere 1,300 miles from Gibraltar .... and on the 11th March, 108 days after our departure from Moorea the Mediterranean was only 1,000 miles ahead.

Only another thousand miles ... six to eight days, if the wind remained free! Meanwhile *Joshua* had started to drag her heels because the breeze had eased, but it was still from the north-west and *Joshua* continued to head straight for Gibraltar. It was a sheer miracle in the Trade wind belt, on latitude 27°, 320 miles west of the nearest of the Canary Islands.

14th March

A swallow circled round the boat in the morning, then it flew off in the direction of Madeira. Later, another one came in through the hatch, flew round the cabin and landed on Françoise's head. It showed no fear when we caught it. We gave it some water mixed with a little evaporated milk to drink, for it seemed tired.

We had now been at sea for 111 days since leaving Moorea. There were still some onions, garlic and lemons left, not to speak of tinned food and Ovaltine (of which we consumed a great deal), and we were both in excellent health, as was *Joshua*. True, this kind of sailing was not tiring: no ships, no fishing vessels, and the boat sailed herself on the steering vane. She had done so from Moorea (except for the gale in the Pacific and the eight hours during which I had steered from inside in the *pampero*).

The swallow was dead in the morning. Another one came and alighted on the main boom. We caught it and took it to the safety of the cabin, and it left us at dawn in the direction of Madeira, which we soon saw some 25 miles to port through a break in the rain squalls.

We had done a daily average of 119·2 miles from Cape Horn (7,510 miles in 63 days) and of 117·5 miles since Moorea (13,167 miles in 112 days). Gibraltar was now 660 miles away, Marseille 1,400 miles ... This was the 15th March, and the children would be starting their holidays at the end of the month!

18th March

A swell from the north-east had built up the day before, then the wind had veered north-easterly. And now we were within 300 miles of the Straits, almost becalmed since 5 p.m., and without a breath of wind during the night. The barometer rose to 1,021. Our luck had ended, but we had to thank the gods for we had gained about 1,200 miles on our schedule. Thanks to these unexpected westerly winds which had blown for a whole week in the Trade wind belt, we were now almost home, after 115 days at sea.

On the next day we woke to a feeble northerly breeze, force 1 in the morning, then freshening to force 2 to 3. The swell was from the east-north-east, dead ahead ...

Our morale fell ... so did the barometer, while the northerly breeze smartened up and we were laughing again, watching *Joshua* romp along with a free wind, making straight for Gibraltar. We were definitely born lucky, all three of us: this drop in pressure indicated a depression far to the north, which meant bad weather in the long run. But a depression to the north was bound to bring westerly winds where we were and not so much bad weather.

Joshua gathered up her skirts in the night, but the barometer looked as though it had fallen a bit too far, which meant that the depression had moved too quickly eastwards.

At dawn on the 20th March we promptly had a gale from the east-north-east. We lowered all sail and lay hove-to, under bare poles and with the helm down to reduce leeway. *Joshua* had covered 124 miles in the past 24 hours, and after 117 days at sea we were 80 miles from Casablanca, 150 miles from the entrance to the Straits of Gibraltar.

The day before, a storm had been forecast for the Mediterranean (an easterly gale, probably), which in the event caused havoc at Nice, Menton and Antibes, and even caused the dams to break. It looked as though we were better off where we were.

For two days the wind never eased, while *Joshua* lay-to quite safely with the helm down and the sea on the beam. In the South Pacific we would have turned turtle several times over: different seas, different means of combating them.

Joshua lost 49 miles in 48 hours, but in the afternoon of the 22nd March the wind decreased and the sea went down. I cast a dejected glance at the masthead and prepared to climb the mast in order to see to the main halyard which had parted in the night having rubbed against the rigging clamp of a runner.

Joshua's main mast has 'mock cross-trees' about 3 feet down from the masthead on which I can sit and work in leisure for replacing a halyard or attending to a sheave. I just have to climb the mast, with my ankles tied together with an end of rope, which permits me literally to *grip* the mast with my feet. This takes no more force than one would apply to a pair of pliers. The technique is based on the nut-cracker principle and enables a practised person to climb a 65 ft high coconut palm in twenty-five seconds.

When the halyard was repaired, around 6 p.m., we set sail towards the east-south-east in a north-easterly breeze force 3,

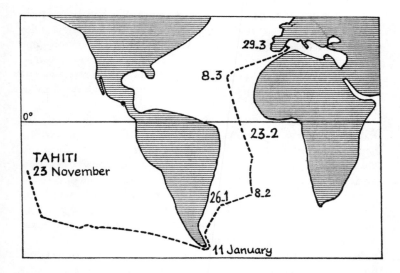

decreasing to force 2 during the night. The sea was still very rough and *Joshua*, battling along close-hauled, complained that our luck had turned. Come on now, *Joshua*, just one last effort and we're home!

23rd March

North-easterly wind, force 2, sea rough. Radio Morocco forecast winds from the north-east for the next 24 hours and there were long faces on board *Joshua*.

Noon position: longitude 8° 38', latitude 34° 08'. Day's run 55 miles.

But ... the current was now taking us directly to Gibraltar and helped us along quite a bit. Then the wind, on its dying breath, backed to the north-north-west early in the afternoon ... and we were a mere 168 miles from the entrance to the Straits while the sea became completely calm and *no swell from the east was noticeable.*

24th March

Light breezes from NW to NNW, force 1 to 2 in the morning, then the wind freshened to force 3 to 4 NW and the swell became steady from the NW. The barometer was high (1023) and Casablanca forecast a north-easter. Would it hold?

Our day's run turned out to be 70 miles. We had been at sea for 121 days since leaving Moorea and were now within 98 miles of the gates to the Mediterranean: Cape Spartel on the right, Cape Trafalgar to the left, and in the middle the Straits, wide open to shipping. We were hoping that we would be spared fog which is very frequent in those parts in westerly winds ... Only 98 miles to go!

Joshua was now flying along as though she had sensed the stable ahead, the sweet smell of the Vieux Port. I was terribly nervous and tried to calm myself by taking a sight in the afternoon and another one after sunset. Françoise, equally nervous, made the coffee with sea water ... and that cheered us up!

The sea was beautiful, the sky promised a steady wind and *Joshua*, with all her canvas set, was rushing along on a broad reach. We were praying that there wouldn't be any fog. If there was, we would have to find our way in blindly, with the aid of a radio beam, a lump in our throats and straining our eyes to penetrate the cold murk to pick out in time the lights of a ship or a fishing boat before getting too close. We would then be glad of our radar reflector fitted to the top of the mainmast. But we were hoping that there was not going to be any fog ...

'That's it, Françoise ... when I say 'stop' you count the seconds on the chronometer ...'

My eyes may have been dimmed with tears at that moment, I cannot remember any more, but I know that my heart nearly burst with the immense joy I felt as I watched the sweep of the powerful beacon of Larrache flickering among the waves low down on the horizon. Yes, that was it alright, the count tallied.

Then the light of Cape Spartel appeared in its turn. *Joshua* sped along towards it, her sails full, and all the while the wind held.

We had been at sea for four months and the time had passed so quickly that we could hardly believe it. We were both in good health, but our family was bound to be worried: four months without news! We decided to call at Gibraltar and send a telegram.

Pushed along by a nice breeze and a fair current, *Joshua* left Cape Spartel to starboard at 3 a.m., and the rock of Gibraltar to port at 6.30 a.m., but the weather was too good to stop, for, in the Mediterranean, it is almost a crime to waste a fair wind. Françoise was the first to say so, beaming with joy at knowing the children were so near, at last. We had covered 164 miles in the past 24 hours. Hurry, *Joshua*, hurry!

Splendid weather, not a cloud in the sky. The air was laden with moisture which obscured the outlines of the coast. The wind eased but remained fair, and the sea was so calm ... We had forgotten what a sea as calm as this looked like. We were happy, and completely relaxed.

But not for long ... The Mediterranean is an exhausting sea, especially for a yacht without an engine: calms ... calms ... faint breezes coming from nowhere ... menacing clouds ... and calms again while the Met Office forecast the end of the world in the Gulf of Lions.

On the night of the 28th to the 29th March we found ourselves almost becalmed off Alicante when we were nearly run down by a trawler steaming towards her fishing grounds at 8 knots. And that in spite of our 250 candle-power pressure lamp!

At around 3 a.m., the wind rose and came fresh from the north-east, precisely the direction in which we wanted to go! We were extremely tired after five nights almost without sleep, troubled by ships, fishing boats, calms and feeble breezes. Our excitement at being so near to our goal was great, but a little voice whispered to me: 'Careful ... careful ...'

'Françoise ... I feel this is becoming risky ...'

'I've been meaning to say to you ... shall we go into Alicante?'

'I think it would be wiser.'

So we had arrived, after 126 days and 14,216 miles between our noon positions. I had lost four pounds, Françoise was as fresh as a daisy. On the following day she took the train to Marseille and was with the children in two days. I stayed behind, waiting for them to join me for the summer holidays.

Shortly after midday *Joshua* entered the inner harbour of Alicante ... where we found moored five other French yachts, five sea birds, like us! They lent a hand in making *Joshua* fast: Jean-Marie, Claude, Jean Louis Martinet, Denis, Jean-Pierre.

'Tell us, truthfully ... : do we look unusual after four months at sea?'

'No more unusual than us ... but you ought to get your hair cut!'

Part III   Appendices

Designer's Notes

When Bernard Moitessier asked me to design a boat for him, he had a very precise idea of what he wanted, gained through experience and the years he had spent sailing his previous boats. He set down these conditions: *Joshua* was to be a double-ended, ketch-rigged, with the following dimensions:

LOA:	34 ft 6 in
Beam:	10 ft 6 in
Draught:	4 ft 6 in

She was to be cold moulded, have two cabins and a centre cockpit and had to meet a number of other requirements:

– She had to go well to windward and be stiff to enable her to gain sea-room off a lee shore in a gale.

– She had to be as easy as possible to handle but carry enough canvas to allow her to make use of light winds such as she was likely to encounter in the Doldrums and between Panama and the Galapagos.

– Boat and rigging had to be strong enough to withstand the heaviest weather, and the boat had to remain manœuvrable under all circumstances.

– Her movement in a seaway had to be as gentle as possible and her stability excellent to ensure good course keeping under a self-steering mechanism.

– It was understood that in the course of the exercise I would raise objections on any point which appeared to me unsatisfactory, but that Bernard would always have the last word.

I was, of course, in agreement with most of the conditions he put forward, even where they were contradictory, like shallow draught and close-windedness. In most cases a boat has to be a compromise in order to satisfy the owner.

The choice of a double-ender seemed to me particularly sensible, considering the purpose to which the boat was to be put. A double-ender had numerous drawbacks: for its size it is a heavy boat, and its overhangs are short. To achieve a large enough sail area the mast must be high, and the type is particularly ill-suited to a ketch rig, which calls for generous deck length over which to spread the sail area to avoid the mizzen being blanketed by the mainsail on the wind. It is for this reason that most ketch-rigged double-enders have adopted the wishbone rig in order to enlarge the sail area between the masts.

The wetted surface of a double-ender is considerable and slows the boat down in light airs.

The curve of the diagonals is awkward towards the stern, which means a poor passage through the water if there is a sea.

It follows that it would never occur to anyone to have a double-ender built to compete in the One Ton Cup, nor could it be said that for cruising on the French coasts the advantages of a double-ender would appear obvious.

But when the boat is intended for ocean cruising where it is bound to meet with strong gales some day, the one consideration which overrules all others is that of staying afloat in an enormous sea, under bare poles. It appears to me that in these conditions the double-ender is clearly superior to other types of hull.

The very strong rudder is well supported by a number of gudgeons along its entire height and is among the least fragile types of rudder, which is as well considering that its loss might be fatal. It is perfectly suited to take a trim tab for the self-steering gear. Finally, it is easier to repair at sea than a rudder passing through a trunk.

But the most important consideration of all is that the boat must remain manœuvrable no matter what the state of the sea, which means its tendency to yaw in a following sea must remain under control in all conditions.

Here I must say something about the factors which influence a boat's tendency to yaw.

When a boat is caught up by a wave coming obliquely from astern several things tend to make it pivot round its centre of lateral resistance:

(a) The inclined plane of water which lifts up the quarter acts as a horizontal component which pushes the part of the boat with which it comes in contact. This creates a couple which makes the boat pivot and is more powerful the more abrupt the wave is and the greater the distance between the point of its attack and the centre of lateral resistance.

Thus, a boat with a counter stern has a much greater tendency to yaw, all the more so since this pivoting force, which acts on the hull until the crest of the wave is level with the centre of lateral resistance, will act on it for much longer.

(b) The motion of the water molecules is quicker at the crest of the wave than in the trough. This means that the after part and the forward part of the hull are moving in currents of different speeds.

(c) Under the effect of the wave the boat heels. The resulting asymmetry of the hull gives it a tendency to come up into the wind (luff).

These three causes combine to make a very powerful couple. The following forces counteract the pivoting motion of the hull:

1. The moment of inertia of the boat in relation to a vertical axis passing through its centre of lateral resistance.

2. The resistance to pivoting of the boat's underwater profile which is stronger the longer the profile is, for it varies approximately as the square of its length.

3. The action of the rudder, which is more effective the further removed from the centre of lateral resistance the rudder is.

It is obvious that all these conditions are best realised in the case of a double-ender, where the stern overhang is insignificant, the underwater profile very long and the rudder right aft.

A transom stern offers almost the same advantages, but has one drawback. When the boat is caught up from behind by the almost vertical crest of a wave advancing at twenty knots, the impetus imparted to the boat by the energy of the wave is so much greater on the large area of the transom, almost perpendicular to the wave, than on the inclined stern of a double-ender. Therefore the boat moves faster and stays in a dangerous position for longer, whereas it is desirable for safety's sake to let the crest pass under the boat as quickly as possible.

Finally, from the point of view of resistance, a transom stern is weaker. Old-timers among yachtsmen may remember the gale of August 1932 when over forty tunny fishing boats were lost with all hands, their long overhangs or wide transoms having been stove in by following seas. Their design was afterwards modified, and the Krebs boatyard was the first to produce a type of fishing boat with a very short scotch stern which offered perfect safety.

Bernard Moitessier's story shows that during the gale in the Pacific, running before the seas under bare poles, the boat remained manœuvrable for six days without once refusing to be stopped from coming up into the wind. This fills us with admiration for the proficiency of Bernard and Françoise as helmsmen, but it also proves that the double-ender is a good type of boat for these conditions and the Bernards had made an excellent choice.

Equally the ketch rig appears to me the most satisfactory type of rig for the anticipated conditions: it is the easiest to handle single-handed. When a ketch is rigged with one foresail only, the only sail changes necessary between wind forces 0 to 7 consist of changing the genoa for No. 1 jib when the wind freshens above 4 and of taking a reef in the mainsail when it reaches force 6.

The fact that the mainmast is placed well forward makes the boat more stable in a following wind. Finally, it is easily balanced on almost all points of sailing. If the sea is not too rough it is even possible to disperse with the self-steering.

The schooner rig, which is also very suitable for cruising, nevertheless has a few drawbacks: the fisherman, which is indispensable in light airs, is difficult for one man to handle by himself, and it is more difficult to stay the mainmast satisfactorily if the deck is short.

Joshua is a ketch with two foresails which makes her more stable at moments when one of them is lowered for a sail change.

The rig was designed after Bernard had decided to have *Joshua* built in steel and have her length increased to 39 ft 6 in. Her displacement, fully equipped for cruising, is 13·4 tons and her wetted surface 472 sq. ft.

To give a boat a satisfactory turn of speed in both light airs and fresh winds one has to aim at a ratio

$$\frac{\text{(Measured sail area) } \frac{1}{2}}{\text{(Displacement) } \frac{1}{3}}$$

of between 3·8 and 4, and a ratio

$$\frac{\text{Measured sail area}}{\text{Wetted surface}}$$

of around 2·3.

A wishbone rig having been rejected for considerations of ease of handling and safety, we decided on a high-aspect ratio rig (the mainmast is almost 50 ft high above the coach roof), a long bowsprit and a mizzen boom which projected beyond the stern quite a bit.

Nevertheless, the ratio $\dfrac{\text{Sail area}}{\text{Wetted surface}}$ does not exceed 2·27.

On the other hand, the other ratio comes to 4·19, which shows that the boat is still generously canvassed in relation to her displacement and requires a quick shortening of sail as soon as the wind freshens.

The other drawbacks are: a very high and narrow mizzen which suffers from a pronounced twist off the wind even with a kicking strap set and will therefore wear more quickly. Finally, the slot between the mainsail and the mizzen is very narrow and the latter consequently reduced in efficiency on the wind.

The considerable height of the rig and the weak staying of the mizzen mast aft, despite a preventer back stay set off the wind, filled me with grave doubts. The fact that Bernard has weathered all the gales he met without suffering any damage gives an idea of how carefully he rigged his boat and what a good seaman he is.

When I designed *Joshua* I had no experience with double-enders. I thought that in the case of this particular boat with its very shallow draught, the effective part of the underwater profile being situated rather far aft, a lead of the centre of effort of the sail plan of 12% LWL forward of the theoretical centre of lateral resistance would be sufficient to balance the boat under sail. I was wrong there, and after having sailed the boat a few times Bernard was forced to reduce the foot of the mizzen by 20 in. and extend the bowsprit by 31 in to balance her.

One point on which we disagreed strongly was the centre cockpit. In the original 34 ft 6 in plan of the boat the after cabin was no more than a rat trap, and, whatever the size of the boat, I hated to see the most agreeable part of it made unusable as living quarters because of a cockpit. We had a lively exchange of letters on this subject and Bernard's obstinacy finally won. I can see now that he was right. In a big following sea the central cockpit gives much more effective protection to anyone who has to come up on deck, and the risk of being knocked out by a breaking sea is much smaller than in a cockpit placed aft.

Joshua has a slight sheer and moderate free-board. There is no doubt that in very heavy seas it would have been reassuring to have a higher free-board, but this would have had an adverse effect on her windward abilities, and since certain other factors, like her shallow draught, were already working in that direction, I thought it wiser to leave the free-board as it was. This was not a happy decision; in fact, as Bernard has pointed out, the boat, which was designed for construction in moulded ply, was eventually built in steel and the weight of the bare hull increased by 2·6 tons. Even after reducing the weight of the ballast from 4·6 tons to 3 tons the freeboard was still lower by almost 2 in with the boat fully laden.

There is no doubt that if it had been planned from the outset to build the boat in steel and for her LOA to be 39 ft 6 in a number of things could have been designed differently. It would probably have been possible, by increasing the sheer and the free-board, to do away with the cabin top and still have adequate headroom, also to accommodate a drop-keel under the floor boards which would have improved the boat's close-windedness. We would have had a choice of cabin lay-outs, a berth never being longer than 6 ft 3 in whatever the length of the boat. Finally, a longer bow overhang would have improved her looks and reduced the length of the bowsprit.

There is nothing more fascinating than to forecast, from her characteristics, the behaviour at sea of a boat one has designed. What could one say about *Joshua*? She would have a gentle movement and be reasonably comfortable at sea. She would go to windward satisfactorily as long as she did not heel too much, when her shallow underwater profile would lie in the water obliquely, and in turbulent water at that. This would cause the boat to make excessive leeway and lose speed. The skipper would then have to reduce sail fast and not seek to point too high.

The boat would have good directional stability and sail well under self-steering.

Her long underwater profile would make her fairly slow to manœuvre, but she would still respond well to the helm and would not have a strong tendency to yaw.

Because of her large wetted surface her speed in light airs would be very modest, and she would only become enjoyable to sail in force 3 to 4. On the other hand her high rig combined with her reduced and shallow ballast would make it necessary to shorten sail rather quickly.

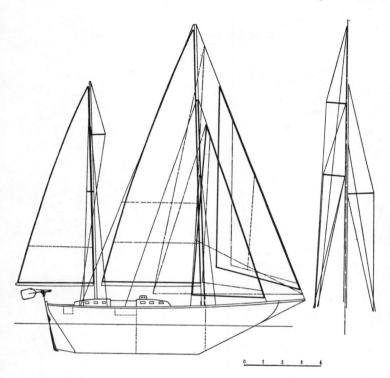

The height of the masts would call for prudence and make it advisable not to carry too much sail on the mizzen mast in a strong free wind.

Since Bernard always likes to please he told me that he was satisfied with the boat despite her faults, but if you should ever meet him he might whisper to you what he did not like to tell me.

Joshua's dimensions are as follows:

LOA	39 ft 6 in
LWL	33 ft 9 in
Beam	12 ft
Draught	5 ft 3 in
Free-board forward	4 ft 3 in
Free-board aft	3 ft
Minimum freeboard	2 ft 6 in
Ballast	6,615 lbs

Displacement . . . . . . 134 tons
Mooring and ground tackle . . . 1,410 lbs

Measured sail area:
Fore triangle . . . . . . 495 sq. ft
Mainsail . . . . 375 sq. ft
Mizzen . . . . 215 sq. ft

J. KNOCKER

Author's Notes

Self-steering

Joshua's self-steering vane is based on the 'Flettner' (trim tab) principle used in aircraft and is, in my opinion, less effective than the Marin-Marie type which was used on *Wanda* and *Marie-Thérèse II*

Wanda and *Marie-Thérèse II* followed an almost straight course, whereas *Joshua* frequently jaws as much as 20 degrees on a broad reach in a fresh wind. I had made provisions, in the construction, for using either type (Marin-Marie or Flettner) and fitted *Joshua* with the necessary ball-bearings and a connecting rod ready to be used in the same way as shown in the sketch on page 134 of *Vagabond des Mers du Sud*. But the projecting mizzen boom would have endangered a vane of the Marin-Marie system, so I opted for the Flettner principle, which is less efficient but nevertheless quite acceptable, especially if the helm is held in place with shock cord to restrict its movement.

Ia Ora Na, Jean-Louis Martinet's 31 ft Bermudian cutter, can make use of both systems by a simple inversion of the connecting rod. Jean-Louis by far prefers the Marin-Marie, and after having been out with him in *Ia Ora Na* I had no doubts: the boat followed a virtually straight course under Marin-Marie steering and a decidedly more wavering course with the Flettner vane set.

I made the same observations during a cruise to the Canaries on board *Vencia*, Pierre Deshumeur's 30 ft boat, which is also equipped to take both systems: straight course with Marin-Marie, less accurate course with Flettner.

Automatic self-steering gear can certainly be dispensed with on a very well balanced boat, fitted if possible with a bowsprit to make her less prone to weather helm. Both the *Snark* and *Marie-Thérèse II* were sailed like this before leaving Capetown. It worked very well, except that the boats often hesitated on course for long periods and also did not make such good speed because, except when hard on the wind, we had to slacken the mizzen sheet and sheet the jib far too hard to balance the boat with the helm lashed. As a result we logged fewer miles and it was much more tiring and worrying, whereas an automatic self-steering vane would have done it all for us and kept the sails full all the time.

But I believe I am trying to force an open door. Yachting magazines have for some years delved into the subject, and many cruising yachtsmen have built or installed one or other type of vane self-steering to dispense with the need for trimming their sails into impossible positions and see them less than full.

Joshua yaws about 15° maximum under self-steering vane, the average being around 10°. This makes her route a little longer, but not as much as one might think. According to the graph we drew during our Atlantic crossing a diversion from the direct course by 10° results in an increase of 2·3% of the distance covered. Thus, a boat that yaws by 10° follows a winding course *whose maximum angle of deviation is* 10°, while intermittent angles range from 0° to 10° progressively in relation to the direct course. The actual increase in distance covered for a boat yawing by 10° would, therefore, probably lie between 1·5 and 1·8%.

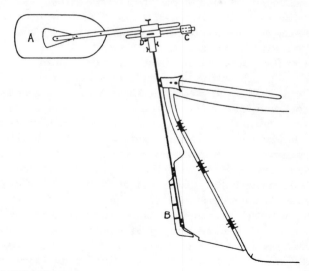

Joshua's *self-steering gear*
A. Vane made from 3 mm ply-wood
B. Articulated Flettner (trim-tab) on the trailing edge of the rudder proper, made from 18 mm ply for the tab and a length of standard galvanised water pipe.
C. Counterweight of vane
D. Connecting device made of lengths of galvanised tube welded in the shape of a double T and fitted with butterfly nuts for tightening.

Mooring tackle

It is better to have too much than not enough ... This is what *Joshua*'s 'mooring wardrobe' consisted of:

Anchors

One 38 lb fisherman's anchor with 7 fathoms of $\frac{1}{2}$ in chain and 33 fathoms of $2\frac{5}{8}$ in Nylon rope. This is the one we normally use.

One 66 lb Danforth anchor with 4 fathoms of $\frac{3}{8}$ in chain. This anchor is lashed on deck against the main mast when we are coastal cruising.

Two fisherman's anchors of 22 and 44 lbs respectively, and one 35 lb Colin Trigrip anchor, all stowed in the hollow keel.

One 55 lb CQR anchor. In my opinion, the CQR is the best anchor of all. It is followed, in order of preference (again, in my opinion) by:

The fisherman's anchor, because it holds in any ground and does not suddenly drag, providing its has a sufficiently long stock and wide, pointed flukes. This is how Chinese fisherman's anchors are made, and the hold extremely well. Those one finds at European ship-chandlers can be modified easily enough by welding new flukes onto the existing stumps. Almost all fishermen do this, and it pays.

The Colin Trigrip, the holding power of which has surprised me and which I prefer to the fisherman's anchor in tidal waters (the latter can get fouled).

But it is definitely the CQR which is way ahead of all other anchors I have ever used.

For safety's sake it is always advisable to have one's main anchor a little too large. Since we have an anchor windlass this causes no extra effort but gives us more peace of mind at night. Twenty pounds extra, for example, make all the difference to the holding power of the anchor because these additional twenty pounds are converted into holding surface.

Chain

7 fathoms of $\frac{1}{2}$ in chain on the permanent anchor.

55 fathoms of $\frac{3}{8}$ in chain in several lengths with a shackle all ready at either end to avoid losing time rummaging through the spare shackles.

Author's Notes

33 fathoms of ½ in chain.
All this chain is stowed in the hollow keel, except for the one on the main anchor.

Warps
33 fathoms of 2⅝ in Nylon warp which is part of the permanent anchor.
55 fathoms of 2 in Nylon warp (wound on a reel).
82 fathoms of 1¾ in Nylon warp (wound on a reel).
55 fathoms of 1½ in Nylon warp.
110 fathoms of 1 in Nylon warp (half of it wound on a reel).
55 fathoms of ¾ in Nylon warp.

Why do I have so much nylon?
The combination of chain and nylon warp is much more elastic than chain alone (but more length is needed to obtain the same holding power). Besides, nylon is so much easier to handle in a really stiff blow: it is easy to carry an anchor 100 yards to windward in a dinghy if it has a nylon warp to it with only 6 to 8 fathoms of ¾ in chain. One can even swim the anchor out, after have made it fast to an empty canister or two, if the wind is too strong for the dinghy to be used.

On the other hand nylon warp does not like rocky ground and needs watching more closely. When there is a risk of the nylon warp getting entangled with a rock or a coral I always buoy it so that it cannot touch bottom in a calm sea. Of course, when I spend the winter in port I moor on chain only.

As for the old rule of anchor cable scope having to be 'three times the depth of water', it is often misinterpreted: it is alright in fine weather in an open roadstead but dangerous in port, especially when the boat is moored stern to quay, for it is then impossible to increase the scope to obtain better holding if the wind should freshen. It is better to let out five or six times the depth of water right away; it will rarely be regretted.

Navigation
Our navigational aids consist of the following:

A. An *Omega* pocket watch of very good quality to serve as a chronometer.

Author's Notes

B. A *Techni-France* radio receiver, model T.R.88M run on round 1.5 v batteries, with which we can pick up the radio time signals and check the chronometer against them. Nowadays, thanks to the radio, it is possible to employ astro-navigation by using an ordinary watch fitted with a seconds sweep hand.

C. A vernier sextant bought second-hand. If I had had a choice (and, above all, more experience before setting out) I would have brought a micrometer sextant, which is quicker to read. This is not important for sun observations, because one sight is nearly always enough for a good fix. Since the telescope magnifies the apparent diameter of the sun the latter can be brought down to the horizon very accurately, so that one sight is quite enough.

But for star observations taken in twilight it is better to take three sights of the same star and take the mean, or even better, five sights and plot them on a graph.

At least two different stars are necessary (three, if possible) to get a fix. With a micrometer sextant, which is so easy to read, the whole series of observations can be completed much more quickly before the last of the daylight is lost. Before a tricky landfall it is reassuring for a skipper to know that he can take several sights of the same star *very quickly* before it is hidden by a cloud. For these reasons a micrometer sextant is to be preferred. But beware of so-called 'small yachtsman's sextants'. With none of the ones I have seen would it be possible to observe a star except in certain exceptional conditions. Even in plain daylight these small sextants are often incapable of giving a decent sun sight if the sky is a little too overcast and the sea rough.

D. The current Nautical Almanac. I believe that the British one is easier to use than the French, because all the figures necessary for calculating the hour angles of all usable heavenly bodies (sun, planets, moon, stars) are given on the same page. This does away with the need to thumb through the book and, in my opinion saves time and cuts down the risk of errors. Besides, the British Nautical Almanac lists the corrections to be applied to observed heights on the endpapers, and this means another saving in time compared with the French Nautical Almanac which involves another thumbing through pages.

E. Dieumegard & Bataille tables. (Later, other yachtsmen told me that, in their opinion, the American HO214 tables or the

243

British HD486 tables are much easier to use than Dieumegard & Bataille, because they give the values for intercept and azimuth at a single glance and require far fewer figures to be jotted down.

F. *Le Guide des Étoiles*[1] (a guide to stars), this marvellous work by Post Captain Pierre Sizaire, from which we learnt inside one week at sea to identify most of the stars used in astro-navigation. While it is easy enough, in theory, to find your position from Sirius, Vega or Capella (for example), you have to be able, first of all, to identify them.

G. *Le Panarama des Étoile*[2] by Admiral Yves Durand de Saint-Front (Marin-Marie's brother). This remarkable book helps you to visualise the movements of heavenly bodies.

H. Later, a friend made us a present of the American *Star Finder*. This is a set of 10 small plastic discs about 9 ins in diameter representing the dome of the sky as seen under all the different latitudes. The *Star Finder* makes it possible to identify all stars used in navigation and to know their approximate height and azimuth in advance. This makes it possible to pre-set the sextant and to look in the right direction. Also, if the sky is overcast, you can quickly take a sight of some brilliant star appearing suddenly in a break in the cloud, without having to know which star it is. You then ask the *Star Finder*: 'Which star is this that I have found at 31° 33', azimuth 306?' and the *Star Finder* replies: 'Only Vega can be found at this hour 31° above the horizon and at 306 azimuth.'

With the help of a naval officer it took Françoise and me five minutes to learn to use this magic device.

Finally here is my advice to those who *really* want to learn what astro-navigation is all about:

1. Study a book on astro-navigation. This will help you to cover a good deal of ground and will stand you in good stead afterwards.

2. Then ... go aboard a ship in harbour (I prefer Navy vessels) and ask a *young* officer to be good enough to explain to you how to calculate the 'hour angle' from the Nautical Almanac and how to

---

[1] *Le Guide des Etoiles*, Grandes Éditions Françaises, 36 rue de Penthièvres, Paris.
[2] *Le Panorama des Etoiles*, Éditions du Moustié, 254 Bd. Haussmann, Paris.

use the Navigation Tables. Young officers can still put themselves into the shoes of a beginner because they are not so far removed themselves from the days when all that sounded like a lot of Greek to them ... I hope they will forgive me for recommending them as the best teachers I have ever met.[1]

The engine

Our engine is very small with its 7 HP, but when the moment comes to replace it I am going to instal one of about 15 HP. This will be quite enough to give us four knots in a flat calm, and if there is any wind ... well, that's what the sails are for.

For the kind of cruising which we want to do I cannot see the need for a large engine, considering the cost, maintenance cost, complications, weight and space needed ...

Maintenance of a steel hull

Joshua is now six years old and her hull is still as good as it was the day she was launched.

Her bottom is painted with Dox-Anode.[2] This is a zinc silicate paint which gives cathodic protection against electrolysis (the zinc is destroyed in protecting the steel). It also possesses anti-fouling properties and can be scrubbed.

The anti-corrosive action of this paint is supported by four zinc anodes of the type 3Z welded to either side of the hull.

The rest of the hull is easy to maintain: two coats of paint twice a year when we cruise.

I believe that once a year would be enough for a steel boat used for one month a year only, for the quality of marine paints has improved greatly in the past few years.

I believe in making a very good job of painting a boat before she is launched (seven or eight coats), to give the hull adequate

---

[1] As I write these lines a friend tells me that there is now a new book which is extremely clearly written: *La Navigation Astronomique a la Portée de tous* by Maurice Oliveau (Éditions du Compas, 71 rue Fondary, Paris), and makes it possible to dispense with advice No. 2. But astro-navigation is full of pit-falls and only a professional can point them out quickly and save you wasting a lot of time.

[2] Dox Anode is made by O.M.E.X.I.M., 1 rue Lord Byron, Paris.

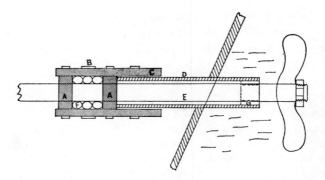

Propeller shaft installed by Henry Wakelam, using a length of rubber pipe, two wooden washers cut from a plank of teak and several tightening bands to make a 'stern gland'. This device, built *in situ* without slipping *Joshua* has worked for five years now.

 A. Washers cut from a 1¼ in teak plank.
 B. Stainless steel tightening bands.
 C. Rubber pipe.
 D. Stern tube welded in place during construction of boat.
 E. Greased packing.
 F. Standard rubber bearing.

protection from the very beginning. I have heard that naval ships are given ten coats of paint before they are first launched.

The interior

This is no problem; *Joshua* was given only four coats of paint inside before she was launched (two coats of anti-rust or zinc chromate and two coats of white).

In six years we have repainted the inside twice except for the galley, which becomes dirty more quickly, and which gets two coats once a year.

The waterline

This is the part of the hull which causes the greatest headaches. But here again things are simple enough if one is not driven mad by the sight of the occasional spot of rust ... or a small blemish caused by electrolysis: the solution is paint, paint and paint again. It is worth remembering that *Shafhai* was twenty-eight years old when Henry Wakelam raised her as a wreck ... and she is still sailing.

Hatches, cleats, mooring bitts, etc.

I regret not having had all the bitts that are welded on deck dip galvanised. This would have prevented the small outbreaks of rust which are so offensive to the eye.

Order in which things are done when *Joshua* is painted:
1. Scrape patches of rust
2. Apply a rust eliminator. This is a liquid based on phosphoric acid (available from chemists or from most makers of marine paints) which destroys *completely* any remaining rust which has escaped the scraper. This procedure also ensures that the first coat of anti-rust paint (red lead, zinc chromate etc.) adheres well.
3. Two coats of anti-rust paint followed by two top coats. We use quick-drying paint which is more convenient if you live on board.

Electrolysis

During the return voyage the hook on one of our fishing lines came off without the transparent nylon line itself having broken. Jean Bluche had told us about the phenomenon of electrolysis which a friend of his had observed in a similar case. One explanation is that the static electricity accumulated in the nylon line through friction with the water is transmitted to the hook which gradually wears away at the point where it is attached to the line.

Electrolysis can lead to various surprises of this kind. I have taken infinite precautions to make sure that they don't happen. *Joshua*'s propeller is of cast iron (instead of the traditional bronze), and there is not a single piece of yellow metal under the waterline. The intake of sea-water for the W.C. is placed more than 12 feet away from the latter, and the water is conducted by a pipe of reinforced *rubber* with a knee above the waterline so that the water can be drawn off eventually. There is also a knee in the outlet pipe which drains ... above the waterline. In this way electrolytic action between the main part of the W.C., which is of bronze, and *Joshua*'s bottom, is made impossible.

As for the risk of electrolysis due to static electricity possibly held by nylon and other plastics, I made a thorough check after what Bluche had told me: one of our fresh water tanks, connected to the sink pump by a plastic pipe, had suffered quite serious damage from electrolytic corrosion after two years' use without maintenance (the corroded patches were 1 mm deep in places), while the other tank, connected to the pump by a rubber pipe (and not touched for two years either) showed only very little normal corrosion and a number of benign patches. Had the plastic pipe anything to do with the difference?

The Echo Sounder

I have known a boat which narrowly missed sinking in port because of electrolytic corrosion caused by the contact of the steel hull with the bronze transducer of the echo sounder.

Joshua has been fitted with an echo sounder (run on batteries) since we slipped her at Martinique. To minimise the risk of electrolysis I have isolated the threaded rod (which houses the electric wire) with a piece of rubber pipe where it passes through the steel hull. Some rubber-based mastic (sold in tubes at ship-chandlers), applied before tightening up the screw, completed the job.

If I *did it again*

Without a second's hesitation: my new boat would be steel again. But there is no question of wanting to change boats; we are very pleased with *Joshua*: she is quite fast on all points of sailing, rides well to a sea close-hauled and her movements are gentle. But one day we will improve her accommodation by cutting an opening through the two watertight bulkheads which restrict the space inside.

The rigging

A stainless steel shroud is a little stronger than a galvanised steel shroud of the same diameter. But in the long run the successive stresses placed on the shrouds by the working of the mast leads to a kind of crystallisation in the stainless steel which makes it liable to fracture. This is why I think it wise to use dispropor-tionately thick shrouds if one chooses stainless steel: less stretch-ing, less vibration, less trouble in the long run.

As for mast fittings, rigging screws, shackles etc. I prefer to stick to galvanised steel, because it does not crystallise and, in my opinion, is safer. A yachtsman I know has seen three of his rigging screws break like glass. Another has had the stainless steel pin of a runner break, which was $\frac{1}{2}$ in in diameter. There are so many types of stainless steel these days that one gets lost. Some are safe, others aren't. How do you know which is which?

Black as a colour

On *Joshua* all the cleats, stancheons, mooring bitts, as well as the inside of the bulwarks are painted black. Black flags, about 16 in × 16 in in size, fly from the shrouds instead of the usual 'tell-tales' that indicate the direction of the wind.

Why all this black? Because black shows up much better than white at night, *at sea*. That is difficult to believe, but it is true. Without our black flags flying from the mizzen shrouds at the height of a man's head we could never have steered to the waves during our last four nights of the big gale.

The 'Logical Route'

The following lines are only a very incomplete testimony ... and perhaps quite mistaken. Just because we have once got away without suffering damage I cannot pretend to talk like an authority on the handling of a yacht in the high latitudes of the South Pacific.

The seas we met with shortly after the 40th parallel have led me to adopt a formal rule: never run with the wind from dead aft in the South Pacific, whether it is blowing a gale or merely a fresh breeze. I have seen *Joshua* surf for some thirty yards and *bounce twice* in the way a s.o.s. might do, in a wind probably not exceeding force six. I know this is incredible, but it is nevertheless true. The weather was quite fine, but there was this peculiar sea running which I have frequently observed in these high latitudes and which is just right for surfing. The boat can then be in real danger of being pitchpoled unless the setting of the self-steering is corrected to take the seas at an angle of 15 to 20 degrees. It all depends on the boat, of course. Fred Debels' boat *Tereva*, which is about *Joshua*'s size but with more beam and a pronounced sheer, could have continued quite safely without altering course in the very same sea. In a stiff blow *Tereva* would probably have to adopt Vito Dumas' technique, or in any case 'do something'. And in a gale the question would no longer arise: whereas *Joshua* would be pitchpoled 15 times in 24 hours, *Tereva* would be pitchpoled only 3 or 4 times (which would amount to the same thing, in the end).

As for lying hove-to, with or without sail up, this is no longer possible in the South Pacific for boats of our size: *Joshua* would have been rolled over several times in 24 hours during the big gale.

In *Joshua*'s case the essential thing in a gale is to remain very manœuvrable, to keep moving at a fair speed (but not so fast as to become hard on the helm, day between 5½ and 6 knots) and to take every wave, *without a single exception*, at an angle of 15 to 20 degrees, even if breaking seas come continuously on board. The danger definitely does not come from breaking seas if they are taken over the quarter, and I was amazed to see with what ease the boat took on enormous seas without flinching.

The real danger comes from very steep waves which, without actually breaking can throw the boat forward at high speed and *pitchpole it into the trough of a secondary wave* approaching at an oblique angle to the direction of the predominant swell.

If a boat is pitchpoled then this is the result of her surfing forward (not of a breaking sea) and being literally rammed into the sea at a speed of 15 to 25 knots. This accounts for the *crushing* impact which ripped off *Tzu-Hang*'s dog-house and two masts with a single blow, as though everything above deck had been struck with a sledge hammer ...

By comparison, a breaking sea, even if enormous and taken on the beam, puts me in mind of a blow from a giant bludgeon, but a foam rubber bludgeon. The blow may be very powerful, but it is still relatively soft, and has little breaking force. Thus, during her second attempt to round Cape Horn, *Tzu-Hang* was rolled over by an enormous breaking sea while lying hove-to under bare poles and broadside-on to the sea. She lost her main mast, half of her mizzen mast, but not the dog-house. When *Joshua* had her masts ducked during the first night of the gale, the blow was strong but definitely soft, almost *gentle*. When *Marie-Thérèse II* was struck by that enormous breaker which turned her over I happened to be on deck, I saw it all, I felt it all. That, too, was a soft blow, despite its tremendous power.

Henry Wakelam once described an episode in *Wanda*: 'I was down below and heard something like a railway engine approaching at great speed but with a muffled sound. Then *Wanda* began to lie over, further and further and I could no longer hear a sound, as though the boat had been wrapped in a ball of cotton wool.

Then she righted herself quietly.' Here, too, the impact was powerful yet soft. I must point out that *Tzu-Hang*'s masts were not snapped off by the breaking sea but by the impact on the sea to leeward, otherwise the mizzen mast would have been broken near the deck, where the breaker struck, and not level with the hounds.

Ventilation in heavy weather

The ventilator pipe on *Joshua* is made of a bent tube cut from the inner tube of a lorry tyre. It works by suction. When a wave comes on deck it flattens the tube, which reopens by itself. (This 'water-tight' ventilation tube can be seen on one of the photographs in this book.)

Fresh water

Joshua's rain awning has a gutter on either side with a length of plastic hose attached to it to collect the rainwater. The most we ever collected was 80 gallons in one night. Never once, all the way from Panama to Tahiti, did we have to go ashore for water.